Technology, War and Independence

1901–Present Day

Aaron Wilkes

Chapter 6: The post-war world

Chapter 7: From empire to Commonwealth

Chapter 8: Into the modern world

Chapter 9: The modern world: what has changed?

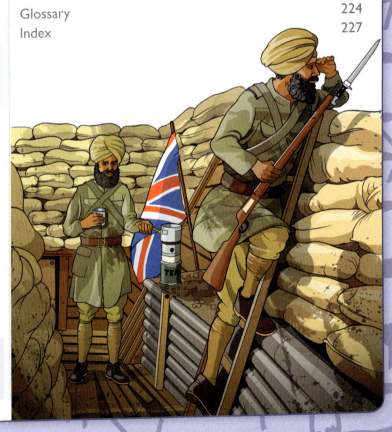

Introducing KS3 History Fourth Edition

So what is history?

History is about what happened in the past. It's about people in the past, what they did and why they did it, and what they felt. To enjoy history you need to be able to imagine what life was like in the past, or what it may have been like to be involved in past events.

How does this book fit in?

This book will get you thinking. You will be asked to look at different pieces of evidence and to try to work things out for yourself. Sometimes, two pieces of evidence about the same event won't agree with each other. You might be asked to think of reasons why that is. Your answers might not be the same as your friend's or even your teacher's. This is OK. The important thing is to give *reasons* for your thoughts and ideas.

How to use this book

Features of the Student Book are explained here and on the opposite page.

Kerboodle support

Kerboodle provides digital Lessons, Resources and Assessment for the classroom and at home. This book contains icons that highlight some of the digital resources available:

 Animation

 Film clip

 Assessment presentation

 Knowledge organiser

Key to features

Objectives All lessons in this book start by setting you objectives. These are your key aims that set out your learning targets for the work ahead.

History Skills These activities test a range of history skills, so each box has its own title. The tasks will challenge you to think a little deeper about what you have been studying. These are also important skills to develop if you are going to study GCSE History.

Over to You This is your opportunity to demonstrate your knowledge, and your understanding, of history skills. In each box the tasks become progressively more challenging.

Meanwhile... 1930s This gives you an idea of what else is going on in the world (perhaps in another country on a different continent) at the same sort of time as the period you are studying in the lesson.

Earlier on... and Later on... 1906 You will be challenged to think how the topic you are studying relates to events, people, ideas or developments that may have happened many years before… or might connect to things in the future.

Key Words These are important words and terms that are vital to help you understand the topics. You can spot them easily because they are in bold red type. Look up their meanings in the glossary at the back of the book.

Fact ✓ These are funny, fascinating and amazing little bits of history that you don't usually get to hear about! They're important because they give you insights into topics that you'll easily remember.

 These sections give you an opportunity to pull all your skills together and investigate a controversial, challenging or intriguing aspect of history. In this book you will consider a question surrounding a well-known event in suffragette history – did Emily Davison mean to kill herself?

 In each book, there is a depth study that focuses on an important event, person or development. This gives you the chance to extend and deepen your understanding of key moments in history.

 Literacy and Numeracy
Throughout the book you will see icons like these when a task is particularly focused on your literacy or numeracy skills.

Have you been learning?

There are different types of assessments at the end of every chapter. These are opportunities for you to showcase what you have learned and to put your ability to recall key information and history skills to the test.

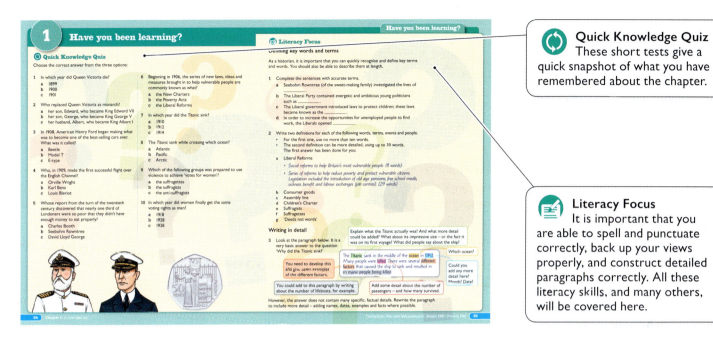

Quick Knowledge Quiz
These short tests give a quick snapshot of what you have remembered about the chapter.

Literacy Focus
It is important that you are able to spell and punctuate correctly, back up your views properly, and construct detailed paragraphs correctly. All these literacy skills, and many others, will be covered here.

History skills assessments

The assessments at the end of each chapter are designed to help you improve the way you think about history, write about history and apply your historical knowledge when you are being assessed. These step-by-step guides will help you write clear, focused answers to some challenging history questions. These concepts and skills are essential if you wish to go on to study History at a higher level, so by tackling these you are giving yourself a good foundation in history.

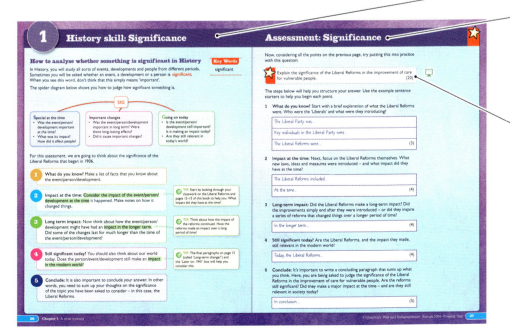

For each assessment: **History skill** pages show you how to approach the question step by step and **Assessment** pages coach you through writing your answer.

Each chapter ends with a **'big question' assessment task** which tests your understanding of historical concepts such as continuity and change, cause and consequence, similarity, difference and significance.

Timeline from 1901 to the present day

At the beginning of the twentieth century Queen Victoria was in her sixty-third year as Britain's queen. Despite increasing competition from other countries, the British controlled the largest empire the world had ever known, covering one quarter of all the land on the planet… and Britain's factories, businesses, shipyards and banks made more money than those of any other nation! Telephones and cars had been invented, but were very rare, and television didn't exist. Most British men could vote, but women couldn't, and the average person could expect to live to about 50 years of age. As the century progressed, many aspects of life began to change considerably.

This book covers this period of change, not only in Britain, but in the world as a whole. The timeline on these pages gives you an idea of some of the key events, ideas and discoveries that have happened since the start of the twentieth century.

1979
Margaret Thatcher becomes Britain's first female Prime Minister

1975
Sex Discrimination Act is introduced in UK, making discrimination against women illegal

1973
Britain becomes a member of the European Union (then known as the European Community)

1969
US astronaut Neil Armstrong becomes the first person to walk on the moon

1901
Queen Victoria dies and is succeeded by her son, Edward VII

1912
The *Titanic* sinks

1918
The vote is given to British women over 30 if they own a home or are married to someone who does; all women get the vote in 1928

1957
The USSR launches the world's first ever satellite into space: Sputnik 1

1906
A new law introduces free school meals for Britain's poorer children

1929
A global financial crisis begins; many banks, businesses and individuals are ruined (known as the Great Depression)

1914
The First World War begins; it lasts until 1918 and around nine million soldiers are killed

1928
Scottish scientist Alexander Fleming discovers the antibiotic properties of penicillin

1989
British computer scientist Tim Berners-Lee invents the World Wide Web; the first website is launched in 1991

1999
Scottish Parliament and Welsh Assembly are set up

2009
Barack Obama becomes President of the USA

1998
The 'Good Friday Agreement' (a peace agreement setting out how Northern Ireland will be governed) is signed and an Assembly (a type of parliament) is set up

2001
Terror attacks in the USA lead to US-led military action in Afghanistan

2016
British people vote to leave the European Union

2019
An outbreak of a severe respiratory disease known as COVID-19 is first identified in China, in December 2019.

1952
Elizabeth II becomes queen of the UK and the other Commonwealth countries

1948
Start of Britain's National Health Service

KEY

⚫ Political		🟣 Invention/Discovery	
🔴 Warfare		🔺 Disease	
⭐ Social			

1947
British-controlled India gains independence and is partitioned (split) into the nations of India and Pakistan

1933
Adolf Hitler becomes leader of Germany

1939
The Second World War begins; it lasts until 1945 and over 50 million people are killed

1937
Coventry-born engineer Frank Whittle invents the jet engine

Over to You

1 Make a list of:

a as many different historical periods as you can. You will have studied many during your time in school, for example, the Victorian period.

b In the future, what might be a suitable name for the period of history we live in today? You could discuss this with a partner or as a group before explaining your choice.

2 Look at some of the inventions on the timeline. Pick out a few that you think have made the greatest impact or change. Explain your reasons.

1.1A Britain and the world in 1901

In 1901, lots of British people had every reason to be proud. Most were better fed, better clothed, healthier and more educated than many people in other nations around the world. Cities were full of shops that contained a wide range of goods, either made in British factories or brought in from parts of the **British Empire**. This was the largest empire the world had ever seen – Britain controlled over a quarter of the world (about 450 million people).

Objectives

- Examine Britain's place in the world at the turn of the twentieth century.
- Explain how and why other countries were catching up with Britain in terms of industry, trade and empire.

The world in 1901

Britain had been the first country in the world to have an industrial revolution. By 1901, it was the world's richest country. Yet Britain's status in the world was under threat. The USA was now making more goods than Britain, and Germany and Japan were quickly catching up. How long could Britain hold onto its position as the country that did more trade (and made more money) than any other?

There were also growing rivals on the military front. Britain had more battleships than any other two countries added together. But several other nations were increasing the size of their armies and navies. By 1901, Germany's army was one of the largest in Europe. Japan, Germany, Russia and the USA greatly increased their numbers of battleships. And these countries were just as proud and **patriotic** as the British were. So could this rivalry lead to conflict?

The end of an era

Queen Victoria died on 22 January 1901. She had been queen for 63 years. Her son became King Edward VII. Through Victoria's marriage to Albert, and the marriages of her children, Britain's royal family was directly connected to the rulers of Russia, Germany, Spain, Norway, Denmark, Sweden, Greece and Romania.

What was Britain like by 1901?

While some people in Britain were very wealthy, and many had enough money to live comfortably, a huge number of people were still very poor. About 3 per cent were very rich (the upper class), 25 per cent were relatively wealthy (the middle class – such as bankers, doctors, accountants and managers), and the rest, the working class, were poor.

The wealthier people of Britain lived a life of luxury. They owned land and homes, and many didn't have to work at all because they made so much money out of investments and rents. But this was not the case for the vast majority of people. Many earned just enough to get by, often working in factories, mills or shipyards. However, others earned nowhere near enough to feed their families. There were no benefits from the state, and the injured and sick paid for their own medical care.

▼ **MAP A** The empires of the world in 1901. Up to this point, empire-building countries had been competing to have the largest empire.

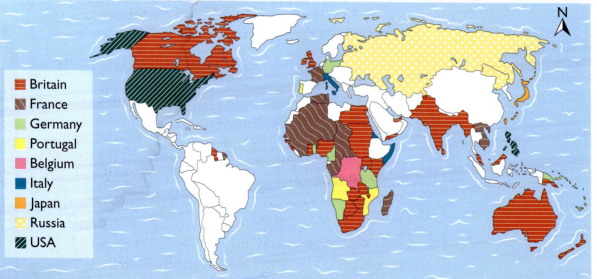

- ■ Britain
- ■ France
- ■ Germany
- ■ Portugal
- ■ Belgium
- ■ Italy
- ■ Japan
- ■ Russia
- ■ USA

SOURCE B & C These photographs highlight the contrast between rich and poor at the start of the twentieth century. The poor slum area shown in **Source B** (below left) is vastly different from the rich Park Lane region of London shown in **Source C** (right).

SOURCE D Adapted from a book called *Sybil, or The Two Nations* (1845) by Benjamin Disraeli. As well as writing books, Disraeli was a politician who twice served as British Prime Minister.

'Two groups; between whom there is no interaction and no sympathy; who are as ignorant of each other's habits, thoughts, and feelings, as if they lived in different times, or were inhabitants of different planets; who are formed by a different breeding, are fed by a different food, are ordered by different manners, and are not governed by the same laws... the rich and the poor.'

INTERPRETATION E From a 2008 book about the history of Britain by history writer Ruth Brocklehurst.

'With its vast empire and far-ranging fleet, Britain was at the peak of its powers at the opening of the new century... But while the rich celebrated, millions of poor British families couldn't escape from poverty or the grinding routines of life in the industrial age. They watched nervously as European nations jostled for supremacy, threatening to drag the world into a new and intense war.'

Fact ✓

Shopping habits were beginning to change in the early 1900s. Instead of selling just a few similar items, shopkeepers would sell a range of different items in separate departments – the department store was born. By 1910, these stores would be able to sell Coca-Cola (which arrived from the USA in 1900), Heinz Baked Beans (1901), Marmite (1902), Gillette razors (1905), Hoover vacuum cleaners (1908) and Persil washing powder (1909).

Over to You

1 Look at **Sources B** and **C**.
   a Write a sentence or two describing each photograph.
   b If you did not know that **Source B** was the poor area and **Source C** was the richer area, what details in the photographs might have helped you decide this?

2 a Why do you think many British people were proud of their nation in 1901?
   b Why were some British people worried about their nation's status by 1901?

Interpretation Analysis

1 Read **Interpretation E**. Describe what point the author is making about Britain's position in the world.
2 How far do you agree with **Interpretation E** about the differences between rich and poor in the early 1900s?

Scientific and technological breakthroughs

The start of the twentieth century saw major developments in three particular areas of discovery and invention. This new technology was to have a major impact on life after 1901.

Transport

By 1901, a vast railway system linked Britain's major towns and cities, and the road network had been improved – there were more roads to more places, and the road surfaces had been upgraded. In 1885, Karl Benz, a German, had made the first successful petrol-driven vehicle, or 'motor car'. It had three wheels and could reach speeds of up to 10mph. In 1886, Gottlieb Daimler, another German, made the first four-wheeled petrol-driven car.

By the early 1900s, building cars had become a big moneymaking industry but cars were still too expensive for most people. Then, in 1908, an American called Henry Ford began making what was to become one of the best-selling cars ever – the Ford Model T. Based in Detroit, USA, the Ford Motor Company had made over one million Model Ts by the end of 1915. Ford used state-of-the-art techniques in his factory to **mass-produce** the cars on an **assembly line**. They would pass in front of the workers on a conveyor belt and each person would have an individual job to do. The cars were made quickly… and cheaply. In fact, in 1908 a Model T cost $900 to buy, but by 1927 Ford was making them so efficiently that the price dropped to around $200 (around £2500 today).

On 17 December 1903, in North Carolina, USA, Orville Wright made the first manned powered flight. It lasted 12 seconds and he flew a distance of 37m. He had built the aeroplane with his brother Wilbur. By 1905, the brothers had made over 150 flights, some lasting nearly 40 minutes. Flying became the latest craze and, in 1909, a Frenchman, Louis Bleriot, flew over the English Channel. By 1910, some countries were investigating the possibility of attaching bombs to planes so they could be dropped on an enemy.

▼ **SOURCE F** A photograph of the Ford Model T assembly line in Highland Park, Michigan, USA. By 1914, the assembly process for the Model T was so efficient that it took only 93 minutes to assemble a car.

Meanwhile...

The Ford Model T was built in Ford factories that were opened in several different countries. In 1911, a Ford factory opened in Manchester (UK), and soon after the car was being built in Germany, Argentina, France, Spain, Denmark, Norway, Belgium, Brazil, Mexico and Japan.

▼ **SOURCE G** The Wright Brothers' 'Baby Grand' plane was built in 1910 and could fly up to 115kph.

Communications

The telephone (invented in 1876) and the radio became increasingly popular after 1901. By the 1920s, they were two of the most popular household items. They spread news quickly and enabled business to be done at a faster rate.

Consumer goods

Other new inventions, such as vacuum cleaners and electric irons, were based on the growing use of electricity. These and other consumer goods, such as wristwatches, phonographs (for playing recorded music) and cameras, became widespread after 1901.

How did people amuse themselves?

Sport remained a popular activity, as it had been in the previous century. Football, cricket, rugby, tennis and golf continued to attract thousands of spectators and participants. Going to the pub was as popular as ever too! The early 1900s also saw the growth of the cinema and 'movie stars' such as Charlie Chaplin, Rudolf Valentino, Buster Keaton and Mary Pickford, who became household names. Later, cartoon characters such as Mickey and Minnie Mouse, Donald Duck and Pluto became well known too.

Over to You

1 What was:

   a   a Model T

   b   the Baby Grand

   c   a phonograph?

2 Why did a Model T cost less in 1927 than in 1908?

3 a   Design a poster that describes Britain and the world at the start of the twentieth century. Your poster should:

   • be aimed at a Year 6 pupil who has never studied Britain in the early 1900s
   • include no more than 50 words
   • mention the rich/poor divide, shopping, the media, sport, and transport developments.

   b   Using the same guidelines, design another poster that describes Britain and the world today.

   c   In what areas and categories are the two posters similar and how are they different?

Key Words

assembly line   consumer goods   mass-produce

Fact ✓

Printed books and newspapers were widely available in the early 1900s. Many books that are viewed as classics today were written at this time such as Beatrix Potter's *The Tale of Peter Rabbit* (1901), Kenneth Grahame's *The Wind in the Willows* (1908) and J.M. Barrie's *Peter Pan and Wendy* (1911).

▼ **SOURCE H** A movie poster from 1912, showing one of the biggest movie stars of the time – Mary Pickford.

Fact ✓

By 1901, Britain's population was around 40 million – and around 80 per cent lived in towns and cities.

Change ⭐

1 In what ways were the lives of people beginning to change at the start of the twentieth century?

1.2A Tackling poverty and public health

When Queen Victoria died in 1901, Britain was a divided nation. The gap between rich and poor was huge. A tiny minority of people enjoyed fine food, large houses and long holidays... but many millions were so poor that they couldn't afford even the most basic necessities, such as enough food. For the poor of the country, life was extremely tough. So just how poor were Britain's poorest? And who chose to help them... and why?

Objectives

- Identify the level of poverty experienced by many in the early twentieth century.
- Outline key events and significant people in the attempt to improve public health at this time.
- Assess the impact of the Liberal Reforms.

Poverty hits the headlines

In the late 1800s and early 1900s, two reports into **poverty** and the lives of the poor shocked the nation. Charles Booth discovered that nearly one third of Londoners were so poor that they didn't have enough money to eat properly, despite having full-time jobs. But the problems weren't just in London. In York, Seebohm Rowntree (of the sweet-making family) found that 28 per cent of the city's wage-earners didn't earn enough to eat healthily, and 40 per cent of children suffered illness and stunted growth from lack of food (see **B**).

Booth's and Rowntree's investigations caused quite a stir – and famous politicians like David Lloyd George and the young Winston Churchill felt that governments should try harder to look after people who couldn't help themselves. Army leaders soon became worried too. Nearly one third of all men who volunteered to join the army failed their medical examination because they were too small, too thin, too ill, or had poor eyesight. Unless something was done about the health of the nation's young men, how was Britain going to fight its wars in the future?

▼ **SOURCE B** An extract from Seebohm Rowntree's *Poverty: A Study of Town Life* (1901).

'These children presented a pathetic sight; all bore some mark of the hard conditions against which they were struggling. Thin and feeble bodies, dirty and often sadly insufficient clothing, sore eyes, filthy heads, cases of hip disease, swollen glands – all these and other signs told a tale of neglect.'

▼ **SOURCE A** Poor children on the streets of London around 1900.

Children were hit hardest

In the early 1900s, hundreds of thousands of schoolchildren were reported as suffering from a disease or poor diet. Millions of children were not getting the good diet they needed because their parents couldn't afford it – and they didn't know much about the benefits of healthy eating. Also, calling a doctor cost money in the early 1900s, so parents rarely did unless they were desperate. By 1901, 15 out of every 100 children died before the age of five. A poor child was, on average, 9cm shorter than a rich child of the same age!

Change at last?

In 1906, the general election was won by a political party (group) called the Liberal Party. David Lloyd George and Winston Churchill were both members of the Liberal Party. They were committed to introducing measures to fight poverty, improve the lives of ordinary people, and raise the general level of public health.

▼ **SOURCE C** David Lloyd George (left) and Winston Churchill in 1910. Both went on to become Prime Minister – Lloyd George during the First World War and Winston Churchill during the Second World War.

Key Words   poverty   public health

Earlier on...

In the eighteenth and nineteenth centuries, most politicians believed that if a person was poor, it was probably their own fault. They said that poverty was a result of laziness or an addiction to alcohol, for example. It was social reformers, such as Booth and Rowntree, who worked to change these attitudes and demand that the government do more to help people.

Fact ✓

A social reformer named Octavia Hill tried to improve the quality of housing for some poorer Londoners in the late 1800s. She created a scheme that bought up poor quality housing, improved it, and rented it out to poor tenants for low prices. By 1874, she had 15 housing schemes with around 3000 tenants. She went on to help create the National Trust in 1895. This organisation still plays a major role in the maintenance of important buildings and parks in the UK.

Over to You

1 **a** Who were
   - Charles Booth
   - Seebohm Rowntree?

   b Why do you think their reports shocked so many people?

2 Why do you think army leaders were so worried about the health of Britain's young men in the early 1900s?

Changing times

In 1906, the newly elected Liberal government brought in a series of new laws, ideas and measures to help some of the most vulnerable people in society. Collectively, the changes they introduced are known as the 'Liberal Reforms'.

Free school meals

The School Meals Act of 1906 allowed local councils to provide free school meals for the poorest children. By 1914, over 158,000 children were having a free school meal every day. **Source D** shows the impact these meals made on children's weights. Other measures were introduced too – free medical checks and treatment, for example (see **E**). A 'Children's Charter' was created, which introduced laws that, even today, still protect young people (see **F**).

> ### Fact ✓
> The school system was also seen as a way of improving children's health and well-being. From 1907, special schools were set up to teach young women about the benefits of breast feeding, hygiene and childcare.

▼ **SOURCE F** The Children's Charter (or the Children and Young Person's Act), 1908. As you can see, many of these reforms are still in place today.

- Children are 'protected persons' – parents can be prosecuted if they neglect or are cruel to them.
- Inspectors are to regularly visit any children who have been neglected in the past.
- All children's homes are to be regularly inspected.
- Youth courts and young offenders' homes are to keep young criminals away from older ones.
- Children under 14 are not allowed in pubs.
- Shopkeepers cannot sell cigarettes to children under 16.

▼ **SOURCE D** This graph shows how children gained and lost weight during part of the year in 1907.

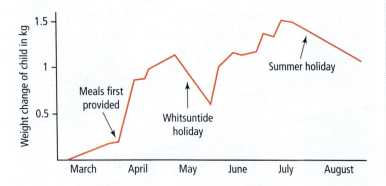

▼ **SOURCE E** An anxious mother watches a doctor examine her son in one of Britain's first free medical checks, 1911.

Other reforms

After helping children, the new Liberal government moved on to help other vulnerable sections of society. It introduced unemployment benefit, sickness benefit, and pensions for the elderly. It opened Britain's first job centres (known then as 'labour exchanges') and banned the building of overcrowded back-to-back housing – so fewer people would have to live in crowded, filthy, disease-ridden slums.

While the Liberal Reforms did not go anywhere near to solving all the problems connected to poverty and ill-health, they established that it was the responsibility of government to look after people who could not look after themselves. They also showed that systems and measures could be created to do this.

Long-term change?

Over the next 30 years, successive governments continued to take measures to improve the welfare and health of Britain's citizens. In 1918, for example, local councils had to provide health visitors, clinics for pregnant women and day nurseries. A year later, councils began to build new houses for poorer families and in 1930 a huge slum clearance programme began, finally clearing away the breeding grounds of so much disease.

Gradually, during the first half of the twentieth century, standards of public health began to improve. Cleaner towns and improved medical understanding had already seen life expectancy rise in the 1800s – but it increased more and more in the 1900s. For example, by 1901, life expectancy had reached 48 for a man and 52 for a woman. By 1931, this had increased to 59 and 63. Infant mortality had started to drop too. For example, in 1900, out of every 1000 babies born alive, 163 died before their first birthday. This rate had dropped to around 60 out of every 1000 by 1930.

Meanwhile... 1900

In January 1900, in Chicago, an ambitious new public health project began. The direction of the Chicago River was reversed, making the water flow into the Chicago Sanitary and Ship Canal. It could then be cleaned before entering Lake Michigan, where the city's drinking water came from.

Fact ✓

In Victorian times, there were two main political parties – the Conservatives and the Liberals. In 1900, a new political party was formed – the Labour Party – to attract workers' votes. Some say the Liberal Party's focus on helping ordinary, working people and children after 1906 was an attempt to pull voters away from the new Labour Party.

Later on...   1941

Seebohm Rowntree, whose report shocked the nation, published another report 40 years later. In it, he claimed that poverty had reduced by 50 per cent since 1901.

Over to You

1 Define the term 'Liberal Reforms'.

2 Apart from free school meals, how else were children helped in the early 1900s?

3 Write a sentence or two to explain how the government helped the following in the early 1900s:
   a the unemployed
   b the sick
   c people living in poor quality housing
   d the elderly.

Source Analysis

Look at **Source D**.

1 What effect did the introduction of free school meals have on the weight of children? Try to use numbers from the graph in your answer.

2 What happened to the weight of the children during the holidays?

3 How useful is this source to a historian studying the impact of free school meals?

1.3 Who or what was to blame for the *Titanic* disaster?

The *Titanic* is probably one of the most famous ships ever built. It was the biggest moving object ever made. But just four days into its first voyage across the Atlantic Ocean from Southampton to New York, on the evening of Sunday 14 April 1912, the *Titanic* collided with an iceberg and sank just a few hours later. There were just over 2200 people on board, but only 704 were rescued.

The sinking of the *Titanic* caused a sensation in Britain and the USA. Your task is to conduct an enquiry into the disaster and write a report for both governments. Your report should be entitled 'The *Titanic* Disaster Enquiry' and you must decide what the main cause was. Use evidence A to E to help you!

Objectives

- Explain why the *Titanic* is such a famous ship.
- Judge who or what caused the *Titanic* disaster.

EVIDENCE A

Captain Smith

Edward Smith was the *Titanic*'s captain, responsible for the ship's safe, efficient operation.

He was due to retire after the *Titanic*'s first voyage and some people think he might have wanted to set a speed record on his last ever trip. He ignored at least seven warnings of icebergs from nearby ships and the *Titanic* was travelling at 20 knots per hour (around 37kph) – close to top speed – when it struck the iceberg. If the ship had been going slower, could it have turned out of the iceberg's way in time? Captain Smith once said, 'I can't imagine anything causing a modern ship to sink. Shipbuilding has gone beyond that.'

EVIDENCE B

Harland and Wolff

The *Titanic* was built at the Harland and Wolff shipyard in Belfast, Northern Ireland. About three million rivets were used to hold it together. When the wreck was finally discovered in 1985, some of the rivets were brought to the surface. Investigations showed that they were made from poor-quality iron. When the ship struck the iceberg, the heads of the rivets snapped off and sections of the ship were torn wide open. If the rivets had been made of more expensive, higher-quality iron, perhaps the hole in the *Titanic*'s side would have been smaller – and maybe it wouldn't have sunk. Further tests showed that the poor-quality rivets shattered easily in extremely low temperatures – as on the night of 14 April 1912.

EVIDENCE C

Thomas Andrews

Thomas Andrews, an architect who worked for Harland and Wolff, designed the *Titanic*. The ship was thought to be unsinkable by many because Andrews created 16 watertight compartments in the bottom of the ship. However, the compartments didn't reach as high as they should have done. Andrews had reduced their height to make more space for first-class cabins. If just two of the watertight compartments had reached all the way to the top, there is a chance that the *Titanic* wouldn't have sunk.

EVIDENCE D

Stanley Lord

Stanley Lord was the captain of a ship called the *Californian*, which was only 30km away from the *Titanic* when it struck the iceberg. Despite being aware of icebergs in the area, Lord let his radio operator go to bed at around 11:15pm. At around midnight, members of the *Californian*'s crew saw what they thought were fireworks being fired into the sky on the horizon. They were, in fact, **distress flares**. They woke Captain Lord and told him, but he decided not to sail towards the lights – he assumed it was just another ship having a fireworks party! Should Lord have raced the *Californian* towards the scene? Should he at least have insisted that the radio be turned on so they could have heard the *Titanic*'s **SOS** signals? How many more people would have survived if the *Californian* had been there to pull them from the icy waters?

Fact ✓

The *Titanic* was more than three football pitches long, weighed 46,000 tons, and was taller than a 17-storey building.

EVIDENCE E

Bruce Ismay

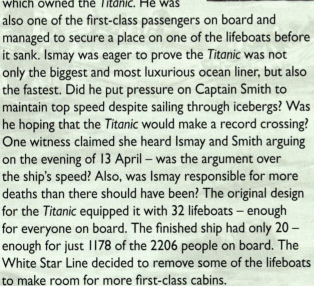

Bruce Ismay was in charge of the White Star Line shipping company, which owned the *Titanic*. He was also one of the first-class passengers on board and managed to secure a place on one of the lifeboats before it sank. Ismay was eager to prove the *Titanic* was not only the biggest and most luxurious ocean liner, but also the fastest. Did he put pressure on Captain Smith to maintain top speed despite sailing through icebergs? Was he hoping that the *Titanic* would make a record crossing? One witness claimed she heard Ismay and Smith arguing on the evening of 13 April – was the argument over the ship's speed? Also, was Ismay responsible for more deaths than there should have been? The original design for the *Titanic* equipped it with 32 lifeboats – enough for everyone on board. The finished ship had only 20 – enough for just 1178 of the 2206 people on board. The White Star Line decided to remove some of the lifeboats to make room for more first-class cabins.

Key Words   distress flare   SOS

Over to You

1 Complete the sentences with accurate terms:
- The *Titanic* was built at the Harland and Wolff shipyard in _____.
- The *Titanic* hit an iceberg on _____.
- There were over _____ people on board, but only _____ survived.
- The *Titanic*'s captain was named _____.
- After sinking to the bottom of the _____ Ocean, the *Titanic* was eventually found in _____.

2 So who or what was the main cause of the huge loss of life in the disaster?

a **Step 1: Analyse the evidence**
Under the following five headings, write a sentence or two outlining how each factor may have contributed to the sinking.
- Captain Smith
- The shipbuilders
- Thomas Andrews
- Captain Lord
- Bruce Ismay

b **Step 2: Prioritise the evidence**
Place the factors in order – put the person/company you think is most responsible for the sinking at the top, down to least responsible at the bottom. Think – did the actions of one contribute more to the sinking? Write a paragraph or two explaining your decision. Did any have nothing at all to do with the sinking? If so, say how you arrived at this conclusion

c **Step 3: Deliver your verdict**
Write up your report and present your findings on what the main cause was to the US and British governments. Structure your report under a series of headings:
- Start with a brief introduction to the disaster.
- Outline the role in the sinking of each factor under investigation.
- Write a conclusion – is one factor to blame or several, or a combination of all?
- Remember, if you don't name one factor as the main cause, it doesn't mean your investigation has failed! There is often more than one factor to consider in most investigations.

At the beginning of the twentieth century, there was a large gap separating the rich from the poor. But there was another gap that separated men from women! Many professions (such as teaching) expected women to leave when they got married: their place was thought to be in the home, looking after their children and husbands. And even if women did the same jobs as men (such as factory work), they were paid less. Also, women could not become politicians in Parliament, nor vote in elections for the politicians that ran the country. Some women (and men) obviously thought this was totally unfair and decided to do something about it. So how did these people try to win the vote? What tactics did they use? And what finally won the vote for women?

Objectives

- Compare suffragettes and suffragists.
- Evaluate what finally won the vote for women.

Time for change?

There had been some changes during the 1800s that had made life better for women. They were allowed to divorce their husbands, for example, and could control their own income and vote in local council elections. But women's rights were far from equal to men's. In 1897, a group was formed that campaigned for women to be allowed the right to vote in nation-wide, government elections. They thought that if women could vote, they might be able to elect politicians who promised to improve their lives – such as making sure women were paid the same as men. This group was known as the **suffragists** ('suffrage' is another word for 'vote') and they held meetings, wrote letters to Parliament, went on protest marches and produced posters (see **B**).

New tactics

Unfortunately, the suffragists were not particularly successful. In 1903, some of the group's members decided to form their own group – and after a couple of years they changed tactics. Known as **suffragettes**, and led by Emmeline Pankhurst and her daughters, the motto of these women became 'deeds not words'!

▶ **SOURCE A**
This 1905 postcard demonstrates what many people thought about a woman's mental abilities. Those who produced this poster would clearly never accept that women should be allowed to vote!

A WOMAN'S MIND MAGNIFIED

▼ **SOURCE B** A poster from 1912 that contrasts the types of work women could do, yet were not allowed to vote, with 'unworthy' male convicts, lunatics, white slave traders, drunkards and those unfit to serve in the army, who still had voting rights.

Spectacular suffragettes!

The Pankhursts decided that the best way to highlight their cause was to commit spectacular stunts that would guarantee newspaper coverage. They disrupted political meetings, chained themselves to railings outside the Prime Minister's home in Downing Street, pelted politicians with eggs and flour, and smashed Parliament's windows with stones. They also set fire to churches and railway stations and some poured acid on golf courses. When they were arrested and fined, they refused to pay and were sent to prison. Soon, they were going on hunger strike and refusing all food in prison. This gave the government a terrible choice – free the suffragettes or let them starve to death. At first, they released all hunger strikers, but soon decided to force-feed them instead (see **D**). All this guaranteed that the suffragettes were front page news.

▶ **SOURCE C**
This 1914 photograph shows a suffragette being arrested outside Buckingham Palace.

Key Words   suffragette   suffragist

▼ **SOURCE D** A suffragette being force-fed in Holloway Prison, London, in 1909. Hunger strikers were force-fed meat and lime juice. The suffragettes tried to use this harsh treatment to gain sympathy for their cause.

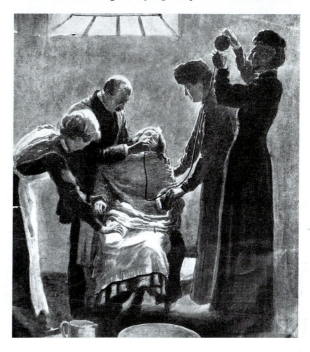

▼ **SOURCE E** Adapted from *My Own Story* by Emmeline Pankhurst (1914).

'What good did all this violent campaigning do us? For one thing our campaign made women's suffrage a matter of news – it had never been that before. Now the newspapers are full of us.'

Over to You

1 Look at **Sources A** and **B**.
   a For each source, explain the point that the cartoonist is trying to make.
   b In what ways are the messages of the cartoons different?

2 Explain two ways in which a suffragist and a suffragette were similar and two ways in which they were different.

3 Read **Source E**.
   a Who was Emmeline Pankhurst?
   b According to Pankhurst, how did the suffragettes intend to win women's right to vote?

Meanwhile...

1890s–1910s

Women were fighting for the right to vote in national elections in other countries at this time. That right was finally given to women in New Zealand in 1893, in Australia in 1902, in Finland in 1906 and in Norway in 1913.

Source Analysis

Look at **Source B**.
1 Describe what is shown in the cartoon.
2 How useful is **Source B** to a historian studying the votes for women campaign?

Why had women not won the vote by 1914?

Some politicians supported the idea of women getting the vote. Between 1909 and 1911 there were several attempts in Parliament to give votes to women, but each time too many politicians were against the idea. As a result, the suffragette campaign grew increasingly violent. In July 1912, a small axe was thrown at Prime Minister Herbert Asquith on a visit to Dublin, missing him narrowly (but injuring a nearby politician). In February 1913, a bomb damaged a house belonging to David Lloyd George, and in May 1913, a bomb was placed in St Paul's Cathedral (it failed to explode).

The increase in violence meant that the suffragettes lost many supporters who did not want to be associated with destructive and dangerous tactics. Prime Minister Asquith (who was personally against votes for women) argued that giving in to violence would only encourage other groups who wanted change (such as miners) to use violent methods. Lloyd George said 'the very worst way of campaigning for the vote is to try and intimidate a man into giving them what he would gladly give otherwise'!

An unexpected opportunity

By 1914, women had still not won the right to vote. When the First World War started that year the suffragettes called off their campaign of violence and asked their supporters to help the war effort instead. In fact, the war brought women an unexpected opportunity! With more and more men leaving work to become soldiers, women got the chance to 'fill in' for them and do jobs they had never done before. They became bus drivers, police officers, mechanics and road menders. Thousands of women worked in munitions factories or became nurses or ambulance drivers near the battlefields in France and Belgium.

Meanwhile … 1918

Constance Markievicz (an Irish politician) was the first woman elected as a British MP in 1918, but she refused to take her seat because she did not want to swear an oath of allegiance to the monarch. Nancy Astor was the second woman elected to Parliament and took her seat in 1919.

▼ **SOURCE F** Women working in a munitions factory during the First World War. This was a dangerous job that could leave workers very ill because of the toxic chemicals in the explosives.

The impact of women

The work done by women during the war was vital (see **F** and **G**). By the end of the war, many people felt that women had earned the right to vote – and many politicians didn't want the suffragettes to restart their violent campaign. In 1918, Parliament changed the law and gave all men over 21 the right to vote. All women over 30 were also given the right to vote, but only if they owned their own property or were married to a man who did. Some people argued that this wasn't enough, while others said it was a move in the right direction. Eventually, in 1928, Parliament reduced the voting age for women to 21, regardless of whether they owned property or were married. Finally, women had the same voting rights as men!

▼ **SOURCE G** A comparison of the quality and output in factories of men and women from the Report of the War Cabinet Committee on Women In Industry (1919).

Quality
- Metal – women's work better than men's
- Aircraft woodwork – women's work equal to men
- Bullet making – women's work equal to men
- Bomb making – women's work poorer than men's

Quantity
- Metal – women's production equal to men's
- Aircraft woodwork – women's production equal to men's
- Bullet making – women's production equal to men's; in some cases, women produce 20 per cent more than men
- Bomb making – women's production behind men

'It is true that women cannot fight with rifles, but they have aided in the most effective way in the war. What is more, when the war comes to an end, don't women have a special claim to be heard on the many questions that affect their interests? I cannot deny that claim.'

SOURCE I The suffragette campaign to gain women the vote is commemorated in this 50p coin from 2003. It features a suffragette chained to a railing and a WSPU banner (the Women's Social and Political Union was the official name of the suffragettes). The WSPU was formed in 1903.

INTERPRETATION J Adapted from *The Effect of Militancy In the British Suffragette Movement* by Marcie Kligman (1996).

'These actions by the WSPU, while attracting huge amounts of publicity, had the opposite effect intended; the public began to disapprove of the suffragettes, as well as their cause... Opponents in Parliament used the terrorist actions the women were using to their advantage in debate, saying that the insane actions were a very good reason why women should not get the vote. Parliament and the suffragettes thus reached a stalemate. The more **militant** the WSPU became, the more reluctant Parliament was to grant women the vote, and the more firmly Parliament stood on the issue of suffrage, the more violent and desperate the suffragettes became.'

INTERPRETATION K From an article on the suffragettes by history and television writer Edward Boyd in a book called *A Pageant of History* (1958).

'The Suffragette movement developed into a tremendous force. Its increase of numbers made it no longer possible for its enemies to dismiss it as the cranky notion of a few women. The Suffragettes were helped, too, rather than hindered by the stupidity and brutality of those in authority. Time and again these brave women were sent to prison where they were treated with less consideration than the commonest and vilest criminal. When they went on hunger strike, they were forcibly fed. A great many people, who had not cared one way or the other about votes for women, changed their minds when they learned of such indignities.'

Over to You

1 What happened to suffragette support in the years leading up to the First World War?

2 What impact did the First World War have on:
   • the suffragette movement   • the roles of women?

3 Read **Sources G** and **H**. In your own words, assess the impact of women during the First World War.

4 Look **Source I**.
   a Why do you think the suffragette movement was commemorated in 2003?
   b Design your own coin commemorating the story of how women won the right to vote.

Interpretation Analysis

Read at **Interpretations J** and **K**.
1 Summarise the view of the writer of **Interpretation J**.
2 Summarise the view of the writer of **Interpretation K**.
3 In what ways do the two interpretations differ about the impact of the suffragettes?
4 Which interpretation do you most agree with? Give reasons for your answer.

The Derby is one of the best-known horse races in the world. Every year, thousands of people flock to Epsom Downs racecourse to watch it. This race has always had plenty of coverage in the newspapers, which is why on 4 June 1913 a suffragette named Emily Davison thought it would make the ideal opportunity for the suffragettes' next publicity stunt. Historians cannot agree over what happened during the race. What we do know is that Davison was knocked down by the king's horse, Anmer, and died of her injuries on 8 June. But did Davison deliberately kill herself for the suffragettes' cause – or did she misjudge the speed of the horses and die in a tragic accident?

Objectives

- Examine the circumstances surrounding the death of Emily Davison.
- Judge whether Emily Davison killed herself deliberately or not.

What does the evidence say? Read through the following sources and interpretations before explaining your conclusions.

▼ **SOURCE A** Part of Emily Davison's prison record. She was a very militant suffragette who believed in 'deeds not words'.

March 1909	One month in prison for obstruction (blocking a road)
September 1909	Two months for stone throwing
November 1910	One month for breaking windows
January 1912	Six months for setting fire to postboxes
November 1912	Ten days for assaulting a vicar whom she mistook for a Member of Parliament

▼ **SOURCE B** From a book by G. Colmore, *The Life of Emily Davison* (1913). The Suffragette Summer Festival was a week-long meeting of hundreds of suffragettes.

'She was able to go to the [Suffragette Summer] Festival on the opening day, Tuesday 3 June. Emily was never brighter than on that day. She stayed long at the fair and said she should come every day, "except tomorrow. I am going to the Derby tomorrow".
"What are you going to do?"
"Ah ha!"
It was her usual answer... when she had planned something. "Look in the evening paper," she added, "and you will see something".'

▼ **SOURCE C** From an eyewitness, John Ervine, who stood near to Emily Davison on the day.

'The king's horse, Anmer, came up and Ms Davison went towards it. She put up her hand, but whether it was to catch hold of the reins or protect herself, I don't know. It was all over in a few seconds. The horse knocked her over with great force and then stumbled and fell, throwing the jockey violently onto the ground. Both he and Ms Davison were bleeding a lot. I feel sure that Ms Davison meant to stop the horse and that she didn't go onto the course thinking the race was over.'

▼ **INTERPRETATION D** From a history website, written by a modern historian.

'Some believed that Davison was trying to cross the racecourse and had failed to see that not all the horses had cleared the course. Other spectators claimed that they heard her shout "Votes for women" before leaping out in front of the king's horse. A crude black and white film was taken that caught the event "live"... and it shows clearly that Davison stopped in front of Anmer (therefore she did not want to simply cross the course) and it appears that she tried to make a grab for the reins of the horse.'

▼ **SOURCE E** A photograph of the incident that appeared on the front page of the *Daily Sketch* newspaper on 5 June 1913 – the day after the Derby. Look closely at the photograph.

Why do you think there were so few reliable witnesses despite the thousands of people who were there?

▼ **SOURCE F** Adapted from the writings of Davison herself. These events occurred in Holloway Prison, on 22 June 1912 during a six-month sentence for arson. She was released ten days later.

'As soon as I got the chance I threw myself over the prison railings. The idea in my mind was that one big tragedy would save many others; but the netting prevented any injury. Then I threw myself down on an iron staircase, a distance of 10 to 13 metres, but the netting caught me again. I felt I had only one chance left, so I hurled myself head first down the staircase, a distance of three metres. I landed on my head with a mighty thud and was knocked out. When I recovered I was in agony.'

▼ **SOURCE G** Part of the official report surrounding Davison's death. She had asked for the flags a few days before the race meeting.

FOUND ON THE BODY OF EMILY DAVISON OFFICIAL POLICE REPORT

2 large suffragette flags (green, white and purple stripes) pinned inside the back of her coat; 1 purse (containing three shillings, eight pence and three farthings); 8 postage stamps; 1 key; 1 helper pass for the Suffragette Summer Festival, Kensington, London; 1 notebook; 1 handkerchief; some envelopes and writing paper; 1 race card; 1 return railway ticket.

Key Words
martyr

▼ **INTERPRETATION H** From Sylvia Pankhurst's book *The Suffragette Movement: An Intimate Account of Persons and Ideals* (1931).

'Her friend declared that she would not have died without writing a farewell message to her mother. Yet she sewed the [suffragette] flags inside her coat as though to make sure that no mistake could be made as to her motive when her body was examined.'

Over to You

Imagine you are part of a government enquiry team that has been given the job of investigating Davison's death in order to arrive at a conclusion. There are two main theories about her death. Consider them both:

Theory 1 She tried to kill herself for the cause of 'votes for women', hoping to turn herself into a **martyr** in the process.

Theory 2 She wanted to make a protest by stopping the king's horse but it went badly wrong and she died as a result, in a tragic accident.

1 Reread the evidence on these pages and consider:
   a why she had two flags
   b why she didn't tell anyone what she planned to do
   c why she chose the king's horse – or did she step in front of Anmer by chance?

2 Make a list of evidence that shows Davison was trying to kill herself.

3 Make a list of evidence to show that Davison did not plan to kill herself.

4 Deliver your conclusion in the form of a report.
   • Remember to give a basic outline of Davison's death. You might include details of Davison herself and the events before she was killed.
   • State clearly if you think Davison planned to make a protest.
   • Decide if you think she planned to kill herself in the process.
   • Back up any of your conclusions with evidence.

🔄 Quick Knowledge Quiz

Choose the correct answer from the three options:

1 In which year did Queen Victoria die?

   a 1899

   b 1900

   c 1901

2 Who replaced Queen Victoria as monarch?

   a her son, Edward, who became King Edward VII

   b her son, George, who became King George V

   c her husband, Albert, who became King Albert I

3 In 1908, American Henry Ford began making what was to become one of the best-selling cars ever. What was it called?

   a Beetle

   b Model T

   c E-type

4 Who, in 1909, made the first successful flight over the English Channel?

   a Orville Wright

   b Karl Benz

   c Louis Bleriot

5 Whose report from the turn of the twentieth century discovered that nearly one third of Londoners were so poor that they didn't have enough money to eat properly?

   a Charles Booth

   b Seebohm Rowntree

   c David Lloyd George

6 Beginning in 1906, the series of new laws, ideas and measures brought in to help vulnerable people are commonly known as what?

   a the New Charters

   b the Poverty Acts

   c the Liberal Reforms

7 In which year did the *Titanic* sink?

   a 1910

   b 1912

   c 1914

8 The *Titanic* sank while crossing which ocean?

   a Atlantic

   b Pacific

   c Arctic

9 Which of the following groups was prepared to use violence to achieve 'votes for women'?

   a the suffragettes

   b the suffragists

   c the anti-suffragists

10 In which year did women finally get the same voting rights as men?

   a 1918

   b 1928

   c 1938

Literacy Focus

Defining key words and terms

As a historian, it is important that you can quickly recognise and define key terms and words. You should also be able to describe them at length.

1 Complete the sentences with accurate terms.

   a Seebohm Rowntree (of the sweet-making family) investigated the lives of _____ .

   b The Liberal Party contained energetic and ambitious young politicians such as _____ .

   c The Liberal government introduced laws to protect children; these laws became known as the _____ .

   d In order to increase the opportunities for unemployed people to find work, the Liberals opened _____ .

2 Write two definitions for each of the following words, terms, events and people.

   • For the first one, use no more than ten words.
   • The second definition can be more detailed, using up to 30 words. The first answer has been done for you:

   a Liberal Reforms

   • *Social reforms to help Britain's most vulnerable people. (8 words)*

   • *Series of reforms to help reduce poverty and protect vulnerable citizens. Legislation included the introduction of old age pensions, free school meals, sickness benefit and labour exchanges (job centres). (29 words)*

   b Consumer goods
   c Assembly line
   d Children's Charter
   e Suffragists
   f Suffragettes
   g 'Deeds not words'

Writing in detail

3 Look at the paragraph below. It is a very basic answer to the question 'Why did the *Titanic* sink?'

> Explain what the *Titanic* actually was! And what more detail could be added? What about its impressive size – or the fact it was on its first voyage? What did people say about the ship?

> The Titanic sank in the middle of the ocean in 1912. Many people were killed. There were several different factors that caused the ship to sink and resulted in so many people being killed.

> Which ocean?

> Could you add any more detail here? Month? Date?

> You need to develop this and give some examples of the different factors.

> You could add to this paragraph by writing about the number of lifeboats, for example.

> Add some detail about the number of passengers – and how many survived.

However, the answer does not contain many specific, factual details. Rewrite the paragraph to include more detail – adding names, dates, examples and facts where possible.

1 History skill: Significance

How to analyse whether something is significant in History

Key Words

significant

In History, you will study all sorts of events, developments and people from different periods. Sometimes you will be asked whether an event, a development or a person is **significant**. When you see this word, don't think that this simply means 'important'.

The spider diagram below shows you how to judge how significant something is.

SIG

Special at the time
- Was the event/person/development important at the time?
- What was its impact? How did it affect people?

Important changes
- Was the event/person/development important in long term? Were there long-lasting effects?
- Did it cause important changes?

Going on today
- Is the event/person/development still important? Is it making an impact today?
- Are they still relevant in today's world?

For this assessment, we are going to think about the significance of the Liberal Reforms that began in 1906.

1 **What do you know?** Make a list of facts that you know about the event/person/development.

2 **Impact at the time:** Consider the impact of the event/person/development at the time it happened. Make notes on how it changed things.

> **TIP:** Start by looking through your classwork on the Liberal Reforms and pages 12–15 of this book to help you. What impact did they have at the time?

3 **Long term impact:** Now think about how the event/person/development might have had an impact in the longer term. Did some of the changes last for much longer than the time of the event/person/development?

> **TIP:** Think about how the impact of the reforms continued. Have the reforms made an impact over a long period of time?

4 **Still significant today?** You should also think about our world today. Does the person/event/development still make an impact in the modern world?

> **TIP:** The final paragraphs on page 15 (called 'Long-term change?') and the 'Later on: 1941' box will help you consider this.

5 **Conclude:** It is also important to conclude your answer. In other words, you need to sum up your thoughts on the significance of the topic you have been asked to consider – in this case, the Liberal Reforms.

Assessment: Significance

Now, considering all the points on the previous page, try putting this into practice with this question:

> Explain the significance of the Liberal Reforms in the improvement of care for vulnerable people.　　　　(20)

The steps below will help you structure your answer. Use the example sentence starters to help you begin each point.

1　**What do you know?** Start with a brief explanation of what the Liberal Reforms were. Who were the 'Liberals' and what were they introducing?

> The Liberal Party was…
>
> Key individuals in the Liberal Party were…
>
> The Liberal Reforms were…　　　　(3)

2　**Impact at the time:** Next, focus on the Liberal Reforms themselves. What new laws, ideas and measures were introduced – and what impact did they have at the time?

> The Liberal Reforms included…
>
> At the time…　　　　(4)

3　**Long-term impact:** Did the Liberal Reforms make a long-term impact? Did the improvements simply end after they were introduced – or did they inspire a series of reforms that changed things over a longer period of time?

> In the longer term…　　　　(4)

4　**Still significant today?** Are the Liberal Reforms, and the impact they made, still relevant in the modern world?

> Today, the Liberal Reforms…　　　　(4)

5　**Conclude:** It's important to write a concluding paragraph that sums up what you think. Here, you are being asked to judge the significance of the Liberal Reforms in the improvement of care for vulnerable people. Are the reforms still significant? Did they make a major impact at the time – and are they still relevant in society today?

> In conclusion…　　　　(5)

2.1A Why did the First World War start?

The memorial below was built to commemorate 60 ex-students of a school now known as St James Academy (in Dudley, West Midlands), who died during the First World War of 1914–1918. Many schools, factories, sports clubs and town councils across Britain built memorials like this to record the names of men who had died fighting for their country. So what caused this war? Why is it sometimes referred to as the 'Great War'? And when, exactly, did war break out?'

Objectives

- Identify short- and long-term causes of the First World War.
- Explain how an assassination led to the outbreak of war.

First World War or Great War?

In the years before the Second World War, the conflict of 1914–1918 was generally known as the 'Great War' (or sometimes simply the 'World War'). After the Second World War began in 1939, the Great War was more commonly referred to as the 'First World War' or 'World War I'.

At the time, it wasn't called the Great War because people enjoyed themselves and had a great time; it was called the Great War because the world had never experienced a war on such a large scale before. Millions of men, split into two sides (or **alliances**), fought in desperate conditions, using the deadliest weapons the world had seen, for over four years. In total, around nine million soldiers were killed – that's over 5000 deaths every day for over four years. Such was the horror felt at this enormous **death toll** that many called it 'the war to end all wars'.

Why and how did the First World War start?

Wars usually have a number of different causes. Some causes go back a very long time, perhaps years or decades. These are called '**long-term** causes'. But some causes may have happened only recently, within days, weeks or months. These are called '**short-term** causes'. Historians often like to divide the reasons why something happened into long-term and short-term causes. The information on these pages outlines the long-term causes of the First World War.

▼ **SOURCE A** The memorial at St James Academy, West Midlands, also includes the name of a teacher who joined up to fight in September 1914. He was killed in action in France two years later, aged 31.

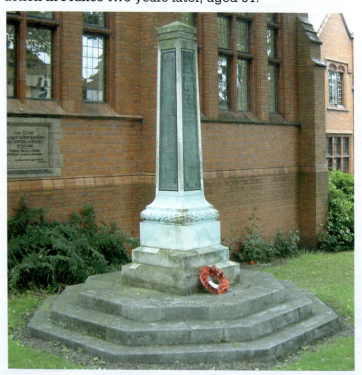

Nationalism

At the beginning of the twentieth century, people started to take great pride in their countries. Some people went a step further and felt that their country was better than others. This is called **nationalism**. Unfortunately, for many leaders of Europe, the obvious way to prove they were the best was to have a war with their rivals.

Militarism

As well as taking pride in their countries, people took great pride in their armies and navies. To make sure that theirs were the best, countries spent more and more money on huge armies and were prepared to use their forces aggressively to defend or promote the country. This is known as **militarism**. Nobody wanted the smallest army, so some countries got caught up in an **arms race**. To many, there was no point in having a big, expensive army if you weren't going to use it, and whenever countries fell out the temptation to use these forces was always there.

Key Words

alliance   ally   arms race   death toll   imperialism   long-term   militarism   nationalism   short-term

Alliances

As each country began to feel threatened, they looked for friends (known as **allies**) to back them up in a war. Europe split into two alliances. Some of the most powerful countries in Europe at this time – Britain, France and Russia – formed the Triple Entente. Other powerful nations – Germany, Austria-Hungary and Italy – formed the Triple Alliance. The idea was to put other countries off starting a war as it would mean fighting against three nations instead of one. Although this made the countries feel more secure, it meant it would only take one small disagreement between two nations in different alliances for much of Europe to be dragged into a war.

▼ **MAP B** The Alliance System in Europe, 1914.

Imperialism

Britain had conquered lots of land all over the world by 1914 and had a vast empire. But other nations wanted big empires too – a desire known as **imperialism**. The race to gain control of other nations, particularly in Africa, led to tension and fierce rivalries among European countries. They began to see each other as a threat to their empires and thought war was the only way to remove this threat.

Over to You

1 Write definitions for the following terms:
   • militarism   • imperialism
   • alliances   • nationalism

2 Look at **Map B**.
   a Make a list of the countries in:
      • the Triple Alliance
      • the Triple Entente
   b If the Triple Alliance attacked France, how could Russia's friendship help France?
   c If Russia attacked Germany, how could Austria-Hungary's friendship help Germany?

3 Some historians have compared Europe in 1914 to two groups of mountain climbers, all tied together with one rope.
   a If one climber slipped and fell, what's the best thing that could happen?
   b If one climber slipped and fell, what's the worst thing that could happen?
   c How does this compare to the situation in Europe at the start of 1914?

The short-term reason for the start of the war

Some historians have compared Europe in 1914 to a barrel of gunpowder in that it only needed a spark to make it explode. On 28 June 1914, the spark arrived. So what exactly happened on that date? And how did it lead to war?

A tragic visit to Sarajevo

On 28 June 1914, the heir to the kingdom of Austria-Hungary – Archduke Franz Ferdinand – visited the Bosnian city of Sarajevo with his wife Sophie. The small state of Bosnia was part of Austria-Hungary – but only since 1908 when it had been **annexed**. Many Bosnians were still deeply unhappy about this. They wanted to join with their neighbours, Serbia, and many Serbians wanted Bosnia to join with them. One gang of Serbians, known as the 'Black Hand', decided to take drastic action to highlight their cause – they planned to **assassinate** the Archduke. His visit to Sarajevo was the perfect opportunity.

1

Archduke Franz Ferdinand and Sophie arrived at Sarajevo train station at 9:28am. They were driven towards the town hall to meet the mayor. Crowds lined the streets and the car drove slowly so that the royal couple could wave to the people.

3

The Archduke cancelled the rest of the visit, but decided to check on those injured by the bomb before he went home. At 11:00am, he again got into the car – but it drove much faster this time! As it passed Schiller's Café, the driver was informed that he'd taken a wrong turn. He stopped to turn around.

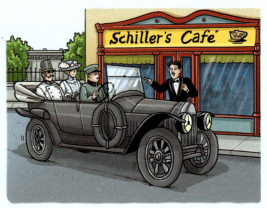

2

Seven Black Hand assassins waited for the car by the Cumurja Bridge. As the car passed, one of the Serbians threw a bomb at the royal couple. The bomb missed its target and exploded beneath the car behind, injuring several people. The Archduke's car sped off to the town hall.

4

After the bomb attack, the assassins had split up and run into the crowds. By coincidence, one gang member – 19-year-old Gavrilo Princip – was standing outside the café. He took out a pistol, walked towards the car and fired two shots. Ferdinand was hit in the throat; Sophie was shot in the stomach. Both were killed.

▶ **SOURCE C** Princip received a 20-year prison sentence for the murders. He died in prison in 1918, from a lung disease called tuberculosis.

Look at the timeline below to see how the assassination led to all-out war.

A timeline to war

28 July: Austria-Hungary blames Serbia for killing the Archduke, and attacks Serbia.

29 July: Russia, which has promised to protect Serbia against attack, gets its army ready to attack Austria-Hungary.

1 August: Germany, which supports Austria-Hungary, hears about Russian preparations for war. Germany declares war on Russia.

2 August: Britain prepares its warships.

3 August: Germany, which is more worried about the French army than about the Russian army, decides to attack France first. It declares war on France, hoping to defeat the French quickly, then turn to fight the Russians.

2 August: Germany asks Belgium to allow German soldiers to march through Belgium to attack France. Belgium says no. Germany marches into Belgium anyway.

4 August: Britain, which has a deal to protect Belgium from attack (dating back to 1839), declares war on Germany.

5 August: France declares war on Germany.

6 August: Austria-Hungary declares war on Russia.

12 August: Britain and France declare war on Austria-Hungary.

▼ **INTERPRETATION D** Adapted from *Catastrophe: Europe Goes to War 1914* (2013) by Max Hastings, a journalist and author of many military books.

'Rather than providing a genuine "cause" for the First World War, the murder of the Archduke Franz Ferdinand of Austria-Hungary was exploited to justify unleashing forces already in play.'

Key Words

annex   assassinate

Fact ✓

Italy didn't stick to the agreements it had made before the murders. Instead it joined Britain, France and Russia's side in 1915. The countries that joined with the Triple Entente members (Britain, France and Russia) together became known simply as the 'Allies'. Those that joined with the remaining Triple Alliance members (Germany and Austria-Hungary) became known as the 'Central Powers'. In total, 32 countries joined the war and the major ones lined up like this:

Allies: • Britain and its empire • France • Belgium • Italy (from 1915) • Serbia • Romania (from 1916) • Portugal (from 1916) • Russia (until 1917) • USA (from 1917) • Japan

Central Powers: • Germany • Austria-Hungary • Turkey • Bulgaria (from 1915)

Over to You

1 Read page 30 and look at the timeline of events. Why did:

  a Austria-Hungary attack Serbia?

  b Russia prepare to attack Austria-Hungary?

  c Germany invade Belgium?

  d Britain declare war on Germany?

2 The outbreak of war has been compared to a 'row of falling dominoes'. Why do you think this comparison has been made?

3 Did Gavrilo Princip start the First World War? Explain your answer carefully – you may want to discuss it and/or plan your answer with a partner first.

4 a Make a list of *all* the causes of the First World War.

  b Divide them into short-term and long-term causes.

Interpretation Analysis

1 Read **Interpretation D**. What point does the author make about the assassination of Archduke Franz Ferdinand?

2 Does the interpretation support the view that the assassination of Archduke Franz Ferdinand was a major cause in the outbreak of the First World War?

2.2 Joining up

As soon as war broke out, the British government asked for male volunteers aged between 19 and 30 to join the **armed forces**. At first, there was a great rush and by Christmas 1914 over a million men had **enlisted**. However, it soon became clear that this wasn't going to be enough. So how did the government encourage more men to join the war? What reasons did these men give for joining up? And how did the government finally solve the shortage of fighting men?

Mission Objectives

- Outline the reasons why men chose to fight.
- Define 'propaganda' and explain how the government used it to attract more volunteers.

Mind control?

A number of techniques were used to encourage and persuade men to join up. At first, a huge **propaganda** campaign was started. This meant that the government closely controlled information (a process known as **censorship**) in order to influence public opinion about the war. It allowed large news articles about battle victories to be printed in newspapers, while defeats were hardly mentioned. British soldiers were always made to look like heroes, while Germans were made to look like cruel savages. The government hoped that if people loved Britain (and hated Germany and its people), they were more likely to support the war and join up to fight. The government printed millions of propaganda posters aimed at making men either love their country and their king, feel guilty about not joining up, or hate the enemy (see **A** and **B**). The propaganda campaign had a remarkable effect: by January 1916, 2.5 million men had agreed to fight.

Pals battalions

The government thought that fighting alongside friends and neighbours, rather than strangers, might encourage more men to join up – and they were right! Rival towns competed with each other to prove how patriotic they were and formed **pals battalions**. Brothers, cousins, friends and workmates enlisted together. There were pals battalions for professional footballers, bankers and railway workers, for example. There were tragic consequences. For example, of the 720 'Accrington Pals' who fought, 584 were killed, wounded or missing during one attack. This robbed entire communities of many of their men, and no new pals battalions were created after 1916.

> **Fact** ✓
>
> Think of propaganda as a bit like advertising in newspapers and on television. However, with advertising, companies try to make you think a certain way and believe certain things about their product. With propaganda, governments and politicians try to get people to believe different things and influence opinions.

> **Fact** ✓
>
> As many as 250,000 under-18s lied about their age and served in the British Army during the war. It is thought that Sidney Lewis was the youngest. He fought at the Battle of the Somme in 1916, aged 13.

▼ **SOURCE A** This British poster shows a romantic version of Britain's countryside and asks people to fight to protect it.

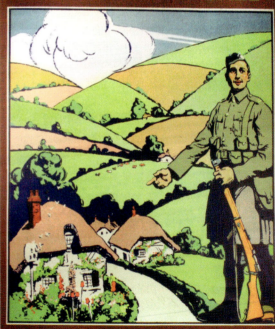

YOUR COUNTRY'S CALL

Isn't this worth fighting for?
ENLIST NOW

▼ **SOURCE B** This British poster shows a German nurse pouring water on the floor in front of a thirsty, injured British soldier. Two Germans laugh in the background. The Red Cross is an organisation that helped soldiers on both sides, and the Iron Cross is a German bravery medal.

Female pressure

Women were encouraged to persuade – or shame – men into joining up. A movement (the White Feather Campaign) was started where women handed out white feathers – a symbol of **cowardice** – to any man who seemed fit enough to fight, but was not in military uniform. This sort of public humiliation was enough to make some men join immediately (see **C**).

Causation

1 By Christmas 1914, how many people had joined the army?

2 By January 1916, how many had joined up?

3 Explain why so many people joined up to fight.

Key Words   armed forces   censorship   conscientious objector   conscription   cowardice   enlist   pals battalion   propaganda

▼ **INTERPRETATION C** S.C. Lang joined up in 1915. Adapted from *Forgotten Voices of the Great War* by Max Arthur (2002).

'I was walking down Camden High Street when two young ladies said, "Why aren't you in the army with the boys?" I said, "I'm sorry, I'm only 17" and one of them said, "Oh we've heard that one before." Then she pulled out a feather and pushed it up my nose. Then a sergeant came out of one of the shops and said, "Did she just call you a coward? Come across the road to the drill hall and prove that you aren't a coward." I told him I was 17 and he said, "What did you say, 19?"... To my amazement, I found I was soon being called Private S.C. Lang.'

Conscription and conscientious objectors

By summer 1916, the flood of volunteers had slowed to a trickle. With thousands dead and many more returning home injured, war didn't seem like such an exciting adventure. But the government still needed more men to join the war, so it introduced a new law that became known as **conscription**. This meant that any man aged between 18 and 41 could be forced to join the army. As a result, an extra 2.5 million were called up – but some men believed that war was wrong under any circumstances and refused to join up. They became known as **conscientious objectors**.

In all, there were around 16,000 conscientious objectors who refused to fight because it was against their moral or religious beliefs. However, most still joined in the war effort by working in factories or mines or carrying stretchers on the battlefields, where some lost their lives. Around 1500 people refused to have anything at all to do with the war and were sent to prison. Conditions were made very hard for them and 69 of them died in prison.

Over to You

1 Write a sentence or two explaining the meaning of:
- propaganda
- conscription
- pals battalions
- conscientious objectors

2 What are the advantages and disadvantages of pals battalions?

3 Study **Sources A** and **B**. For each one, write a sentence explaining:
- who the poster was appealing to
- how it was trying to appeal to them
- how successful you think it might have been.

4 Read **Interpretation C**.
   a What was the White Feather Campaign?
   b What was the impact of this campaign on S.C. Lang?

2.3A The First World War: an overview

The First World War was fought mainly in Europe. The areas where the armies fought each other were called **fronts**. One of the longest was the Western Front (in Belgium and France) where French, Belgian and British soldiers tried to stop the Germans advancing to the coastline of northern France. But how did they do this? What was it like fighting under these conditions? And where else did fighting take place?

Mission Objectives

- Examine the typical experience of a soldier in the trenches.
- Identify the main areas of conflict and the main features of trench warfare.

Digging in

As enemy soldiers faced each other they dug holes in the ground to protect themselves. These soon turned into deep **trenches** as they dug deeper. Soon, long lines of trenches stretched for over 640km between the English Channel and Switzerland (see **A**).

▼ **MAP A** A map of the Western Front.

Where else?

There was also fighting in the east (the Eastern Front), where Russians faced Germans and Austro-Hungarians, and in Turkey (Turkey was on Germany's side). Italy (which joined Britain's side) fought Austria-Hungary on the Italian border. The war spread to Africa and the Pacific too, as Germany's colonies were attacked by Allied forces. It was mainly a war fought by soldiers on foot (known as **infantry** soldiers), but there were a few battles at sea, and in the skies between newly invented fighter planes.

Trench warfare

The infantry soldiers spent most of their time in the trenches they had dug out to protect themselves (see **C**). The trenches were protected with sandbags and barbed wire. They were defended by men with rifles, machine guns and **hand grenades**. A few hundred metres away, the enemy did the same. In between was an area called **no man's land**, a wasteland full of bomb craters and the rotting remains of dead soldiers.

Meanwhile...

1915–1918

There were many other key battles in the war taking place around the world:

- **Gallipoli (1915–1916):** Soldiers from Britain, Australia and New Zealand unsuccessfully fought Turkish troops in Turkey.
- **Battle of Jutland (1916):** The largest naval battle of the war, between British and German battleships.
- **The Brusilov Offensive (1916):** Russian soldiers fought Austro-Hungarians on the Eastern Front.
- **The Battle of Megiddo (1918):** British-led attack on German and Turkish troops in Palestine.

▼ **SOURCE B** A painting by William Barnes Wollen showing Canadian soldiers (who fought on Britain's side) taking part in the Battle of Ypres on 8 May 1915.

Key Words front   hand grenade   infantry   no man's land   stalemate   trench

▶ **SOURCE C** These British soldiers are in a German trench they have captured in 1918.

Over to You

1 Some of the following sentences are false. Copy them all out, correcting the false ones.

   a A 'front' is an area where fighting takes place.

   b All the fighting took place in Europe.

   c The largest naval battle was the Battle of Jutland.

   d The Western Front stretched for 100km through France and Belgium.

Attack!

Occasionally, the soldiers would try to capture the enemy's trenches. The attackers would move across no man's land towards the enemy trenches and the defenders would try to pick them off with rifle fire and machine guns. For the loss of thousands of lives, one side might move forward for a week or two and gain a few hundred metres of muddy, useless ground. A week later, for the loss of even more men, they might be pushed back to their original trenches. Despite the millions of deaths, the Western Front didn't move more than a few kilometres either way in over four years of war. This was stalemate – a complete inability to move forward and a solid determination not to be pushed back.

Source Analysis

1 Look at **Source B**. Write a paragraph to describe this painting. You must write more than 20 words, but no more than 100 words.

2 How useful is **Source B** to a historian studying trench warfare?

On the front line

A soldier's basic training did nothing to prepare him for life on the front line. The deadly fire of the enemy guns forced entire armies to live almost underground for month son end. As well as the mud, the cold and the wet they lived with the knowledge that they could lose their lives at any moment.

Look at these pages and see how the First World War soldiers on the Western Front fought, lived and died.

Key battles on the Western Front

- **First Battle of the Marne (1914).** Germans fight French and British troops.
- **Battle of Verdun (1916).** Longest battle of the war, Germans fight French troops.
- **Battle of the Somme (1916).** British and French forces attack German positions near the River Somme.
- **Third Battle of Ypres (1917).** Also known as Passchendaele after the village nearby. Troops from Britain and the empire fight German soldiers.
- **German Spring Offensive (1918).** Huge German attack on British and French positions.
- **Battle of Amiens (1918).** British and French attacks on German positions.

Knowledge and Understanding

1 Write a brief definition of the term 'trench warfare'. Use no more than 15 words.
2 Describe two features of trench warfare.

Key Words   censor   shell   trench foot

① Duckboards: Placed on the ground to stop troops sinking in the mud
② Fire step: Soldiers stood on these to look and fire 'over the top'
③ Dugouts: Rooms dug out of the back wall of trenches
④ Periscope: Enabled troops to see 'over the top' without being shot
⑤ Barbed wire: Slowed down attacking troops
⑥ Machine gun: Mowed down attacking troops
⑦ Concrete bunker: Reinforced and underground
⑧ Artillery: Huge guns that fired enormous shells (bombs)
⑨ Machine gun nest: Protected machine-gunner
⑩ Sandbags: Reinforced walls, muffled explosions and soaked up moisture
⑪ Aeroplanes: Helped spot targets for artillery, dropped bombs on the enemy and shot down enemy planes
⑫ Communication trench: Linked front line trench to reserve trenches
⑬ Reserve trenches: Where soldiers went to rest or to wait to go to the front line
⑭ Gas bell: Rung to tell troops to put on gas masks
⑮ No man's land: Around 50m to 200m wide
⑯ Soldiers went 'over the top' to face the enemy on the front line
⑰ Soldiers also did guard duty, collected food, wrote letters, cooked, cleaned their weapons and repaired the trenches
⑱ Soldiers would be boiling hot in summer… and freezing cold and wet in winter; many became ill – ulcers, boils, pneumonia, dysentery and bronchitis
⑲ Spending days knee deep in water could lead to trench foot, a painful condition where the foot swells up and develops open sores, and can even rot
⑳ Keeping clean was tough, so soldiers were infested with lice, and rats roamed the trenches
㉑ Food was basic – stew, bread and hard biscuits; bacon, cheese and jam were treats but the water tasted of chlorine (used in swimming pools) which killed germs

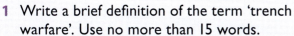

Over to You

1 a Write ten questions you would like to ask a soldier in the trenches. Cover at least:
   - daily work
   - food
   - health
   - living conditions

  b Write the answers a soldier may have given you.

2 Before any report could appear in a British newspaper, a government official would censor (cut out or delete) any information that might damage morale back home, lead to fewer people joining up to fight, or alert the enemy to British troops' movements. With a pencil or red pen, underline any information in the answers that you think would be censored.

3 In what ways has this censorship changed your answers?

2.4 Weapons of war

In the years leading up to the First World War, there had been advances in science, design and invention. Motor cars and aeroplanes had been invented and there had been breakthroughs in physics and chemistry. However, lots of these new ideas were used to create new weapons that killed and injured millions of people in the war. What were these new weapons?

Mission Objectives

- Explain why the weapons used in the First World War were so deadly.
- Judge which weapons were most effective.

Rifle

RANGE: 6/10
KILLING POWER: 6/10
DEFENSIVE ABILITY: 4/10

This long gun was lightweight so could be carried easily by soldiers. It was accurate up to 600m. A 40cm knife, called a bayonet, could be fitted onto the end. Highly trained soldiers could fire between 15 and 20 bullets per minute.

Machine gun

RANGE: 4/10
KILLING POWER: 8.5/10
DEFENSIVE ABILITY: 9/10

Invented in the mid-1800s, machine guns became recognised as one of the First World War's deadliest weapons. They could fire up to ten bullets per second. In just one day of fighting (22 August 1914), the French reported losses of 27,000 men, mostly through machine gun fire. According to British estimates, machine guns caused about 40% of all wounds inflicted on British troops during the war.

Poison gas

RANGE: 1.5/10
KILLING POWER: 3/10
DEFENSIVE ABILITY: 0.5/10

The first ever major poison gas attack was in April 1915. The Germans released gas from cylinders and allowed the wind to carry it over French

soldiers on the front line. The French panicked and ran. A 6km gap opened up in the French lines but the Germans didn't have enough men to mount a major attack. An opportunity like this never happened again but gas proved its worth as a weapon of terror. Soon both sides were using gas. There were two main types:

Chlorine gas – suffocated the lungs and left the victim gasping for air.
Mustard gas – rotted the body: skin blistered, eyes bulged. A victim would cough up the lining of his lungs in clots.

Later in the war, gas became less of an effective weapon because gas masks protected troops from the worst effects of the poison.

Grenade

RANGE: 1/10
KILLING POWER: 5/10
DEFENSIVE ABILITY: 2.5/10

These are small, hand-held bombs. After removing a pin, a soldier had to immediately throw the grenade towards the enemy, as it would explode in a few seconds. When it exploded the outer case would shatter into razor-sharp fragments, causing horrific injuries.

Flamethrower

RANGE: 1/10
KILLING POWER: 6/10
DEFENSIVE ABILITY: 0.5/10

A canister was strapped to a soldier's back which forced fuel through a nozzle. The petrol was ignited by a spark to create a sheet of flame that could travel up to 15m. These were deadly in small spaces, like dugouts, and caused panic if one was spotted during an attack. Defending soldiers would try to shoot the canister of petrol before it got close.

Earlier on...

There are accounts of soldiers using some sort of flame-throwing devices to destroy forts in wars in Ancient Greece.

Key Words

bomber   fighter
shrapnel

Tank

RANGE: 4.5/10   (if it didn't break down)
KILLING POWER: 6/10
DEFENSIVE ABILITY: 6.5/10

A British invention, tanks were bulletproof vehicles that could travel over rough ground, crush barbed wire and cross trenches. At first they were called 'landships' but were code-named tanks in an attempt to convince the Germans they were water tanks and so keep the invention secret. The name stuck! Although they caused panic and terror on the battlefield, they were very slow (6kph) and unreliable. All sides saw potential and built their own tanks, but it wasn't until the next world war that tanks became battle-winning weapons.

Fighter and bomber planes

RANGE: 10/10
KILLING POWER: 2.5/10
DEFENSIVE ABILITY: 1/10

Aeroplanes had first appeared in 1903. When fighting began, planes were very slow, clumsy and unreliable, and were used for keeping an eye on what the enemy was doing and spotting artillery. At first, pilots fired pistols and even threw bricks at each other, but soon 'fighter' planes armed with machine guns were developed. Not long after, 'bombers' were developed to fly over enemy trenches and attack them from the air.

Artillery

RANGE: 10/10
KILLING POWER: 7.5/10
DEFENSIVE ABILITY: 2/10

Artillery is another word for the large, heavy guns that could shoot bombs (shells) over long distances. It was common to bombard the enemy trenches for several hours before an attack in the hope you might kill lots of soldiers as they sheltered in their dugouts. In 1915, 400,000 shells (some as big as soldiers) were fired every month on the Western Front. Some big guns could fire shells over a distance of 21km. When the shells exploded, the red-hot metal splinters (shrapnel) would cut an enemy to pieces.

Knowledge and Understanding

1 Describe two features of First World War weapons.

Over to You

1 Copy and complete a larger version of this chart in your book.

Weapon: List the eight major weapons	Range: Short, medium or long range?	Killing power: Low, medium or high?	Is it used mainly for attack, defence or both?

2 In your opinion, which was the First World War's most deadly weapon and why? Back up your opinion with facts and figures.

3 In general, did the weapons used in the First World War make it easier for an army to attack or defend?

2.5A Why was Harry Farr killed?

The horror of trench warfare was too much for some soldiers to cope with. The constant danger of death, the relentless noise of shelling, and seeing friends being killed in terrible ways all took their toll. More and more men were diagnosed with a condition called **shell shock**. Some shook uncontrollably, while others became paralysed despite suffering no physical injury. Many had panic attacks, cried constantly or couldn't speak. How did the British Army deal with this? And what were the consequences for Private Harry Farr?

Mission Objectives

- Examine how victims of 'shell shock' were treated during the First World War.
- Decide whether Harry Farr was a coward or the victim of cruel injustice.

Diagnosis and treatment

Shell shock was first diagnosed as an illness in 1915, but doctors struggled to find a way to treat it. They tried rest, hypnosis, counselling, and even electric shocks through the brain. Many men just needed time away from the front line to recover. Unfortunately, when they did get better, they were often sent straight back to fight. Their symptoms soon returned and many ran away – unable to cope any longer. When these men were caught they were charged with **desertion** or cowardice, which were categorised as 'crimes' by the army, and some were executed (see **B**). In total, Britain shot 306 of its own soldiers for cowardice and desertion during the war. The French shot 600, but the Americans and Australians shot none of their own men. Official figures show that the Germans shot fewer than 50.

▼ **SOURCE A** A victim of shell shock photographed in a British hospital c1917–1918.

▼ **B** The sort of 'crimes' for which British soldiers could go on trial. Punishments varied, but soldiers could be executed if found guilty. This was usually done by **firing squad** – a group of soldiers who are ordered to shoot and kill prisoners.

- Being a coward (cowardice)
- Leaving a trench or position without permission (desertion)
- Disobeying orders
- Falling asleep on guard duty
- Going on strike
- Throwing away a weapon

The case of Private Farr

Your task over these four pages is to consider the case of Private Harry Farr (see **C**). He was put on trial (known as a **court martial** in the army) charged with cowardice and was found guilty. He was shot dead by firing squad at 6:00am on 18 October 1916. Was the verdict correct? Was Farr suffering from shell shock? Should he have been in hospital instead?

Farr's background

Private Harry Farr, who lived in London with his wife and baby daughter, had been a soldier since 1908. He had been fighting in France for nearly two years and, in that time, he had reported sick with his 'nerves' three times. Each time he had been sent to hospital – once for five months – and he shook so violently that a nurse had to write his letters to his wife. But, as he wasn't physically injured, he was returned to the front line each time he recovered. These adapted notes are from his court martial.

The details of Farr's trial:

- **Court Martial** at Ville-Sur-Ancre, 2 October 1916.
- **Alleged Offender:** No. 8871 Private Harry T Farr 1st Battalion – West Yorkshire Regiment.
- **Offence Charged:** Section 4. (7) Army Act: Misbehaving before the enemy in such a manner as to show cowardice.
- **Plea:** Not Guilty.

The Prosecution

(acting on behalf of the army; trying to show that Farr was guilty)

1st witness: Sergeant Major H. Haking

'On 17 September, Farr reported to me well behind the front lines. He said he was sick but had left his position without permission. He said he couldn't find his commanding officer. I told him to go to the dressing station [a small temporary hospital near the trenches]. They sent him back saying he wasn't wounded. I sent him back to the front lines.'

'At about 8:00pm, his commanding officer (Captain Booth) told me Farr was missing again. Later on I saw Farr back where I'd first seen him well behind the line.
I asked him why he was there. He said, "I cannot stand it". I told him to get back to the front line and he said, "I cannot go". I then told Booth and two other men to take him back by force. After going 500 metres, Farr began to scream and struggle. I told him that if he didn't go back he would be on trial for cowardice. He said, "I'm not fit to go to the trenches". I then said I'd take him to a doctor but he refused to go saying, "I will not go any further". I ordered the men to carry on but Farr again started struggling and screaming. I told the men to leave him alone and Farr jumped up and ran back to where I'd first seen him early in the day. He was then arrested.'

2nd witness: Captain J. W. Booth

'On 17 September 1916 at 3:00pm I told Farr to get back up to his trench. Later that evening, I could see he was missing without permission. At about 9:00pm, I saw him well away from where he should have been. Sergeant Major Haking ordered me to take him back to his trench under escort. After about 500 metres, Farr became violent and threatened the three of us. Farr was later arrested.'

3rd witness: Private D. Farrar (one of the soldiers ordered to take Farr back to his trench)

'On 17 September 1916, at about 11:30pm, I was ordered by Captain Booth to take Farr back to the trenches. After going 500 metres, he started struggling and saying he wanted to see a doctor. The Sergeant Major said he could see one later. Farr refused to go any further. I tried to pull him along. The Sergeant Major told me to let go and Farr ran off.'

4th witness: Lance-Corporal W. Form

Lance-Corporal Form said exactly the same as Private Farrar, the third witness.

Key Words

court martial   desertion
firing squad   shell shock

▼ **SOURCE C** Private Harry Farr who was executed for cowardice near the Somme, France in 1916.

Over to You

1 Write a sentence or two to explain these terms:
   - desertion
   - cowardice
   - court martial

2 How many people did the British shoot for cowardice and desertion during the First World War?

3 Up to this point, what is your impression
   - Sergeant Major Haking
   - Private Harry Farr?

After the army presented its prosecution case, it was time for Harry Farr to try to defend his actions.

The Defence

(acting on behalf of Farr; trying to show that he was not guilty)

Harry Farr was not given an opportunity to ask someone to help him with his defence. Instead, he defended himself.

1st witness: The accused, Private H Farr

'On 16 September 1916, I started to feel sick. I tried to get permission to leave the trenches but couldn't because people were asleep or unavailable. Eventually, I found Sergeant Major Haking on 17 September at 9:00am and he told me to go to the dressing station. They said I wasn't physically wounded and sent me back to my trench. I started to go but felt sick again so I told an ordinary officer where I was going and went back well behind the front line again.'

'When I saw Sergeant Major Haking, I told him I was sick again and couldn't stand it. He said, "You're a f****** coward and you'll go back to your trench. I give f*** all for my life and I'd give f*** all for yours so I'll get you f****** well shot". I was then escorted back to my trench. On the way, we met up with another group of soldiers and one asked where I'd been. Sergeant Major Haking replied, "Ran away, same as he did last night". I said to Haking that he'd got it in for me.'

'I was then taken towards my trench but the men were shoving me. I told them I was sick enough already. Then Sergeant Major Haking grabbed my rifle and said, "I'll blow your f****** brains out if you don't go". I called out for help but there was none. I was then tripped up so I started to struggle. Soon after, I was arrested. If no one had shoved me I'd have gone back to the trenches.'

Court question: 'Why haven't you been sick since you were arrested?'

Answer by Farr: 'Because I feel much better when I'm away from the shell fire.'

2nd witness: Sergeant J. Andrews

'Farr has been sick with his nerves several times.'

Character witness: Lieutenant L. P. Marshall

'I have known Farr for six weeks. Three times he has asked for leave because he couldn't stand the noise of the guns. He was trembling and didn't appear in a fit state.'

Character witness: Captain A. Wilson

'I cannot say what has destroyed this man's nerves, but on many occasions he has been unable to keep his nerves in action. He causes others to panic. Apart from his behaviour when fighting, his conduct and character are very good.'

What happened next?

The entire court martial took about 20 minutes. Soon after, the judging panel gave its verdict… guilty. They said, 'The charge of cowardice is clearly proved and the opinion of Sergeant Major Haking is that Farr is bad. Even soldiers who know him say that Farr is no good.'

On 14 October 1916, Harry Farr's death sentence was confirmed by Sir Douglas Haig, the man in charge of the British Army. He was shot at dawn on 18 October 1916. He refused to be blindfolded. According to his death certificate, 'death was instant'. He has no known grave and doesn't appear on any war memorials. At first, his widow was told he had been killed in action, but was later told the truth when her war pension was stopped. Widows were not entitled to a pension if their husband had been shot for cowardice.

The Shot at Dawn campaign

In the years after the war, many relatives of the executed men campaigned to clear their names and reputations. They believed it was the army's lack of understanding about shell shock – not cowardice – that had led to many of the men's deaths. In June 2001, a memorial to the 306 British soldiers killed by their own side was unveiled by Mrs Gertrude Harris, Private Farr's daughter. In 2006, the British government looked into the cases again and pardoned all the men who had been 'shot at dawn'.

▼ **SOURCE D** The 'Shot at Dawn' memorial at Alrewas, near Lichfield, Staffordshire, is based on a young soldier named Herbert Burden. He lied about his age to join up and, when he ran away after seeing all his friends killed in a battle, he was executed for desertion. He was only 17 years and 10 months old – still officially too young to have been in the army.

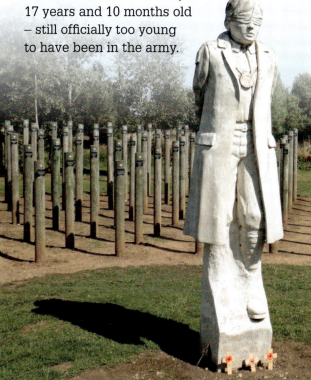

▼ **INTERPRETATION E** Adapted from a report presented at a conference in 1939, written by an official in charge of a mental health hospital in south London. The official is saying why he thinks that men suffering from shell shock should not receive compensation for their war injuries.

'There should be no excuse for believing that a nervous illness means people have a right to compensation. This is hard saying. It may seem cruel that those whose sufferings are real, whose illness has been brought on by enemy action and very likely in the course of serving the country, should be treated so harshly. But there can be no doubt that in most cases, these patients have "shock" because they get something out of it. To give them this reward is not good for them because it encourages the weaker tendencies in their character. The nation cannot call on its citizens for courage and sacrifice and, at the same time, be seen to reward unconscious cowardice or an unconscious dishonesty.'

Key Words pardon   war pension

▼ **SOURCE F** As a result of the 'Shot at Dawn' campaign, many soldiers whose names were missing from their local memorials have been added. This soldier, Joseph Bateman, who was shot for desertion in 1917, was added to the memorial in his home town of Wordsley, West Midlands, in 2008.

Over to You

1 a Write a definition of the word 'contradict'.

   b In what ways does Harry Farr's version of events on 17 September 1916 contradict Sergeant Major Haking's?

   c In what ways are the two versions similar?

   d Why do you think it is difficult for two versions of the same event to agree with each other all the time?

2 Why might Sir Douglas Haig think it was important to execute soldiers for crimes such as 'cowardice' and 'desertion'?

3 In your opinion, was Harry Farr a coward or was he suffering from shell shock? Include details from some of the witnesses in your answer.

Interpretation Analysis

1 Read **Interpretation E**. What point is being made in the report?

2 Do you think this interpretation is a fair comment on all the men suffering from shell shock? Why?

2.6 How did the First World War change medicine?

During the First World War, new and deadly weapons – high explosive shells, gas bombs, hand grenades and machine guns – were used on a massive scale for the first time, inflicting terrible injuries. Over 10 million people were killed, and even more were injured. Yet, despite the great suffering caused by the war, a number of improvements in medicine were made as a direct result. So how did the First World War change medicine?

Mission Objectives

- Examine and explain the links between war and medical progress.
- Assess the impact of the First World War on surgery, health and medicine.

Medical advances

Medicine and medical services usually develop at a greater rate during wartime than in peacetime. Governments of fighting countries spend lots of money on developing ways to get their injured soldiers back 'fighting fit' as soon as possible. If medical techniques and services are good, more soldiers have a chance of survival – and the more soldiers there are available, the greater the country's chances of victory.

Doctors and surgeons work incredibly hard in wartime, often in battlefield situations, to develop their ideas to treat the injured. The huge numbers of wounded soldiers give them more opportunity to try new techniques than is available in peacetime.

Study the image and labels carefully. They outline the impact on health and medicine brought about by the First World War.

X-rays

X-rays were discovered in 1895 and soon hospitals were using them to look for broken bones and disease. However, it was during the First World War that they became really important. Marie Curie, a Polish-born physicist and chemist, helped create mobile X-ray machines which were used in field hospitals near the battlefields. Doctors used them to find out exactly where bullets or pieces of shrapnel were in the soldiers' bodies – so they could be removed quickly and easily.

Shell shock

The horrors and exhaustion of war could cause shell shock. Some shell-shocked soldiers had panic attacks, others shook all the time and some couldn't speak or move. At first the army refused to believe that shell shock existed, and many of the men were treated as cowards. However, by the end of the war there were so many cases that shell shock was officially recognised. Today the condition is known as PTSD, or Post-Traumatic Stress Disorder.

Fact ✓

Some historians have argued that war prevented the development of medicine in some ways. After all, thousands of doctors were taken away from their normal work to treat casualties, and lots of medical research was stopped.

Plastic surgery

During the war, army doctor Harold Gillies worked out how to attach a healthy piece of skin to an injured place on a patient's body (known as a **skin graft**). His work led to the development of what we now call 'plastic surgery'. Gillies was one of the first surgeons to think about a patient's appearance when treating their wounds. Queen's Hospital in Kent opened in 1917 and provided over 1000 beds for soldiers with severe facial wounds by 1921. Over 5000 servicemen had been treated by 1921.

Blood transfusions

Injured soldiers can lose a lot of blood, which sometimes needs to be replaced. However, one of the great medical problems of the time was how to store blood properly. Doctors simply couldn't store blood for long because it clotted (formed lumps) so quickly. Then, in 1914, Albert Hustin (a Belgian doctor) discovered that glucose and sodium citrate stopped blood from clotting on contact with air. Other advances meant that blood could be bottled, packed in ice and taken to where it was needed by surgeons operating on soldiers.

Key Words   skin graft

Later on...

Archibald McIndoe (the cousin of Harold Gillies) continued to develop plastic surgery techniques. During the Second World War he used new drugs to prevent infection when treating pilots with horrific facial burns. He developed new ways of reconstructing damaged faces and hands and was known all over the world for his work.

Over to You

1   Write a sentence or two explaining the following:
    • shell shock
    • blood transfusions
    • skin graft

2   Imagine you were an army surgeon during the war. Write a short letter home explaining how the latest scientific and technological developments have helped you in your work.

3   Rank the developments in order of how much of an impact you think they made on saving soldiers' lives.

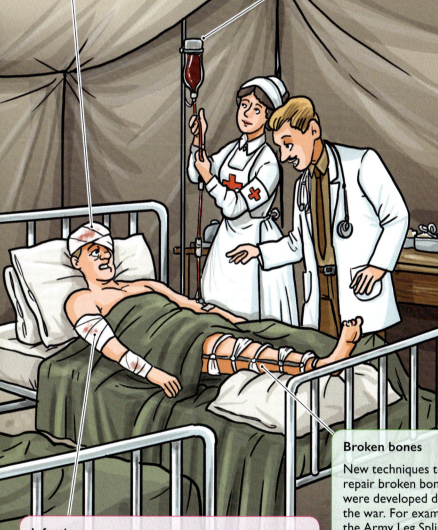

Infection

Battlefields are incredibly dirty places and deadly wound infections were common. Surgeons worked out that the best way to stop the spread of infection was to cut away any infected flesh and soak the wound in salty water. It didn't always work, but as a short-term solution in front line hospitals, it helped save many lives.

Broken bones

New techniques to repair broken bones were developed during the war. For example, the Army Leg Splint (or Keller-Blake Splint) was developed. This raised and extended the broken leg 'in traction', helping the bones join back together more securely. The splint is still in use today.

Consequences

1   Explain why wars often result in major advances and developments in health and medicine.

2   'The First World War made a huge impact on developments in surgery and medicine.' How far do you agree?

Meet Khudadad Khan – a very brave person (see **A**). So courageous, in fact, that he was awarded Britain's top bravery medal, the Victoria Cross, during the First World War. Khan was one of millions of people who weren't born in Britain, and had never even been to Britain, but joined up to fight in Britain's army. So why did Khan and millions of other people from India, Canada, Australia and the West Indies risk their lives to fight for Britain? What contribution did they make to the British forces?

Mission Objectives

- Examine why soldiers from the British Empire fought for Britain.
- Judge the contribution of these 'soldiers of Empire'.

▼ **SOURCE A** Khudadad Khan was born in what is now Pakistan. He gained the Victoria Cross in October 1914 after he was wounded, fought off a German attack with his rifle, and managed to get back to the trenches after being left for dead.

Fighting for the empire

When the First World War broke out in 1914, a great rush of men in Britain volunteered to fight 'for king and country'. But there was also lots of enthusiasm in countries that were part of the British Empire (see **B**). The British Empire was a collection of countries that were ruled by Britain, and when the war started places such as Canada, Australia, New Zealand, India, the West Indies, South Africa and other parts of Africa were all under British rule. These places were known as colonies. As a result, many thousands of people from these areas decided to join up to fight with the British (see **C**). In fact, the British forces would have struggled without them, because when war broke out there were ten times as many soldiers in the German Army as there were in the British.

▼ **SOURCE B** A wounded Sikh soldier writing home from England to his brother in Punjab, India, 15 January 1915.

'Brother, I fell ill with pneumonia and have come away from the war. In this country it rains a great deal: always day and night it rains. So pneumonia is very common. Now I am quite well and there is no occasion for any kind of anxiety … If any of us is wounded, or is otherwise ill, Government or someone else always treats him very kindly. Our Government takes great care of us, and we too will be loyal and fight. You must give the Government all the help it requires. Now look, you my brother, our father the King-Emperor of India needs us and any of us who refuses to help him in his need should be counted among the worst sinners. It is our first duty to show our loyal gratitude to Government.'

SOURCE C Sir Robert Borden, the Prime Minister of Canada, speaking on 19 August 1914. Four years earlier, Canada's previous Prime Minister had said, 'when Britain is at war, Canada is at war. There is no difference at all.'

'As to our duty, we are all agreed. We stand shoulder to shoulder with Britain and the other British colonies in this quarrel and that duty we shall not fail to fulfil as the honour of Canada demands. Not for the love of battle, not for lust of conquest, not for greed of possession, but for the cause of honour, to maintain our promises, to stand up for freedom and stop forces that would convert the world into an armed camp.'

SOURCE D A First World War recruitment poster, sent out to the British colonies. By autumn 1914 one in every three soldiers fighting for Britain in France was from India.

THE EMPIRE NEEDS MEN!

AUSTRALIA
CANADA
INDIA
NEW ZEALAND

All answer the call.
Helped by the YOUNG LIONS
The OLD LION defies his Foes.
ENLIST NOW.

Fact ✓

Some empire countries offered food to Britain in case supplies ran short because of the war. Canada offered a million bags of flour, about two million kilograms of cheese, over a million tins of salmon and 100,000 large bags of potatoes. Some offered money – the West Indian colonies handed over nearly £2 million from taxes and voluntary donations, while India contributed £150 million.

Key Words   Anzac

SOURCE E An Australian recruitment poster. The Australians and New Zealanders (collectively known as **Anzacs**) fought in some of the toughest fighting of the war, against Ottoman forces in Gallipoli, for example.

Australia has promised Britain 50,000 MORE MEN WILL YOU HELP US KEEP THAT PROMISE

Over to You

1   a   Who was Khudadad Khan?

   b   What do you think is meant by the term 'soldier of Empire'?

   c   Can you think of reasons why men like Khudadad Khan and other people from the British Empire might have joined up to fight? You might want to use **Sources B** and **C** to help you.

2   Look at **Source D**. Write a sentence or two explaining:

   a   who the 'old lion' and the 'young lions' were

   b   who the poster was meant to appeal to

   c   how it tried to do this

   d   how successful you think it was in getting men to join the British forces.

Source Analysis

1   Look at **Source E**. Which nation produced this source?

2   What was the purpose of **Source E**?

2.7B Soldiers of Empire

How many empire soldiers were there?

Around 2.5 million men from Britain's colonies fought for Britain during the war. It meant that Britain's army contained soldiers from Europe, North America, South America, Australasia, Asia and Africa.

▼ **MAP F** The British Empire at the time of the outbreak of war.

Australia: Over 400,000 Australians fought in the war. Many were involved in the fighting at Gallipoli in Turkey in 1915, alongside troops from New Zealand, Britain and France. Australian soldiers (including an estimated 1,000 **Aboriginal** and **Torres Straight Islander people**) also fought on the Western Front and in the Middle East, and some played an important role in attacks on German positions during the last few months of the war.

Canada: Over 600,000 Canadians served in the war and Canadian soldiers fought in most of the major battles, such as the Second Battle of Ypres (1915), the Battle of the Somme (1916), and at Vimy Ridge (1917) and Passchendaele (1917).

India: At the time, India included modern-day Pakistan and Bangladesh. Around 1.4 million Indians volunteered as both soldiers and labourers – the largest volunteer army the world had yet seen! Indian soldiers fought on the Western Front, in the Middle East and alongside British and Anzac troops at Gallipoli in Turkey.

West Indies: Around 15,000 West Indians joined up, including nearly 10,000 from Jamaica. Soldiers also joined up from other places in the region, including Trinidad and Tobago, Barbados, the Bahamas, Grenada, St Lucia and St Vincent. West Indian troops were mainly used as labourers – carrying ammunition, digging trenches, building roads and loading ships and trains. This work was often done under heavy fire within range of German artillery and rifles. Towards the end of the war some West Indian soldiers also fought in the Middle East against Turkish troops.

The British Empire

Africa: British colonies in Africa provided over 120,000 soldiers to fight in the war. Troops from colonies including Nigeria, Gambia, the Gold Coast (now Ghana), Kenya and Sierra Leone played a key role in fighting the Germans in East Africa and defeating them in West Africa. The colonies also supplied food and materials to the troops.

South Africa: At this time, South Africa was a very racially divided country. Around 130,000 South Africans fought in the war, with white South African troops fighting in German South West Africa (now Namibia) and East Africa. White South African soldiers also fought on the Western Front. Around 25,000 black South Africans also served on the Western Front, but mainly as labourers, working in ports and railway stations.

New Zealand: Around 100,000 New Zealanders (around one tenth of the entire population) fought in the war, including 2,700 **Māori** and **Pacific Islanders**. Soon after the war started, New Zealand troops (alongside Australians) helped in the capture of German colonies in the Pacific Ocean.

The ultimate sacrifice

At the end of the First World War, Britain's war dead numbered about 700,000. The total number of dead from around the empire was over 200,000: India lost up to 64,000 soldiers, Australia and New Zealand lost 75,000 and Canada lost 56,000. Colonial troops were involved in some of the bloodiest battles of the entire war – Ypres, the Somme, Gallipoli and Passchendaele. Colonial troops also won hundreds of medals during the war, including over 150 Victoria Crosses – the highest bravery award in the British Empire.

▼ **SOURCE G** West Indian troops stacking shells, October 1917.

Meanwhile... 1914

There was also a battle in China during the war. The Chinese port of Qingdao (Tsingtao) had been controlled by the Germans since 1898, but when war broke out British and Japanese troops attacked the Germans, determined to drive them out of the region. After intense fighting, the Germans surrendered. China supported Britain and France during the war and sent around 140,000 workers to the Western Front to dig trenches, repair machinery and transport supplies.

Key Words
Aboriginal people   Māori
Pacific Islander   Torres Strait Islander people

▼ **INTERPRETATION H** From a 2009 Channel 4 television programme presented by Ian Hislop called *Not Forgotten: 'Soldiers of Empire'.*

'Two and a half million soldiers from the Empire fought in the First World War. They made a vital contribution to the British war effort and to eventual victory. More than a quarter of a million men made the ultimate sacrifice... Before the war, people had referred to the colonies as "dependent" – but during the war, Britain became dependent on them! Without them, without the "soldiers of Empire", the British could not have won.'

Over to You

1 Complete the sentences with accurate terms:
   a Around _____ million men from Britain's colonies fought for Britain during the war.
   b Britain's army contained soldiers from five different continents. They were Europe, North America, Australasia, Asia and _____.
   c The colony that contributed most soldiers and labourers was _____.
   d Australians and New Zealanders who fought in the war are collectively known as _____.
   e _____ troops were mainly used as labourers.

2 Many people today don't know about the contribution of troops from all over the British Empire in the First World War. Why do you think this is?

3 a Read **Interpretation H**. What point is the presenter making about the contribution of the British Empire during the First World War?
   b Do you agree with him? Give reasons for your answer.

Consequences

1 Make a list of colonies, areas and regions that fought as part of the British Empire.
2 Explain the part played by British Empire colonies in the First World War.

Depth Study

2.8 What was it like on the home front?

The First World War didn't just involve soldiers, sailors and airmen. The armed forces may have been the ones who went off to fight the enemy on foreign soil, but the people left at home had their part to play too. Huge numbers of civilians had jobs that were directly involved in producing items for the armed forces, and everyone was affected by the war in some way. Some were even at risk of injury or death. So what impact did the war have on people in Britain on the **home front**?

Mission Objectives

- Describe how the First World War affected everyday life in Britain.
- Assess the effect of the First World War on the lives of women in Britain.
- Explain how and why British civilians were at risk between 1914 and 1918.

Bombs over Britain

The Germans flew huge inflatable airships – called **Zeppelins** (see **A**) – over the eastern parts of Britain, dropping bombs on towns and cities there. By the end of the war over 50 Zeppelin air raids had dropped over 5000 bombs, killing 557 people and injuring over 1300. German bomber planes attacked Britain too, and German battleships shelled seaside towns such as Scarborough and Whitby. The government issued posters showing people how to tell the difference between British and German aircraft – and warning them to take shelter if they spotted an enemy aircraft.

Less food and higher taxes

Britain was short of food during the war because German submarines and battleships were sinking the boats that brought food into the country. So the government introduced **rationing** to make sure that the food that was available was equally shared out. Each person was allowed a set amount of butter, sugar, bacon, ham, and so on.

Some goods, such as sugar, flour and meat, were in very short supply – so prices went up. The government also had to borrow millions of pounds from the USA to pay for the war, so taxes went up to pay back the loans.

▼ **SOURCE A** A German Zeppelin airship, photographed around 1916.

Women in the war

With so many men away fighting, women were needed to do men's jobs. Before long, there were lots of female bus drivers, chimney sweeps and steel makers. Thousands of women found work in shipyards, in weapons factories and with the ambulance, police and fire service. In 1915, a Women's Land Army was created so women (known as Land Girls) could work in farming, replacing men called up to the military.

Fact ✓

In 1917, Helen Gwynne-Vaughan helped to form the Women's Army Auxiliary Corp (WAAC), which supported the war effort through non-combat roles such as mechanical and office work. She went on to manage female workers in the air force, and was later made a Dame of the British Empire in recognition of her work.

▶ **SOURCE B**
A poster from 1917 urging women to join the Women's Land Army.

NATIONAL SERVICE WOMEN'S LAND ARMY

GOD SPEED THE PLOUGH AND THE WOMAN WHO DRIVES IT

APPLY FOR ENROLMENT FORMS AT YOUR NEAREST POST OFFICE OR EMPLOYMENT EXCHANGE

▼ **SOURCE C** Female aircraft engineers at work during the war.

Key Words

home front   rationing   Zeppelin

▼ **SOURCE D** Some rules set by the DORA. The rules were designed to protect sensitive information, improve production and preserve vital supplies.

It is forbidden to:
- talk about military matters in public
- spread rumours about military matters
- buy binoculars
- melt down gold or silver
- trespass on railway lines or bridges or loiter near bridges and tunnels
- whistle for a London taxi in case it is mistaken for an air raid warning
- give bread to horses or chickens
- keep homing pigeons without a permit
- buy drinks for other people in a pub

A new law

When war broke out the government introduced a new law called the Defence of the Realm Act (DORA). It gave the government the power to do whatever it felt was necessary to win the war. It could take over mines, railways and shipyards, and control what was published and said in newspapers and on the radio. To limit drunken behaviour, for example, it introduced strict pub opening hours… and even allowed beer to be watered down!

Losing a generation

Around 70 million men around the world fought in the First World War. Over eight million fought for Britain and its empire, and almost one million of these men were killed. Around two million were injured, some with injuries that changed their lives forever. By the end of the war, it was estimated that there were only 12 towns or villages in Britain that hadn't lost a man in the fighting. Some communities lost nearly a whole generation of men entirely.

Meanwhile...

1914–1918

In Russia, Bulgaria, Romania and Serbia, women served as combat troops and took part in the fighting. Maria Bochkareva, for example, created the 'Women's Battalion of Death', a Russian military unit that served at the front line from 1917.

Over to You

1 What is meant by the term 'home front'?

2 What was DORA and why do you think the British government thought it was necessary?

3 Look at **Sources B** and **C**. In what ways do they show how women contributed in the war?

4 Describe how Germany directly attacked British civilians in the war.

Change

1 In what ways did the lives of people in Britain change during the First World War?

2.9 How did 'Poppy Day' start?

1917 was a key year in the course of the war. Ordinary Russian people rebelled against their leaders and stopped fighting the Germans. Germany now focused all of its forces on the British and the French. By then, however, the USA had joined the war on Britain and France's side after (among other reasons) German submarines had sunk American ships. So what brought about the end of the war? When, exactly, did the war end? And how do we remember the conflict each year?

Mission Objectives

- Outline how the war came to an end in 1918.
- Explain how and why 11 November is remembered today.

Final attack

The Germans now tried desperately to defeat the British and French before fresh American soldiers arrived at the front line. But, despite an all-out attack and large advances, the Germans were eventually forced to retreat. Back in Germany, the ordinary civilians had reached breaking point. British battleships had been blocking supply ships from delivering food into German ports, and people were starving. There were riots all over Germany, and sailors in the German navy refused to follow orders. Then in September and October 1918, the countries on Germany's side in the war began to surrender. Eventually, Germany's king (Kaiser Wilhelm II) realised he had lost control of his country and abdicated. The government that replaced him called for a ceasefire (also known as an armistice). At 11:00am on 11 November 1918, the First World War came to an end.

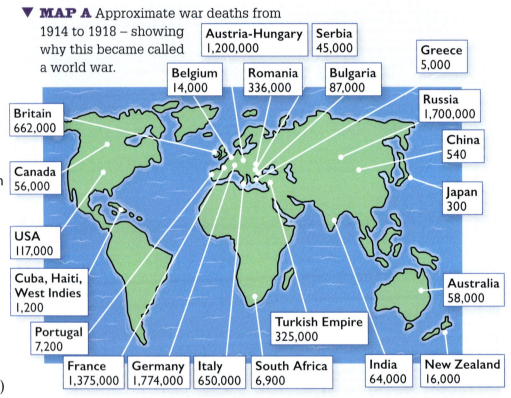

▼ MAP A Approximate war deaths from 1914 to 1918 – showing why this became called a world war.

Austria-Hungary 1,200,000
Serbia 45,000
Greece 5,000
Belgium 14,000
Romania 336,000
Bulgaria 87,000
Russia 1,700,000
Britain 662,000
China 540
Canada 56,000
Japan 300
USA 117,000
Cuba, Haiti, West Indies 1,200
Australia 58,000
Portugal 7,200
Turkish Empire 325,000
France 1,375,000
Germany 1,774,000
Italy 650,000
South Africa 6,900
India 64,000
New Zealand 16,000

Counting the cost

The war did terrible damage to the land on which it was fought. In France, where most of the fighting took place, an area the size of Wales was ruined. Buildings, roads, trees and hedgerows were destroyed. Only one living thing seemed to flourish – the poppy. For many soldiers, the poppy had become a symbol of life and hope among all the fighting. The poppy also inspired one of the most famous poems of the war (see C).

▼ SOURCE B People in London celebrating the end of the war on 11 November 1918.

► **SOURCE C** Part of the poem 'In Flanders Fields' (Flanders is an area of Belgium where fierce fighting took place). It was written in May 1915 by John McCrae, a Canadian doctor who was serving in the trenches. He was inspired to write it after attending the funeral of a friend who was killed in battle.

> In Flanders fields the poppies blow
> Between the crosses, row on row,
> That mark our place; and in the sky
> The larks, still bravely singing, fly
> Scarce heard amid the guns below.
> We are the Dead. Short days ago
> We lived, felt dawn, saw sunset glow,
> Loved and were loved, and now we lie
> In Flanders fields.

Remembering the dead

Inspired by McCrae's poem (see **C**), an American teacher named Moina Michael campaigned to make the poppy a symbol of remembrance of the war dead. Her idea caught on and by 1921 artificial poppies were sold in Britain to raise money for war widows and injured soldiers. In 1922, a factory opened to make the poppies. It was staffed by disabled ex-soldiers, and still operates today. Many people still wear poppies during the month of November every year.

Another tradition started soon after the end of the war. In November 1919, Britain's King George V received a letter from Percy Fitzpatrick, a South African author and politician whose eldest son had been killed in France in 1917. Fitzpatrick suggested that a period of silence be observed on the anniversary of the end of the war. The king agreed. Today, the two-minute silence is held on the second Sunday in November. It is called Remembrance Sunday and poppies are distributed in return for donations to help people affected by any war. Some people call it 'Poppy Day'.

▼ **SOURCE D** Poppy wreaths being made at the Royal British Legion Poppy Factory in Richmond, Surrey, 2006. Every year over 35 million poppies are distributed. The Poppy Appeal raises almost £40 million a year, which goes to help members of the British Armed Forces, past and present, and their families.

Key Words   abdicate   armistice

Later on...

The White Poppy was introduced in 1933 as a symbol of lasting peace. A Purple Poppy was introduced in 2006 to remember the animals who serve during war. In 2010, the Black Poppy was launched to highlight the contribution of black, African and Caribbean communities to the war effort. In 2018, the Khadi Poppy (khadi is a cotton cloth used in Pakistan and India) was created to recognise the contribution of soldiers from this region.

Fact

Soon after the end of the war, an outbreak of influenza (flu) swept across Europe and killed an estimated 25 million more people.

Over to You

1 a Why was 1917 such an important year in the war?

b When exactly did the war end?

c How do we remember the end of the First World War today?

2 Look at **Map A**.

a Identify the main countries that fought in the war and turn these figures into either a bar chart or a pie chart.

b Approximately how many people were killed in the war in total?

3 Look at **Source D**.

a Why did the poppy become a symbol of the First World War?

b Have you ever bought a poppy? If not, say why not. If so, explain why you bought one. Did you know how your money was used?

2.10A How did countries try to avoid any more wars?

The First World War ended in November 1918. In January 1919, the leaders of Britain, France and the USA met with other winning countries to talk about maintaining peace now that the war was over. It soon became clear that they had very different ideas about how to avoid more wars. So just what were these ideas? What did the winners decide? And did their ideas work?

Mission Objectives

- Explain who the 'Big Three' were and how they contributed to the peace settlement.
- Judge whether the League of Nations was a success or a failure.
- Examine opinions about the League of Nations.

The 'Big Three'

In January 1919, politicians from the winning countries met at the Palace of Versailles, near Paris, to decide what was to happen to the defeated countries.

The three most important politicians at the Paris Peace Conference were the leaders of France, Britain and the USA. They were nicknamed the 'Big Three' because they represented the three most powerful winning countries. Russia was not invited to the peace talks. It had dropped out of the war in 1917 after a revolution that led to a new type of government there. Most of Europe's leading politicians refused to recognise this new government. Germany was not allowed to send any politicians, nor were the other defeated nations – Austria-Hungary, the Turkish Empire and Bulgaria. At the conference, Germany was dealt with before the other losing nations.

So what did they decide?

The 'Big Three' argued about what was going to happen for many months. Eventually, in June 1919, they came to a decision. Germany's punishments were written out in a huge document called the **Treaty** of Versailles (see **B** for a summary). German politicians, sent over for the day, were told to sign the treaty… or Germany would face invasion. They signed.

▼ **SOURCE A** The 'Big Three' at Versailles

Georges Clemenceau – Prime Minister of France

- Around 1.4 million Frenchmen had been killed in the First World War and huge areas of France had been destroyed. He wanted revenge on Germany for all of this suffering.
- Wanted Germany to pay for all of the damage caused by the war.
- Wanted to weaken Germany's armed forces so they could never attack France again.

Woodrow Wilson – President of the United States of America

- The USA joined the war in 1917 and didn't suffer as much as Britain and France. Wilson wanted to prevent Germany becoming aggressive again but didn't think it should be punished too much.
- Wanted different national groups to have the right to rule themselves – this is known as 'self-determination'.

David Lloyd George – Prime Minister of Great Britain

- Wanted to keep Germany weak; but he also wanted to avoid humiliating the Germans.
- Wanted to end the German threat to the British Empire and reduce Germany's navy so it was no longer a threat to Britain's navy.

▼ **B** The treaty with Germany was signed on 28 June 1919. The other losing countries signed different treaties in which they were also fined and lost land and weapons.

Key Words treaty

Germany must pay for the war in money and goods. The figure was set at £6.6 billion. They must sign to agree that they had started the war too.

Germany to hand over colonies to Britain and France.

Parts of losing countries cut off to make new countries that wanted to run themselves.

Treaty of Versailles

League of Nations set up (1920). This was a bit like an international club that would meet regularly to talk about problems rather than fight over them. It would also work on strategies to improve the world. The winning countries would join at first – the losing countries might be allowed to join later.

Germany to have no air force, submarines or tanks. Only a tiny army (of 100,000 soldiers) and navy (6 battleships). No German soldiers allowed in the Rhineland (an area near the French border).

▼ **SOURCE C** From a German newspaper, *Deutsche Zeitung*, 28 June 1919. Vengeance means to get revenge for the harm done to you.

'Vengeance! German nation! Today in the Hall of Mirrors in Versailles the disgraceful treaty is being signed. Do not forget it. The German people will reconquer their place among nations to which it is entitled. Then will come vengeance for the shame of 1919.'

▶ **SOURCE D** A cartoon called 'Clemenceau the Vampire'. It appeared in a German newspaper in July 1919. The figure lying on the bed represents Germany. Clemenceau is shown as a vampire, sucking the blood out of Germany.

Over to You

1 Who were the 'Big Three'?

2 Why do you think these men made most of the important decisions after the war ended?

3 **a** Make your own version of the Treaty of Versailles diagram.

b Overall, which of the 'Big Three' do you think would have been most happy with the Treaty of Versailles? Explain your answer very carefully.

4 Give three reasons why the Germans may have been unhappy with the Treaty of Versailles.

Source Analysis

1 Give two things you can infer from **Source C** about German reactions to the Treaty of Versailles.

2 How useful are **Sources C** and **D** for an enquiry into attitudes in Germany towards the Treaty of Versailles?

Reactions to the Treaty of Versailles at the time

Reactions to the treaty were mixed. The 'Big Three' had conflicting ideas about what to do with Germany. By the time the treaty was signed, none of them were completely happy with it. Clemenceau wanted the treaty to be much tougher on Germany, perhaps splitting it into smaller states – but Wilson stopped this from happening. Wilson thought the treaty was far too harsh and even said that, if he were a German, he wouldn't sign it! Lloyd George, despite coming home from France to a hero's welcome, wrote that if Germany 'feels unfairly treated she will find a way of getting revenge'.

Ordinary Germans hated the treaty and the people responsible for it. They hated being forced to sign it, without having a chance to discuss its terms. Some Germans even hated their government for signing it. They said it showed how weak it was and accused their politicians of 'stabbing their own country in the back'.

Later reactions

The Treaty of Versailles has continued to divide opinion. The following interpretations are examples of these different opinions:

▼ **INTERPRETATION E** Margaret MacMillan, the great-granddaughter of David Lloyd George and a professor of international history at Oxford University, in a communication with a history website in 2004.

'It is my own view – and a number of historians who have been working in this area for some years – that the treaty was not all that bad. Germany did lose the war after all. **Reparations** apparently imposed a heavy burden but Germany only paid a portion of what it owed. Perhaps the real problem was that the treaty was never really properly enforced so that Germany was able to rebuild its military and challenge the security of Europe all over again.'

▼ **INTERPRETATION F** From a book called *Guilt at Versailles: Lloyd George and the Pre-history of Appeasement* by British historian Anthony Lentin, published in 1984. To 'pacify' is to bring peace to a country in a time of war.

'The Treaty of Versailles should have made the victors either to conciliate [settle their differences with] the enemy or destroy them. The Treaty of Versailles did neither. It did not pacify Germany, or permanently weaken her... but left her humiliated and resentful.'

The League of Nations

After the defeated countries were punished, the victorious ones turned their attentions to trying to stop wars forever. As agreed in the Treaty of Versailles, they set up a League of Nations, a kind of international club for settling problems peacefully. Its headquarters were in Geneva, Switzerland. About 40 countries joined up straight away, hoping to solve any disputes by discussion rather than war. If one nation did end up declaring war on another, all of the other member nations would stop trading with the invading country until a lack of supplies brought the dispute to an end.

The League of Nations would aim to help in other ways too. Countries would work together to fight diseases, stop drug smuggling and slavery, and improve working conditions. However, fewer than half the countries in the world joined – Germany wasn't allowed, and politicians in the USA voted against it. One major problem with the League was that it didn't have its own army to handle disputes if necessary. Yet, for a few years into the 1920s, it seemed to work well. By the end of the 1930s, however, it had failed to maintain peace in a number of areas.

Later on...

The League set up a 'Health Organization' to improve public health and combat disease. This was later renamed the World Health Organization (WHO), which still exists today.

▶ **SOURCE G** A British cartoon from a magazine published in December 1919. It is called 'The Gap in the Bridge'. The figure on the right represents the USA. A 'keystone' is one of the most important parts of a bridge because it holds all the other stones in position and supports their weight.

Key Words

reparations

THE GAP IN THE BRIDGE.

Successes of the League:

- It freed around 200,000 slaves.
- It helped over 400,000 prisoners of war return home.
- It worked hard to defeat diseases such as leprosy, cholera and smallpox.
- It sorted out a dispute between Finland and Sweden in 1920.
- It sorted out a dispute between Greece and Bulgaria in 1925.

Failures of the League:

- The League never had its own armed forces.
- The USA never joined, which made it weaker from the start, because America was so powerful.
- Japan and Italy joined at first, but eventually left. And Germany was allowed to join in 1926… but left in 1933!
- It couldn't stop Japan invading China in 1931.
- It couldn't stop Italy invading Abyssinia (Ethiopia) in 1935.
- It couldn't stop Germany from building up its weapons again and expanding its territory in Europe between 1933 and 1939.

Over to You

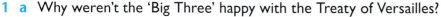

1 a Why weren't the 'Big Three' happy with the Treaty of Versailles?

  b How did the League of Nations try to stop wars?

  c Describe two weaknesses of the League of Nations.

  d In its early years up to 1939, was the League of Nations a success or not? Give examples to support your answer.

2 a Look at **Source G**. Which country is represented by the figure on the right?

  b What is a keystone?

  c Why is this keystone missing?

  d What can be learned from **Source G** about Britain's concerns about the USA failing to join the League of Nations?

Interpretation Analysis

1 Read **Interpretations E** and **F**. For each interpretation, summarise the author's opinion.

2 How does **Interpretation F** differ from **Interpretation E** about the treaty?

Quick Knowledge Quiz

Choose the correct answer from the three options:

1 The First World War was fought between which years?

   a 1914 to 1916
   b 1912 to 1914
   c 1914 to 1918

2 Which of the following countries were allies in the First World War?

   a Britain, France and Germany
   b Germany, Austria-Hungary and Turkey
   c France, Italy and Austria-Hungary

3 A person who refused to serve in the armed forces because it was against their moral or religious beliefs was known by what term?

   a conscripted objector
   b conscientious objector
   c military deserter

4 What were 'pals battalions'?

   a men who joined up together with their friends and ended up in the same group in the army
   b a special unit of the army that specialised in trench building
   c men who refused to fight and were sent to prison together

5 The areas where the armies fought each other were called 'fronts'. Which was the longest in the First World War?

   a the Western Front
   b the Eastern Front
   c the Southern Front

6 The area between the lines of trenches dug by the opposing armies was known by what term?

   a the wasteland
   b nobody's land
   c no man's land

7 Which weapon was first used in the First World War in April 1915?

   a machine gun
   b tank
   c poison gas

8 The work of which army doctor led to the development of what we now call 'plastic surgery'?

   a Albert Hustin
   b Harold Gillies
   c Alexander Fleming

9 Approximately how many people from Britain's colonies fought for Britain during the war?

   a 2.5 million
   b one million
   c 400 million

10 What was the name of the list of rules and punishments imposed on Germany at the end of the war?

   a League of Nations
   b Treaty of Versailles
   c Pact of the Somme

Literacy Focus

Chronology and spelling

1 Look at the following six statements about the events in Sarajevo on 28 June 1914. You may notice that the order of events is all mixed up and each statement contains two spelling mistakes. Write them out in the correct order, making sure you correct the spelling errors.

- Seven Black Hand assassins waited four the car by the Cumurja Bridge. As the car passed, one of the Serbians threw a bomb at the royal couple. The bomb missed its target and exploded beneeth the car behind, injuring several people.

- Archduke Franz Ferdinand and Sofie arrived at Sarajevo trane station at 9:28am.

- At 11:00am, he again got into the car – but it drove much faster this time! As it passed Schiller's Café, the driver was informed that he'd taken a wrong turn. He stopt to turn around.

- They were driven towards the town haul to meet the mayor. Crowds lined the streets and the car drove slowly so that the royal couple could waiv to the people.

- By coincidents, one gang member – 19-year-old Gavrilo Princip – was standing outside the café. He took out a pistol, walked towards the car and fyred two shots.

- The Archduke's car sped off to the town hall. The Archduke cansselled the rest of his visit, but decided to check on those injured by the bom before he went home.

Vocabulary check

2 In each group of historical words, phrases or names below, there is an odd one out. When you think you have identified it, write a sentence or two to explain why you think it doesn't fit in with the other words in its group. The first one has been done for you:

a   France   (Germany)   Russia   Britain

I have chosen Germany because this country was not in an alliance with the others. France, Russia and Britain were in the Triple Entente alliance at the beginning of the war.

b   parapet   sandbag   duckboard   France
c   volunteer   conscription   recruitment   conscientious objector
d   shell   hand grenade   bayonet   bullet
e   mud   tank   machine gun   rifle
f   Somme   Verdun   Jutland   Passchendaele
g   Austria-Hungary   India   Australia   West Indies

> **TIP:** Remember though, there might be other answers! For example, you might say that Russia is the odd one out because the other three countries stopped fighting in 1918, whereas Russia pulled out of the war in 1917. The point of this exercise is not just to get you to think carefully about the First World War, but to get you to *justify* your choices with a reason.

2 History skill: Source analysis (historic environment)

Historians need to be able to think deeply about a particular place at a particular time in history. This is sometimes known as a study of the 'historic environment'. For example, historians might examine the relationship between a place and the historical events and developments that happened there. You might be shown images of the historic environment, or sources from the time that describe it or were written by people who lived in these places or visited them.

Responding to questions about sources and the historic environment

You might get asked the following types of questions on the historic environment:

1 You might be asked to describe the features of a place, or something connected to the place.

> **TIP:** For example, name an important characteristic or part of a place or an event, and include supporting information for each.

2 You might be shown several sources, and be asked 'how useful' they are for an enquiry into the historic environment. The following steps can help you judge this:

Content: What does the source say – or show? What does it tell you about the event or person? What does it not tell you?

Caption: Where does the source comes from, or where does it originate from (also known as the 'provenance')? Use the provenance to get you thinking about the reasons why the source was created.

Context: Is the source accurate? Does it match with what you already know?

Conclude: Now judge how useful the source is.

> **TIP:** A source might be useful because it reveals something new, explains why events turned out the way they did, or reveals why people acted or thought in a particular way at the time.

3 You might also be asked how you might investigate a topic, or a place, in greater detail.

> **TIP:** Here, it might be worth pointing to other sources that you might use in your enquiry:
> - Think carefully what other sources you might you use to find out more.
> - You would also need to explain why the sources would be useful and help you in your studies.
> - Make sure you pick sources that reveal something different from the sources you have already been given.

Assessment: Source analysis (historic environment)

Your challenge is to answer three questions about sources and the historic environment:

1   Describe two features of everyday life for British soldiers serving in the trenches on the Western Front.   (4)

2   How useful are **Sources A** and **B** for an enquiry into everyday life for British soldiers serving in the trenches on the Western Front? Explain your answer, using both sources and your knowledge of the historical context.   (12)

3   How could you find out more about life in the trenches of the Western Front during the First World War? Name two sources (other than **Sources A** and **B**) you could use, and explain your reasons.   (4)

▼ **SOURCE A** A British look-out in a captured German trench in 1916; note the other soldiers asleep in the trench.

▼ **SOURCE B** Adapted from an article written by Robert Donald for the British newspaper the *Daily Chronicle*, August 1915. Donald was the paper's editor and visited the Western Front several times, reporting back on his findings.

> 'The soil is soft clay, suitable for building trenches, tunnelling, and mine warfare – when it is dry. As an outside observer, I do not see why the war in this area should not go on for a hundred years, without any decisive result. What is happening now is precisely what happened last year. The only difference is that the trenches are deeper, dug-outs better made, tunnels are longer, and the charges of explosives heavier.
>
> Everywhere there are trenches, barbed wire, machine guns where they are least expected, and all the complicated arrangements for defence. The trenches are very deep, very narrow, and very wet. Streams of water run at the bottom.
>
> You are allowed to peer through an observation post towards the German trenches a few hundred yards away. You see absolutely nothing but a mass of broken trees, hanging branches and barbed wire.'

The steps below show one way to structure your answers to each question. Use the sentence starters to help you begin each point.

1 Describe two features of everyday life for British soldiers serving in the trenches on the Western Front. **(4)**

Feature 1:	(1)
Feature 2:	(1)
Supporting information:	(1)
Supporting information:	(1)

2 How useful are **Sources A** and **B** for an enquiry into everyday life for British soldiers serving in the trenches on the Western Front? Explain your answer, using both sources and your knowledge of the historical context. (12)

Source A/B

Content:

From the content, I learned that... This is useful because... (2)

Caption:

The caption tells me... This is useful because... (1)

Context:

One thing I already know about everyday life for British soldiers serving in the trenches on the Western Front is... This (matches/doesn't match) with what the source says about... (1)

Conclude:

In conclusion, Source... is... to a study into everyday life for British soldiers serving in the trenches on the Western Front because... (2)

> **TIP:** Copy and complete the tables *for each source*. Each source is worth 6 marks.

> **TIP:** You can pick one of the phrases below that you think fits best in the sentence:
> very useful
> quite useful
> useful in some ways
> not very useful

3 How could you find out more about life in the trenches of the Western Front during the First World War? Name two sources (other than **Sources A** and **B**) you could use, and explain your reasons. (4)

I would find out more about life in the trenches of the Western Front during the First World War with this source... (1)
I would use this source because... (1)
Another source I would use is... (1)
I would use this source because... (1)

> **TIP:** It is important that you don't just think of any source – you need to think carefully about the value (or usefulness) of that source to a historian studying life in the trenches.

> **TIP:** Explain how the source would help you find out more about life in the trenches.

3.1A Was the First World War worth winning?

A few weeks after the First World War ended, Prime Minister David Lloyd George made a speech in which he promised to make Britain 'fit for heroes to live in'. Was he able to deliver what he promised? What was Britain like in the years after the war? Was the First World War worth winning?

Objectives

- Examine the state of Britain in the decade after the First World War ended.
- Judge the extent to which Britain changed.

What changed?

After the war, life in Britain would definitely never be the same again. For a start, well over half a million British men had been killed and a further two million were wounded. Many women had lost their husbands and children had lost parents. Many communities, workplaces and even sports teams must have seemed empty. In addition, many of those who came back physically fit were unable to forget the horrors they had witnessed. However, for a short time, some things appeared to return to normal. People rushed out to buy the things they hadn't been able to get during the war and some businesses did very well. But this didn't last long.

▼ **INTERPRETATION A** Adapted from the 1933 autobiography of Vera Brittain, a nurse during the First World War. Here, she tells of her sorrow after finding out about the death of her fiancé, Roland, who died during the war.

'I wondered how ever I was going to get through the weary remainder of life. I was only at the beginning of my twenties; I might have another forty or fifty years to live. The prospect seemed appalling, and I shuddered with cold and loneliness.'

Britain in decline

During the war, British factories and businesses had been totally dedicated to winning the war. They built guns, bombs and bullets, produced food and made ships. There were many jobs, and business and factory owners made lots of money. However, things started to change when the war ended. Industries that had done well in Britain during the war – coalmining, ship-building and steel-making – were not doing as well now the war was over, since there was less demand for their products. Also, countries such as Japan and the USA had started to make the things that Britain had traditionally made – so other nations started buying from these rivals, rather than Britain. All this meant that Britain's factories needed fewer workers to make the goods.

Japan and the USA had also started to produce new goods that were becoming popular, such as rayon (an artificial fibre used in clothing) and motor cars – and Britain's factories were not making these goods in huge numbers. Within a few years of the end of the war, unemployment began to rise because British factories did not need as many workers. By 1921, two million people were unemployed. This meant that one in five workers had no job (see C). In 1922, a group of unemployed ex-soldiers marched through London on Remembrance Day with a banner that read: 'From the living victims to our dead comrades – you died for nothing'.

▼ **B** The percentage of the world's resources made in the USA by around 1920. By this time the USA had become one of the world's leading producers and suppliers of raw materials.

Wheat	Iron	Electricity	Coal	Wood	Cotton	Petrol	Corn
30%	40%	42%	42%	50%	55%	70%	78%

Did things improve for British people at all?

The government *did* try to improve the lives of British people in the years after the war:

- The Education Act of 1918 set a minimum school-leaving age of 14, and children with special educational needs were recognised for the first time.

- Old age pensions were increased from 1925.

- Great effort was put into finding work for ex-soldiers, particularly those whose war injuries had left them with disabilities.

- More people than ever before could claim benefits if they lost their job.

- New laws protected tenants against large rent increases.

- Teachers' and farm workers' wages were increased.

- A 'Ministry of Health' was set up in 1919 to coordinate and improve healthcare across the country.

- Around 200,000 new homes were built that could be rented from local councils (see **D**). However, the original idea had been for 500,000 new houses to be built within three years, but this target was missed. Also, in some cases the rent was too high for the poorest people.

▼ **SOURCE C** An unemployed man on the streets of London, displaying medals he won in the war. Part of his sign reads 'ex-soldiers starve'.

▼ **SOURCE D** Some of Britain's new 'council houses', built in the 1920s.

▼ **INTERPRETATION E** Dr Gerry Oram, director of Swansea University's War and Society programmes; adapted from a BBC report dated 12 November 2018.

'Lloyd George had promised "Homes Fit for Heroes", though in reality less than 50% of the planned half a million houses were ever built. Perhaps the true legacy of the post-war reforms was to change political thinking, and set out a blueprint for future governments. The expansion of the health insurance scheme is arguably laying the groundwork for the NHS, whilst pension and unemployment provision form the foundations on which the Beveridge reforms were built a quarter of a century later.'

Fact ✓

The Tudor Walters Report (1918) listed recommendations to Parliament for new housing. For example, it set guidelines for buildings to allow enough space between them so that houses could receive enough daylight and direct sunlight.

Over to You ▪▫▫

1. a What is meant by the term 'unemployed'?
   b Why did the number of unemployed people increase in the early 1920s?

2. Summarise the ways in which the British government tried to improve the country in the years after the war. Use no more than 50 words.

3. Look at the man in **Source C**. Do you think he would have thought the war was worth winning?

4. Read **Interpretation E**. What point does the writer make about the changes made after the war?

Were there any reforms that affected women?

Perhaps the biggest change after the war was to the lives of women. Before the war, women had limited rights – and no right to vote in elections to Parliament. But during the war women took over a lot of the jobs left open when men went away to fight… and in 1918 women aged over 30 who owned property were given the right to vote (this totalled around 8.5 million women). Also, a new law made it illegal to exclude women from jobs because of their gender. As a result, more jobs became open to women and they became lawyers and politicians, for example. Then in 1928 all women over 21 were given the vote. Now women had the same voting rights as men.

However, these political reforms didn't really change the *everyday* lives of many women. After the war, when the men returned from battle, they simply went back to the jobs they had been doing before. And most of the women who had replaced the men during wartime went back to looking after the home and children. In fact, by the 1930s, women were doing much the same work as they had done before the war (see **F**), and even if they were doing the same work as men, their wages were always much less.

Good times and bad times

There were some important social changes in the years after the war – in entertainment, leisure and fashion, for example – but there was still a large amount of unrest. Unemployment remained high throughout the 1920s and there were protests and strikes over pay and conditions by shipbuilders, railway workers, engineers, and even the police. The situation was not helped by the fact that the country had borrowed lots of money to pay for the war (£1 billion from the USA) and was trying to pay it back. This meant that the government could not spend as much as it perhaps wanted to on reforms.

A General Strike

In 1926, there was a nine-day 'General Strike' when people from a range of industries went on strike in support of coal miners who were about to have their pay *reduced* and their hours of work *increased*. On 4 May, huge numbers of workers stayed at home, including bus, rail, steel and dock workers, as well as people with printing, gas, electricity, building and chemical jobs. Factories, docks and power stations came to a standstill and most buses and trains stopped running. Volunteers drove buses and trains and unloaded ships in an attempt to keep the country running (see **G**). However, before long the strikers were struggling because they weren't receiving wages any more – and so all workers (except the miners) went back to work. The miners fought on until November… and then returned to work for less pay and longer hours. In 1927, the government introduced a new law making general strikes illegal – a similar law is in force today.

▼ **F** A chart showing the proportion of women and men employed in certain industries in 1914 and in 1931.

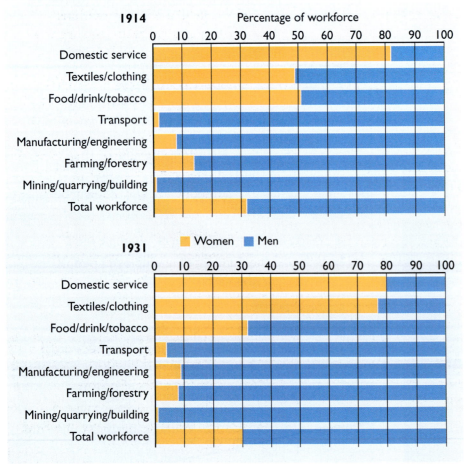

▼ **SOURCE G** A volunteer driver during the General Strike, protected by a police escort. Many middle-class British people helped out during the strike in order to fulfil their childhood dreams of being a train or bus driver!

▼ **INTERPRETATION H** Adapted from a book written by Jennie Lee in 1980. At the time of the strike she was a student at Edinburgh University. Her father, a miner, was involved in the strike. Lee later became a Scottish Labour politician who played a leading role in the foundation of the Open University.

'Although the General Strike lasted only ten days, the miners held out from April until December. Until the June examinations were over I was chained to my books, but I worked with a darkness around me. What was happening in the coalfield? How were they managing? Once I was free to go home to Lochgelly my spirits rose. When you are in the thick of a fight there is a certain exhilaration that keeps you going.

Stanley Baldwin [the Prime Minister at the time] promised the striking miners would be treated fairly when they went back to work. That was not true. My father did not get his job back – for four months he trudged from mine to mine, turned away everywhere. Uncle Michael was also treated unfairly, and so sadly he came to the decision that the only thing to do was to go off to America.'

Key Words　　　　strike

Meanwhile...

General strikes took place in several countries. In Germany, in 1920, a group of battle-hardened ex-soldiers, led by a journalist called Wolfgang Kapp, tried to take over the country – but were stopped when workers went on a general strike and refused to support them.

Over to You

1 a What was the General Strike?

   b Why did the strike take place?

   c Why can't a general strike happen again?

2 Read **Interpretation H**.

   a What happened to Lee's father as a result of him supporting the strike?

   b How useful are interpretations like this to a historian studying the impact of the General Strike?

3 a In your opinion, do you think the following people would think that all the sacrifices made during the First World War were worth it?

   • a property-owning woman in 1918
   • an unemployed worker in 1922
   • someone living in a newly built council house.

   Give reasons for your opinions.

   b Why might people have different opinions as to whether the war was worth winning or not?

Change

1 What does the chart (**F**) show?

2 How far did new policies change the lives of women in Britain after the First World War?

The 'Roaring Twenties'

The years after the war are known for periods of high unemployment, strikes and general unrest. But as memories of the war faded, many younger people were determined to live life to the full and enjoy themselves. As a result, the 1920s is sometimes referred to as the 'Roaring Twenties'. So what was life like for some at this time?

Objectives

- Define the term 'Roaring Twenties'.
- Outline why and how society changed for some people in the 1920s.

Good times?

Many people tried to forget the horrors of the First World War with nights out in dance halls, trips to local pubs and visits to cinemas. The popularity of cinemas (often called 'picture palaces') grew in the 1920s with around half the population going twice a week. Some people enjoyed spending time outdoors. Walking and camping holidays became common and large open air swimming pools (called lidos) were built in many towns and cities. The Boy Scout and Girl Guide Movements became very popular, too. Trips to the seaside were as popular as ever in the 1920s, with Blackpool in the north-west of England, for example, attracting eight million visitors a year.

▶ **SOURCE A** A photograph from 1900 of Blackpool seafront, one of Britain's most popular seaside resorts at this time. Can you see: i) key attractions – the pier, Blackpool Tower, the 'big wheel'; ii) the very crowded beach with people paddling; iii) the bathing huts near the sea where people got changed?

The BBC is born

A new source of entertainment entered many British homes in the 1920s – the radio. In 1922, the BBC was set up to 'educate, inform and entertain' and soon the radio became the 'must-have' home appliance; people listened to news, music, drama, children's shows and sports events.

The birth of the 'flapper'

During the war, many women had taken on roles traditionally done by men. After the war, most men returned to their pre-war jobs, and many women had to return to their roles as wives and mothers. For some, however, the war had given them greater confidence and they felt more able to live independent lives. This was even reflected in the way they behaved and dressed. Some women cut their hair short and wore shorter dresses. Many smoked and drank openly, drove motorbikes and wore heavy make-up. These fashionable young ladies of the 1920s were known as **flappers** (see B), possibly because of the way their arms moved when they danced.

▶ **SOURCE B** A typical flapper's clothing from the 1920s. Flappers were usually middle- and upper-class women who copied the styles and behaviour of American women of the time. For working-class women, life continued pretty much as before – they looked after families and went to work.

An American invasion?

Many of the social changes taking place in Britain in the 1920s were heavily influenced by the USA. In 1920s America, times were good for lots of people. American factories were busy and many Americans were making lots of money. This period of US history is sometimes called the 'Roaring Twenties' – and the name caught on in many countries around the world. For the first time, people in Britain began to copy American entertainment and fashions. Soon, American jazz music could be heard in British nightclubs as people danced the 'Charleston' and 'One Step' on packed dance floors. Film stars like Charlie Chaplin, Rudolph Valentino and Gloria Swanson became household names (see **C**). A few years later, cartoon characters such as Mickey Mouse and Betty Boop (a flapper) prompted a whole generation of younger viewers to flock to their local cinemas.

Meanwhile... 1920s

The Roaring Twenties is also recognised as an era in countries such as Germany, France and Australia. In France it is sometimes referred to as the 'années folles' ('crazy years').

Fact

Until 1927, all movies were silent. Words appeared at regular intervals and a piano player provided background music. Then *The Jazz Singer* was released, the first 'talking film' or 'talkie' as they were known.

▼ **SOURCE C** Gloria Swanson was one of the most famous film stars of the 1920s. This is the poster for her 1924 film *Her Love Story*.

Over to You

1 Complete the sentences with accurate terms:
   a The BBC was founded in _____.
   b Large open air swimming pools, called _____, were very popular in the 1920s.
   c The One Step and the _____ were popular dances in the 1920s.
   d The first 'talkie' was called _____.

2 What was a flapper?

3 In what ways did America influence British culture in the 1920s?

Source Analysis

1 Describe **Source A** in no more than 75 words.

2 How useful is this source to a historian studying the popularity of seaside resorts in the early twentieth century?

Independence in Ireland

Great Britain and Ireland have been closely linked for many hundreds of years. However, for a large part of this time, relations between the two places have been difficult. There has frequently been bloodshed, violence and brutality. So what exactly is the history of the relationship between Britain and Ireland? How and why did this relationship become violent? And how did Ireland end up divided in two in the 1920s?

Objectives

- Define a 'nationalist' and 'unionist'.
- Analyse how and why Ireland was divided.

Part of Britain

People from England and Scotland had been settling in and trying to rule over parts of Ireland since the twelfth century. In 1800, British politicians voted that the whole of Ireland should become part of Britain. On 1 January 1801, Great Britain and Ireland officially united to become the United Kingdom of Great Britain and Ireland. Soon all the major decisions about Ireland were being taken by Parliament in London. There was even a new flag to symbolise this 'union' (see **A**).

A united kingdom?

Many Irish people wanted more control over their country. They wanted Ireland to have its own Parliament and run itself. These people became known as **nationalists** (because of their strong desire for an independent nation). However, there were other Irish people who wanted Ireland to stay part of the United Kingdom. They were known as **unionists** (because they supported the 'union' between Ireland and Britain). The unionists lived mainly in the northern part of Ireland, called Ulster.

Easter Rising, 1916

During the First World War, some Irish nationalists saw a chance to gain independence from Britain. In April 1916, during Easter week, a group of nationalists took control of the city of Dublin (Ireland's capital) and declared independence (see **B**). The British sent in troops to deal with the situation and after five days the Easter Rising (as it was known) had been stopped.

▼ **A** The English and Scottish flags were joined after 1603 when the Scottish King James came to rule England after Queen Elizabeth I died. The red diagonal cross was added in 1801 to represent Ireland, making up the current Union flag.

Earlier on...

1801

The newly merged Parliament of the United Kingdom had its first meeting on 22 January 1801. It was made up of all 558 members of the former Parliament of Great Britain and 100 of the members of Parliament in Ireland.

▶ **SOURCE B**
The Irish nationalists used the General Post Office in Dublin as their headquarters during the Easter Rising in 1916. The building was badly damaged in the fighting.

After the Easter Rising

At the time of the Easter Rising, the nationalist rebels had little widespread support, but after 15 of them were executed by the British Army, public opinion in Ireland began to change. The Easter Rising rebels were seen by some as national heroes who had died for their beliefs and their country. An Irish nationalist political party called Sinn Féin (Irish for 'Ourselves' or 'We Ourselves') increased in popularity, and in the 1918 British general election Sinn Féin politicians won 73 seats in the British Parliament. However, they refused to go to London to sit in Parliament and instead set up their own parliament (called the Dáil), based in Dublin.

In 1919, a new armed group emerged called the **Irish Republican Army** (IRA). Supported by Sinn Féin and led by Michael Collins, the IRA's aim was to use force to drive the British out of Ireland. The IRA carried out attacks on British police and government buildings. The British government responded by sending in tough ex-soldiers known as 'Black and Tans' (because of their uniform colours) to keep order. The IRA and the Black and Tans attacked each other – and sometimes innocent civilians were wounded and killed. This period in Irish history is known as the Irish War of Independence, the Anglo-Irish War, or even the Black and Tan War.

The Anglo-Irish Treaty

Eventually, in December 1921, a treaty was agreed, ending the War of Independence. Six counties in the north of Ireland (where most people were unionists) would remain part of Britain, and be called Northern Ireland. The remaining 26 counties (where the majority were nationalists) would form the Irish Free State, which would run its own affairs, but still remain part of Britain's empire (see **C**).

The Irish Free State

The Irish Free State was established in 1922. Now Ireland was divided – and some people were happy… while others weren't. Some felt that all of Ireland should be united, while others thought the split was a sensible compromise. However, the major divisions relating to the split sparked many years of political issues and conflict.

Later on... 1949

The Irish Free State (by then, known as Éire – Irish for 'Ireland') remained **neutral** during the Second World War. In 1949, it became the fully independent Republic of Ireland and not part of Britain's empire.

Key Words

Irish Republican Army
nationalist   neutral   unionist

▼ **MAP C** Ireland after it was divided in 1921.

- • Capital city
- — Northern Ireland border

Londonderry
Antrim
Atlantic Ocean
Tyrone
Belfast
Down
Armagh
Fermanagh
Lough Neagh
Dublin •
IRISH FREE STATE (now called Éire)
Irish Sea
0   80 km

Over to You

1 **a** Explain the origins of the Union flag. You can use a diagram to help you.

   b Many people in Scotland and Ireland were not happy with the Union Flag when it was designed. Can you think of reasons for this?

2 **a** What were the key differences between a nationalist and a unionist?

   b What was the Easter Rising?

   c The Easter Rising is remembered with pride by many Irish people. Do you think it is mainly nationalists or unionists who remember it with pride? Explain your answer.

3 Explain why there are two countries within the island of Ireland.

The 'Hungry Thirties'

Today, if you asked two different people what their lives were like, you would almost certainly get two very different answers. People's lives are different, even if they live in the same country (or even the same town) in the same period of history. This was very much the case in Britain in the 1930s – a period often called the 'Hungry Thirties' because of the high levels of unemployment and poverty at the time. But is this an accurate label? Who, exactly, was 'hungry', and what caused their problems? And did some people actually live well in the 1930s?

Objectives

- Define the term 'Hungry Thirties'.
- Assess the diverse range of experiences of ordinary British citizens in the 1930s.

Look at the following views of people who lived in Britain in the 1930s.

An unemployed coal miner, 1935

Some industries haven't really recovered after the First World War. If nations want to buy coal, iron, steel or cloth they get it from other countries, or produce it themselves, rather than buy from Britain. Places where these materials were produced, like the north of England, Wales and Scotland, have been badly hit. In 1932, nearly one in five workers had no job.

Unemployed young man, 1936

The government is still paying for the war, so they have tried to save money by cutting unemployment benefit. They introduced a Means Test, sending officials to check if you had savings or any other money coming in. If you did, they cut your dole money even more! My granddad lives with us and has a small pension coming in every week. But his pension counts as income… so now we receive less dole money.

The wife of an unemployed shipbuilder, 1937

In 1929, there was a financial crisis in America that led to banks going bankrupt, factories closing and millions losing their jobs. As a result, Americans stopped buying British goods – so British factories closed and people lost their jobs. My husband lost his job as a shipbuilder – and now we can barely afford to eat.

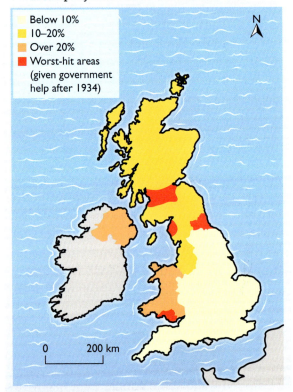

▼ **MAP A** Percentage of workers unemployed in 1937 across the UK.

Below 10%
10–20%
Over 20%
Worst-hit areas (given government help after 1934)

N

0   200 km

▼ **SOURCE B** Adapted from a BBC radio interview, 1934.

'If only he had work. Just imagine what it would be like. On the whole, my husband has worked about one year out of twelve and a half. His face was lovely when I married him, but now he's skin and bones. When I married, he was robust and had a good job. He was earning eight to ten pounds a week. He's a left-handed ship's riveter, a craft which could be earning him a lot of money.

He fell out of work about four months after I was married, so I've hardly known what a week's wage was. We don't waste nothing. And there's no enjoyment comes out of our money - no pictures, no papers, no sport. Everything's patched and mended in our house.'

▼ **SOURCE C** The 'Jarrow March', in which 200 unemployed people from Jarrow in the north-east (where two thirds of the workforce had no job) took a petition to Parliament demanding that new industry be introduced in the town. Their local MP, Ellen Wilkinson, is leading the marchers.

▼ **INTERPRETATION D** From an interview with Dr Matt Perry who is a historian of labour history and the author of a biography about Ellen Wilkinson.

'In the short term, the Crusade did not succeed in its stated goal... The response that they received in the House of Commons bitterly disappointed the marchers... In the longer term, the Jarrow Crusade along with the other protests of the unemployed during the interwar years led to a change in attitudes... The Jarrow Crusade forms part of the long tradition in this country of progress coming through the struggles for rights to work, to have a voice, to not simply accept injustice and inequality. That tradition remains relevant today.'

Key Words

dole
Great Depression

Meanwhile...

1930s

The period in history when American banks, businesses and individuals hit hard times financially is known as the **Great Depression**. And when Americans could not buy goods from abroad, factories in other countries shut down too. Millions lost their jobs in France, Italy, Germany, Japan and Britain.

Over to You

1 Look at **Map A**.
   a Which areas of Britain had the highest levels of unemployment?
   b Suggest reasons why these areas were hit harder than others.

2 Read **Source B**.
   a How has unemployment changed this family?
   b Choose five words that might best describe how the woman interviewed here might feel.

3 Look at **Source C**.
   a Why did the Jarrow March take place?
   b Why do you think the protesters chose to walk to London?

Interpretation Analysis

Read **Interpretation D**.
1 Who was Ellen Wilkinson?
2 According to the author, what was the impact of the Jarrow March?
3 If you were asked to do further research on one aspect of **Interpretation D**, what would you choose to investigate? Explain how this would help you to analyse and understand the Jarrow marchers.

As you have seen on pages 72 and 73, times were hard for many people in Britain in the 1930s… but was it the same for everyone?

▶ **SOURCE E** Car production in Coventry in the 1930s. Towns such as Coventry thrived during this time.

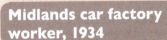
Midlands car factory worker, 1934

I hear things are bad in some areas of Britain, but I have had a steady job for years now! I work in the Midlands and make cars, which are becoming very popular and more affordable. My cousin in the south has a factory job too — he makes radios. His wages have even gone up recently. Some industries are doing very well indeed at the moment, mainly new ones that make things like cars, plastics and electrical goods.

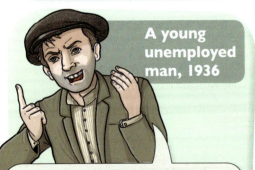
A young unemployed man, 1936

There are a few new political parties starting up that have caught my eye. One is called the British Union of Fascists and they have ideas similar to the Nazi Party in Germany. They always talk about having a stronger government that can deal with Britain's problems and reclaim our position as one of the most powerful nations in the world!

A young female doctor, 1937

All women over 21 gained the vote by 1928. It's also now illegal to exclude women from jobs because of our gender — but this law only applies to single women. A woman can still lose her job if she marries. However, thousands of women now attend university (if we can afford it) and have careers that only men were allowed to have before the war — in politics, law or medicine, for example. However, we still get paid less than men for doing the same job, and some jobs, like banking, insist on employing unmarried women.

A government official, 1938

The government is planning to remove the cuts we made to dole money and make more money available to poor areas like the north-east of England and parts of Wales. We know these areas that contain some of the more traditional industries — coal, iron, steel and cloth — are struggling because of foreign competition. We've also built nearly half a million new homes that people can rent from their local council. But we can only do so much — the war cost millions and the Great Depression means that world trade has slowed down — countries aren't buying and selling things from each other like they used to.

J.F. Aylett, a modern history writer, describing Britain in the 1930s in *In Search of History: The Twentieth Century*, written in 1986.

▼ **SOURCE G** A photograph of the fascist leader Sir Oswald Mosley giving a Nazi salute to his followers. The British Union of Fascists (BUF) never became particularly popular in Britain… but it showed that some people could be persuaded to listen to extreme ideas if they were desperate enough.

'Some industries were doing well, too, and a number of new ones had started up creating new jobs. Plastics, artificial fabrics and the electrics industry were all new and thriving.

But many of the new factories were built in southern England so job prospects were much better there than in the north. Many people in the south had no idea of how deeply the depression was affecting the other half of Britain.'

Meanwhile... `1939`

In America, the 'Golden Age' of Hollywood really got going with the first full-colour films. Dozens of classic films were made in this decade, including *Gone with the Wind* and *The Wizard of Oz* (both 1939). Also, by the end of the 1930s, around 200 movies per year were produced by the Indian Hindi-language film industry (known as Bollywood).

Fact ✓

From its beginning in 1900, the Labour Party supported social justice (fairness for all people) and was strongly supported by working-class people. The Labour Party increased in popularity in the 1920s and 1930s – and was briefly in power in 1924 and from 1929 to 1931.

Over to You

1 Look at **Source E** and read the comments of the Midlands car factory worker. Can you suggest reasons why some industries, like car manufacturing, were doing better than others in the 1930s?

2 Which areas of Britain were less affected by the depression of the 'Hungry Thirties'?

3 a What was the British Union of Fascists?

  b Why do you think it became more popular at this time?

  c Suggest reasons why the Labour Party also attracted support in the 1920s and 1930s.

Interpretation Analysis

Read **Interpretation F**.

1 Summarise how the writer describes British industry in the 1930s.

2 To what extent do you agree with this interpretation?

🔄 Quick Knowledge Quiz

Choose the correct answer from the three options:

1   Who was Britain's Prime Minister at the end of the First World War?
   a   David Lloyd George
   b   Winston Churchill
   c   Woodrow Wilson

2   Approximately how many women aged over 30 were given the right to vote in 1918?
   a   100,000
   b   3.5 million
   c   8.5 million

3   The fashionable, independent-minded young women of the 1920s, who cut their hair short and wore shorter dresses, were known by what name?
   a   objectors
   b   flappers
   c   jazzers

4   In which year was the General Strike?
   a   1929
   b   1926
   c   1923

5   In Ireland, which of the following groups supported the political unity of Ireland and Great Britain?
   a   unionists
   b   nationalists
   c   Sinn Féin

6   The Easter Rising of 1916 took place in which city?
   a   Dublin
   b   Belfast
   c   London

7   What agreement was signed in December 1921 to formally divide Ireland into Northern Ireland and the Irish Free State?
   a   Treaty of Versailles
   b   Belfast-Dublin Agreement
   c   Anglo-Irish Treaty

8   What name is commonly given to the world financial crisis that took place in the 1930s?
   a   the Big Apple
   b   the Great Depression
   c   the Roaring Twenties

9   The 1936 Jarrow March, known as the 'Jarrow Crusade', was led by which Jarrow MP?
   a   Oswald Mosley
   b   Gloria Swanson
   c   Ellen Wilkinson

10   Which British political party became increasingly popular among many working-class voters and was briefly in power in 1924 and from 1929 to 1931?
   a   Labour Party
   b   Conservative Party
   c   Liberal Party

 **Literacy Focus**

Note-taking

Note-taking is a vital skill. To do it successfully, you must pick out all the **key words** in a sentence. These are the words that are vital to the meaning (and your understanding). For example, in the paragraph:

> 'During the First World War, British factories and businesses had been totally dedicated to winning the war. They built guns, bombs and bullets, produced food and made ships. There were many jobs, and business and factory owners made lots of money. However, things started to change when the war ended. Industries that had done well in Britain during the war – coalmining, ship-building and steel-making – were not doing as well now the war was over, since there was less demand for their products. Also, countries such as Japan and the USA had started to make the things that Britain had traditionally made – so other nations started buying from these rivals, rather than Britain. All this meant that Britain's factories needed fewer workers to make the goods.'

… the important words are: During war; factories/businesses dedicated to winning; built weapons; produced food; lots of jobs/£; war ended; coalmining, ship-building, steel-making not doing as well; less demand; other countries (Japan/USA) making goods; other countries bought from them; fewer Brit. workers needed.

The original paragraph was 125 words long – but the shortened version is around 40 words long and contains abbreviations. Note-taking like this will help your understanding of events – and provides you with a great revision exercise.

1   Write down the **key words** in the following sentences. These key words are your notes.

   a   During the 1920s, the government tried to improve the lives of British people. For example, the Education Act of 1918 set a minimum school-leaving age of 14, and children with special educational needs were recognised for the first time.

   b   Old age pensions were increased from 1925 and great effort was put into finding work for ex-soldiers, particularly those whose war injuries had left them with disabilities. More people than ever before could claim benefits if they lost their job and new laws protected tenants against large rent increases.

   c   A 'Ministry of Health' was set up in 1919 to coordinate and improve healthcare across the country. Around 200,000 new homes were built that could be rented from local councils too. However, the original idea had been for 500,000 new houses to be built within three years, but this target was missed. Also, in some cases the rent was too high for the poorest people.

3 History skill: Interpretation analysis

In History, an **interpretation** is evidence from the past that is created much later than the period you are studying. Interpretations are produced by people with a particular opinion about an event in the past. For example, a historian could write an interpretation to share his or her view about a particular moment in history. Or a person (non-historian) might paint a picture, make a film, write a story or carve a sculpture that shows a particular viewpoint after the events have happened.

Analysing an interpretation

When analysing an interpretation, a good historian should firstly work out what is being said, or what message the person who created the interpretation is trying to get across. You may then be asked how far you agree with the interpretation. To do this, you will have to think about all you have learned about the topic mentioned in the interpretation, and then decide how much you agree with what the person creating the interpretation has written. Here is one way to do this:

1 **Think about the content:** First you need to understand what the person is saying and/or showing in the interpretation. What is the content of **Interpretation A** saying?

TIP: Read through the interpretation carefully. What point is the author making about the subject?

2 **What do you already know?** Now that you understand what the interpretation is saying, think about what you already know about the topic, event or person that the interpretation refers to.

TIP: You could approach this question in different ways. You could:
- make a mind-map or spider diagram of the topic, event or person
- make a quick list of what you can recall about the topic, event or person.

3 **Judge how far you agree:** This is about how much (or to what extent) you agree with an interpretation. You should use information from the interpretation and your own knowledge to help you judge and explain your answer.

TIP: You could pick one of the phrases below that you think fits best with your judgement of how much you agree with the opinion in the interpretation:

strongly agree…

agree a little…

agree to a certain extent…

don't agree very much…

agree somewhat…

TIP: Does the content of the interpretation 'fit' with what you know?

TIP: It's OK if you don't agree with the interpretation – it's just important that you explain why.

Assessment: Interpretation analysis

Your challenge now is to answer this question about analysing an interpretation:

 How far do you agree with **Interpretation A** about the impact of the Depression on ordinary people in Britain? **(20)**

▼ **INTERPRETATION A** Josh Brooman, a historian, writing in a GCSE school history textbook, *People in Change*, published in 1994.

'The 1930s is often remembered as a period of depression but it was also a period when people in Britain were able to expand their experiences and improve their lives. The BBC gave people radio and then television, and by 1939 there were 80,000 television sets in London alone. The number of people going on holiday increased immensely. Hotels and boarding houses, fish and chip shops, ice-cream stands, fairgrounds and dancehalls all expanded. The holiday camps flourished, the most famous being Butlins in Skegness.'

The steps and sentence starters show one way to structure an answer to this question.

1 **Think about the content:** First you need to understand what the person is saying and/or showing in the interpretation. What is the content of **Interpretation A** saying?

> In Interpretation A, the author writes...   (5)

2 **What do you already know?** Now that you understand what the interpretation is saying, think about what you already know about the topic, event or person that the interpretation refers to.

> Britain in the 1930s was a time when...   (5)

3 **Judge how far you agree:** This is about how much (or to what extent) you agree with the interpretation. You should use information from the interpretation and your own knowledge to help you judge and explain your answer.

> My overall impression of the 1930s is that...   (4)
>
> This (does/does not) fit with what the author of Interpretation A writes because...   (3)
>
> Therefore I (strongly agree/agree) with Interpretation A because...   (3)

TIP: When answering assessment questions, especially the ones worth lots of marks, it is important to think carefully about spelling, punctuation and grammar.

TIP: Think about the author. He is a historian who has studied this period in detail.

TIP: What do *you* know about the 1930s? This is where you refer back to your studies of this period.

TIP: Here, the author challenges the typical view of the 1930s. Do you agree with the author? If you do, how far do you agree? If not, what do you think?

TIP: What impression does the author try to give of 1930s Britain?

TIP: Try to summarise their view.

TIP: You can quote the interpretation if you like, but make sure you use your own words as well.

TIP: In the same way that the author of the interpretation has done, try to sum up your own view of the 1930s. Look at your notes/pages 72–75 to help you.

TIP: What do you know from what you have studied about this? Does the interpretation back up what you know, or not? You are using your own knowledge here.

TIP: This is where you sum up 'how far' you agree. Do you agree 'fully' or 'partly', for example? Explain why. What makes you think what you think?

Democracy and dictatorship

No two countries in the world are run in exactly the same way. For example, Britain's laws and ways of doing things are different from France's, and both are different from the USA's. It's not just laws that are different; there are also different punishments (some countries have the death penalty, for example), currencies, systems of education and healthcare – even the side of the road you drive on! But despite the differences, it is possible to place most countries into one of two categories. So what are these categories? What are the main differences between the two? And which would you prefer to live in?

Objectives

- Describe the differences between a democracy and a dictatorship.
- Identify the main features of each type of government.

Post-war problems

The major powers that were on the winning side in the First World War (Britain, France and the USA, for example), all had something in common – they had similar types of government. They were all **democratic** countries. These nations hoped that democracy would spread to most countries in the world.

However, many other countries struggled to remain democratic. They were in such a mess after the war that politicians were not able to sort out the major issues facing them. Their politicians seemed to spend more time arguing with each other than solving problems. As a result, in some countries, one person would gain the support of a political party – or even seize power in a rebellion against other politicians – and take complete control. This person is known as a **dictator** – and a country that is controlled by a dictator is called a **dictatorship**.

So what are the key differences between a democratic government and a dictatorship?

Type of government

Democracy

Origins: The word 'democracy' is from the Greek word dēmokratiā (*demos* meaning 'people' and *kratos* meaning 'rule'). The idea of democracy started in Ancient Greece in the middle of the fifth century BC. It developed gradually over hundreds of years, mainly in Europe and the USA.

Beliefs: The basic idea is that ordinary people have a say in how their country is governed. They vote in regular elections in which there are several political parties to choose from. The people are represented by the organisations they elect – for example, Parliament or councils.

Rights: The people usually have a number of 'freedoms' or rights:

- freedom of speech (the right to say what you think)
- freedom of information (the right to read, listen to and watch what you want)
- freedom of belief (the right to follow any religion)
- freedom in law (the right to a fair trial – if arrested, you have the 'right to remain silent' too!)
- freedom of association (the right to join or form a political party, or join a trade union or any other organisation).

Examples of democracies in the 1920s and 1930s: Britain, France and the USA

This government is a joke!

I completely disagree with you – but I'd fight to the death to defend your right to say it!

Type of government

Dictatorship

Origins: The word 'dictatorship' is from the Latin word 'dictare' (meaning 'dictate' or 'to give orders, or tell someone exactly what they must do'). The position of dictator first came about during the Roman Empire. It gave a person absolute power to rule in times of emergency, such as during a rebellion. But after the empire ended, it wasn't until the late nineteenth century that some countries were recognised as 'dictatorships'. Dictators are usually backed up by large numbers of supporters (and weapons).

Beliefs: In a dictatorship, ordinary people have no say in how their country is run. There are no regular elections because the country is run by one political party or one person – the dictator (usually helped by a close circle of people and a personal army).

Rights: People have very few 'freedoms' or rights:

- no free speech (if you criticise your leaders, you are likely to be arrested)
- no freedom of information (the dictator controls the newspapers, books, magazines, films, and so on)
- not all religions are allowed
- no legal freedom (the police can arrest you if they want, when they want and keep you in prison without trial)
- people can only join groups or associations allowed by the dictatorship.

Examples of dictatorships from the 1920s and 1930s: Italy, Spain, USSR (Russia) and Germany

This government is a joke!

NO ELECTIONS (this year or any other) signed The Dictator

Key Words   democratic   dictator   dictatorship

Meanwhile...   1919–1939

Between 1919 and 1939, over 30 countries became dictatorships, including Hungary (1920), Portugal (1926), Brazil (1930) and Cuba (1933).

Over to You

1 a Work with a partner. You must each choose to describe either a dictatorship or a democracy. Explain to your partner the political system you have chosen. They must fully understand what a dictatorship or a democracy is by the end of your presentation. You can use only 20 words, but you can also use drawings or mime to help you.

   b Now write up two descriptions, using a maximum of 20 words to describe a democracy and 20 words to describe a dictatorship.

2 Compare a democratic system with a dictatorship. In what ways are they different?

3 a Which political system best describes the country you live in? Explain your answer.

   b Do you know a country with the opposite political system?

Knowledge and Understanding

1 Describe two features of the democratic system of government.

Britain, France and the USA were the major victorious nations in the First World War. They were all democratic countries. They hoped that other countries around the world would become democracies too. But many countries rejected democracy and turned to dictatorship – two types of which emerged. So which countries became dictatorships? What were the two types of dictatorship called? And what are the differences between the two?

Objectives

- Define both 'fascism' and 'communism'.

- Explain where and how these two extreme political beliefs took hold.

Theory of communism

Communism is a theory about how to run a country. It was thought up by two Germans, Karl Marx and Friedrich Engels, in the 1840s. They wrote several books about their ideas, and over the years these have been read by many millions of people.

Marx and Engels believed that conflict between the different classes in society has been one of the most important things in history. They said that in recent times, the powerful, rich owners of factories, land and businesses had been treating the ordinary working classes like slaves. They felt that the workers did all the hard work, while the rich got richer and even more powerful.

They went on to say that one day, the workers would rise up and get rid of the rich, landowning class. Then, they said, there would be no different classes – no very rich and no very poor. Money and goods would be shared out equally and countries would be run so that everyone was equal too. There would be no need for money, or even laws, because everyone would live a simple life, sharing all they had with each other.

Not surprisingly, many poor ordinary workers liked the ideas of Marx and Engels – a communist life sounded a lot better than the one they had! In fact, in the 1800s people in several countries rebelled against their leaders and tried to set up communist countries – but they all failed. And then the Russians tried in 1917…

▼ **SOURCE A** A French picture from 1891. It shows Marx holding his book, *Das Kapital*, and pointing to a bright communist future.

Case study 1: The USSR/Russia

Key Words communism

The first country in the world to adopt the communist system was Russia (which from 1922 was known as the USSR). During the First World War, nearly two million Russian soldiers had been killed and there had been massive food shortages in the cities. In 1917, a turbulent year of revolution (in which Tsar Nicholas II abdicated) resulted in a communist takeover. Russia officially became a communist country on 1 September 1917, and the Tsar and his family were executed in 1918.

Although Marx and Engels had written a great deal about how a communist society would work, they didn't explain exactly how one could be set up. Not everyone in Russia was keen on the changes taking place so the communists forced people to be equal and to share. They ran the country as a dictatorship.

- No other political parties were allowed to exist, only the Communist Party.

- Newspapers, books, films and radio broadcasts were controlled by the communists. Anyone who spoke out against the party could be sent to prison (or executed). Millions of people 'disappeared' in communist Russia.

- Nobody was allowed to have any open religious beliefs. People were encouraged to believe in the communist way of life only.

- Most work, housing, healthcare and education was controlled by the communists. Jobs, houses, hospitals and schools were provided for all Russians. The state owned everything… and provided for everyone.

For many Russians, this was a much better way of life than what they were used to. Everything was provided for them as long as they were prepared to work and didn't complain. However, communism terrified many people in other countries – especially the rich and members of royal families. Their worst nightmare was that communism would spread to their countries. As a result, the USSR had few friends around the world and became more isolated.

▼ **SOURCE B** Marx died in 1883 and Engels died in 1895, both in London. An inscription on Marx's grave reads: 'Workers of all lands unite'. In the years following their deaths, Marx and Engels' ideas became more and more popular around the world – these statues are in Berlin, Germany.

▶ **SOURCE C** The flag of the USSR. In 1922, Russia, together with the smaller countries it controlled, was renamed the Union of Soviet Socialist Republics (USSR). 'Soviet' is the Russian word for council and 'socialist' is similar in meaning to 'communist'.

Fact ✓

The flag of the USSR (see **C**) tells a story: the red background represents the revolution and the golden star represents power. This power is now controlled by the factory workers (represented by the hammer) and the farm workers (represented by the sickle). In reality, the power was controlled by one person – the leader of the Communist Party.

Over to You

1 What led to the end of the Russian royal family?

2 a Sum up communism in no more than 50 words. You could work with a partner if you like.

  b Define what is meant by the term 'dictatorship' (see page 80 – or use the glossary).

  c Why was communist Russia/USSR classed as a dictatorship?

3 Write a sentence or two about the symbolism on the USSR flag. You could draw the flag in your books and label it with your ideas.

4 Why do you think richer people across Europe feared the spread of communism?

As you know, there are two main ways to run a country – as a democracy (where the people vote for leaders) and as a dictatorship (where there is one strong leader or group). So far (on pages 82 and 83) we have looked at one type of dictatorship – communism (in the USSR) – so now it's time to look at another, known as **fascism**.

Case study 2: Italy

Italy had fought on the winning side in the First World War. Over 600,000 Italians had been killed and the government hoped that this sacrifice would be rewarded with land from the losing countries. They were wrong – Italy gained hardly any new land at all.

In the years after the war, Italy suffered with high unemployment and rising food prices. A series of different governments seemed unable to do anything about this. Added to this, groups of armed bandits (many of them ex-soldiers) roamed the countryside stealing and murdering. Those Italians who weren't suffering were terrified that communists might take over and confiscate their money and belongings.

A new leader

Increasingly, Italians began to turn to a young politician called Benito Mussolini – a former soldier and schoolteacher. He promised to bring discipline, glory and pride back to Italy, but at a price. He believed in an idea called fascism and formed a political group, the Fascist Party, in 1919. The idea behind fascism was that the country would be much stronger if everybody worked together – under the leadership of one person – rather than for themselves or the class they belonged to.

A takeover

In 1922, Mussolini (who wanted to be called 'il Duce' – the Leader) announced he was marching to Rome to take over the country. His supporters – known as 'blackshirts' because of their uniforms – marched with him and made a strong impression on the king. The king gave in and made Mussolini Italy's new Prime Minister. Soon, all opposition was banned and anyone found to be a communist was beaten or murdered.

Controlling the people

Mussolini's new fascist government controlled every aspect of people's lives – clearly working as a dictatorship, but in a different way from Russia's communist government. Education, newspapers, films, radio and even sport all carried the same message: the needs of one person are not important; it's what Italy needs that counts. People were still free to run their own businesses and make money, but there were tight controls on the workers and strikes were banned. In return, the Fascist Party would 'look after' Italy and build roads and railways, which gave people jobs. Those still unemployed could join the army, which would be greatly increased in size.

Unlike communists, fascists didn't believe in equality. They believed that men were superior to women and that some races and nations were superior to others. Mussolini argued that Italians were superior and used the Ancient Romans – whom he viewed as a great civilisation – as evidence to support this. People seemed to like being told they were the best and the Fascist Party was very well supported.

Meanwhile... 1922

Mussolini's tactics didn't go unnoticed by a 34-year-old up-and-coming politician living in Germany. His name was Adolf Hitler. A year later, Hitler would attempt to take over Germany.

▶ **SOURCE D** Italy's fascist flag used during the Second World War. The eagle is a traditional symbol of power and alertness, while the bundle the eagle is clutching is called a 'fascio'. The bundle of sticks represents strength in numbers, unity and law – the axe symbolises power.

▼ **SOURCE E** Mussolini making a speech to a huge crowd in Rome, Italy, January 1935.

Key Words   fascism

Over to You

1   Write a sentence or two about the symbolism on Italy's fascist flag. You could draw the flag in your books and label it with your ideas.

2   Match up the names on the left with the correct description on the right.

- fascism
- communism

- Mussolini
- USSR

- Karl Marx
- fascio

- the fascist leader of Italy who took control in 1922
- from 1922, this was the new name for Russia and the areas it controlled
- one of the symbols of Italy's Fascist Party
- a political system where all people are equal and all property and business is owned by the state and run for the benefit of all
- writing partner of Friedrich Engels
- a political system where the government controls all aspects of people's lives in an attempt to make the nation stronger than others

3   **a**   Explain two ways in which the dictatorships in the USSR and in Italy were different.

   b   Explain two ways in which they were similar.

Fact   ✓

The word 'fascism' comes from 'fascio' meaning 'a bundle of sticks', often tied up together with an axe. In 1919, Mussolini founded a fascist political party in Milan, which became the National Fascist Party two years later.

Causation

1   Which side was Italy on in the First World War?

2   Explain why Mussolini became popular in Italy after the end of the First World War.

4.3A What was Germany like in the 1920s?

In November 1923, in Germany, a 34-year-old ex-soldier who had fought in the First World War tried to take over the country. His name was Adolf Hitler. With around 2000 loyal supporters, he took control of government buildings in Munich (in southern Germany) and made plans to march to the country's largest city (Berlin) and take over the nation. However, the attempted takeover (which became known as the Munich **Putsch**) was a complete failure. Hitler was arrested and sent to prison. But why did Hitler choose that moment to attempt his revolution? What was Germany like at this time? And how did Germany change in the 1920s?

Objectives

- Describe the changes taking place in Germany in the 1920s.
- Examine Hitler's attempted takeover of Germany.

Germany after the war

Towards the very end of the First World War, Germany's all-powerful emperor (Kaiser Wilhelm II) ran away from the country, never to return. Many ordinary Germans were now thoroughly sick and tired of the war into which he had taken Germany. There were riots and rebellions across the country, and millions were close to starvation.

After the Kaiser left, a new government took over and immediately asked for an end to the war. However, despite the war coming to end, the new government still faced a series of major problems. For a start, the country's factories, farms and mines had been exhausted by the war and the country was almost bankrupt. A series of bad harvests meant that there was little food – and the riots continued.

The government was also criticised for agreeing to the Treaty of Versailles, a series of punishments imposed on Germany by the winning countries (see pages 54–57). The punishments meant that Germany had to pay compensation (reparations) to the winning countries. It also had valuable land taken away and its armed forces were greatly reduced.

Enemies of the government

The new government was not popular with many people, who felt that it was doing little to solve the country's problems. Several groups felt they could improve things – and tried to remove the government by force.

The Spartacists

A small group of communists (see pages 82–83) called **Spartacists** tried to take control in January 1919. For a short time they took over important buildings in Berlin, but the government sent in a group of 2000 tough ex-soldiers known as the **Free Corps** to attack the Spartacists and end the revolt. After three days of brutal street fighting, the Spartacist leaders were arrested and murdered, and the revolt was over.

Fact ✓

Christianity was the biggest religion in Germany at this time. Around one third of Germans were Catholic (20 million people) and two thirds were Protestant (40 million). The Jewish community was small (less than one per cent). Jewish people had been living in German lands for around 1600 years and they were fully integrated into Germany society. They tended to be middle class (doctors, lawyers etc.) and many were **secular** in practice.

The Kapp Putsch

In March 1920, a journalist named Wolfgang Kapp managed to convince the Free Corps to help him try to take over Germany. This rebellion against the German government became known as the Kapp Putsch ('putsch' is a Swiss German word meaning 'a sudden blow' or 'rebellion'). Kapp and the Free Corps managed to get control of Berlin, but didn't have the support of ordinary workers, who went on strike and refused to help him. After just a few days, Kapp gave in and fled abroad – and the government was back in control.

More problems

Despite the fact that the German government had managed to stop the rebellions and remain in power, the problems continued. In 1923, a severe financial crisis in Germany meant that prices increased very, very quickly (known as hyperinflation). German money became practically worthless. People had to carry their wages around in shopping bags and wheelbarrows, but still couldn't really afford a cup of coffee or a loaf of bread (see **B**). It was at this time that Hitler tried to take over Germany.

▼ **INTERPRETATION A** Frieda Wunderlich, a German journalist, economist and politician, speaking in 1960.

'As soon as I received my salary I rushed out to buy the daily necessities. My daily salary, as editor of the periodical *Soziale Praxis* [a weekly magazine], was just enough to buy one loaf of bread and a small piece of cheese or some oatmeal. An acquaintance of mine came to Berlin with his monthly salary to buy a pair of shoes for his baby; he could only buy a cup of coffee.'

▼ **SOURCE B** Children playing with packs of paper money notes in Germany, 1923. The money had so little value that they could use it as building blocks, since it would hardly buy anything at all.

Key Words   Free Corps
hyperinflation   putsch
secular   Spartacist

Weimar Germany

Each time the different groups tried to take over Germany, the government left Berlin for the safety of a small town called Weimar, around 300km southwest of the city. As a result, between the end of the First World War and up to the time that Hitler eventually took over Germany (1933), Germany is often known as 'Weimar Germany'.

Over to You

1 Define the following terms:
   a Free Corps
   b Spartacists
   c putsch

2 What was 'hyperinflation'?

3 Read **Interpretation A**. According to the writer, what impact did hyperinflation have on her (and her friend)?

4 a Look at **Source B**. What is happening in the photograph?

   b How useful is this source to a historian studying the impact of hyperinflation?

Knowledge and Understanding

1 Describe two problems faced by the German government in the years 1919 to 1923.

2 Describe two problems faced by ordinary Germans in the years 1919 to 1923.

Who was Adolf Hitler?

Adolf Hitler was born in Austria, near to the German border, in 1889. He had wanted to be an artist, so he moved to Vienna (Austria's capital) but failed to get into the famous art school there. For a short time, he lived in a homeless hostel and earned money any way he could – painting houses, cleaning windows and drawing and selling small postcards in the streets. In 1913, he left Austria to avoid being forced to join the Austrian army, and went to live in Munich, Germany. However, a year later, he decided to join the German army and fight in the First World War. Many people saw him as a brave soldier – he won several medals, including the Iron Cross, Germany's highest award for bravery.

Hitler was in hospital when the war ended in 1918 (he had been temporarily blinded in a gas attack) and was disgusted with the German government for surrendering. He called them 'November Criminals' and claimed that they had 'stabbed Germany in the back' by giving up and agreeing to the punishments set out by the winning countries (see **C**).

▼ **SOURCE C** From the first volume of a book written by Hitler called *Mein Kampf* (meaning 'My Struggle'), published in 1925.

'Everything went black before my eyes; I... threw myself on my bunk, and dug my burning head into my pillow. So it had all been in vain. In vain all the sacrifices; in vain the hours in which, with mortal fear clutching at our hearts, we did our duty; in vain the death of two million who died. Had they died for this? Did all this happen only so that a gang of wretched criminals could lay hands on Germany? ... hatred grew in me, hatred for those responsible for this deed. Miserable and degenerate criminals!'

Hitler's hatred

Hitler did not invent the hatred of Jews, but this hatred dominated his thinking. He exploited anti-Jewish feelings that had been around for a long time. Whilst Hitler lived in Vienna between 1907 and 1913, hatred of Jews was very common in the city – and Vienna's mayor was openly anti-Jewish. At the end of the war and without foundation, Hitler blamed Jews for Germany's defeat. He was obsessed with a false belief that Jewish bankers and businessmen had not done enough to help the country. By blaming the Jews, Hitler created a stereotypical enemy that he continued to blame for all of Germany's problems in the coming years.

The Nazi Party

After the war, Hitler joined one of the many political groups in Germany that claimed they could make the country strong and powerful once more. The group was called the German Workers' Party and Hitler soon became its leader. He changed the name to the National Socialist German Workers' Party (or Nazi Party, for short). Soon Hitler made the swastika the Nazi symbol and used brown-shirted 'storm troopers' to beat up those who disagreed with him when he made speeches (see **D**).

▼ **SOURCE D** Hitler with his storm troopers. Like many political organisations at this time, the Nazi Party had its own private army. The 'brownshirts', as they were nicknamed, beat up people who criticised Hitler and the party. Note the 'crooked cross' or swastika symbol on their arms. It became Germany's official symbol in 1935.

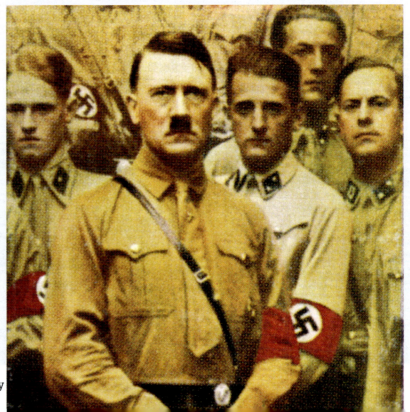

The Munich Putsch

Hitler's views made him popular and in November 1923, when the country was suffering badly from the hyperinflation crisis, he tried to take over Germany. Helped by around 2000 storm troopers, he attempted to seize control of Munich and then go on to Berlin to gain control of the whole country. However, the Munich Putsch (as the attempted takeover became known) wasn't organised properly and failed. Hitler was arrested and sentenced to five years in prison for treason – a crime which usually carried the death penalty. He was released after 9 months.

Hitler, the writer

While in prison, Hitler wrote a book about his life and his ideas called *Mein Kampf* (German for 'My Struggle'). When he was released in 1924 (for good behaviour), Hitler went back to running the Nazi Party. After the failure of the Munich Putsch, he decided that he needed to get into power legally so he tried to get people to vote for him in elections, rather than taking over through revolution. But over the next few years, Hitler and the Nazi Party failed to attract many votes or get elected. This was mainly down to the changes taking place in Germany at this time.

Germany recovers

From the mid-1920s onwards, Germany had slowly begun to recover. The government organised large loans from America, and new factories, houses, hospitals, schools and roads were built. Some US companies (such as Ford and Gillette) set up factories in Germany. By the late 1920s, unemployment figures in Germany were lower than in Britain!

There were no attempts to take over the government between 1924 and 1929. Hitler found it increasingly difficult to persuade Germans they needed him as their saviour when the country was doing so well. In 1924, about three per cent of Germans voted for the Nazis. By 1928, their support had dropped again, and they were even less popular with voters. But this would all change.

Weimar culture

Some people called the late 1920s a 'golden age' for Germany. German artists, writers, poets, designers and performers became known for their creativity and style. A night out in Berlin – cinemas, nightclubs, beer halls, theatres and galleries – was meant to be one of the finest experiences in the world!

▼ **INTERPRETATION E** From *Germany* by Jon Nicol and Robert Gibson (1985). This piece was written by a German poet who lived in Berlin in the 1920s.

'Theatres, opera and concert houses were filled to capacity. European artists from Paris, London and Rome who came to Berlin were excited by it and didn't want to leave. The atmosphere was electric.'

▶ **SOURCE F**
German-born actress Marlene Dietrich became a worldwide star playing glamorous, strong-willed women. This poster is from a 1930 film called *Der Blaue Engel* ('The Blue Angel').

Over to You

1 Complete the sentences with accurate terms.
   a Hitler was born in 1889, in _____ .
   b In 1913, Hitler left Austria and moved to _____ .
   c After the war, Hitler joined a small political party called _____ .

2 Who were the 'brownshirts' and how did they help Hitler?

3 Read **Source C**.
   a According to the source, how did Hitler react to Germany's surrender?
   b Suggest a reason why Hitler might call the politicians who ended the war 'November Criminals'.

4 Suggest reasons why the Nazi Party failed to gain much support between 1924 and 1929.

Change

1 In what ways did Germany change during the 1920s?

4.4 Why did Hitler become so popular?

In 1928, Hitler and the Nazis were the eighth most popular political party in Germany. They got only 800,000 votes in elections, with less than three per cent of the population voting for them. Few Germans would have thought that Hitler could ever become leader of Germany. Yet, by July 1932, the Nazis got nearly 14 million votes. A year later Hitler became Chancellor (Prime Minister). How did Hitler and the Nazis become so popular?

Objectives

- Explain the growth of the Nazi Party in the late 1920s and early 1930s.

- Examine key factors in Hitler's rise in popularity.

There was no single reason why Hitler and the Nazi Party's popularity grew. A number of different factors (or reasons) combined to help Hitler become Germany's Chancellor.

1 Hitler was a brilliant speaker

Hitler held large public meetings (sometimes called 'rallies') to tell people about his ideas for a better Germany. These had magnificent marching displays, loud music and powerful speeches. Hitler's booming voice, piercing stares and fearsome temper thrilled his audiences.

▼ **INTERPRETATION A** Adapted from a book by Alan Bullock called *Hitler: A Study in Tyranny* (1962).

'As a speaker, Hitler had obvious faults. His voice was harsh, he went on too long, he lacked clarity and sometimes lost himself. However, this didn't matter because of the force and passion in his voice, the intensity of hatred, fury, and menace conveyed by the sound of the voice alone without regard to what he said. One of his secrets was his ability to sense the mood of a crowd. He was skilled at finding their hidden passions, hatreds and desires.'

▶ **SOURCE B** Hitler would often film and photograph himself practising speeches, without an audience. He would then spend lots of time studying the pictures. These images were taken in 1933.

2 The Great Depression hit Germany hard

In 1929, world trade began to slow down and a 'Great Depression' started, as countries stopped buying from and selling to each other. German factories closed and millions lost their jobs. Lots of people lost their homes and streets were full of starving people looking for work. Hitler started to propose solutions to all Germany's problems. He promised jobs to those who voted for him. As more and more people lost their jobs, the Nazis got more and more votes.

3 Hitler and the Nazis were well organised

After Hitler failed to take over Germany by force in 1924 (the Munich Putsch – see page 89), he decided to change tactics. He wanted to win power legally, by winning votes in elections – but first he had to turn the Nazis into a proper political party. So:

- Nazi Party offices were set up all over Germany to recruit more followers.

- The Nazis used new media like radio broadcasts and cinema news reports to spread their beliefs. They also bought newspapers and printed millions of leaflets and posters.

- The Hitler Youth Organisation was set up in 1926 to encourage younger followers.

4

German voters were unhappy with the Weimar government

Hitler and the Nazi Party gained votes because many ordinary Germans were unhappy with the current politicians. Several different Chancellors were appointed, but they couldn't solve Germany's problems and unemployment remained high. For many people, the democratic system did not seem to be working. They started to be drawn towards political parties with more extreme ideas about how to run the country.

▼ **C** A graph showing unemployment in Germany and the number of votes the Nazis were receiving in elections.

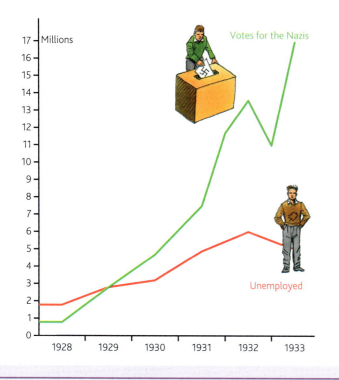

5

Hitler gained support from worried Germans

In 1917, there had been a communist revolution in Russia. The Communist Party took over all businesses, factories and farms. Many ordinary Germans were frightened of communists taking over Germany too. Hitler said he would fight communism, which gained him support from the middle and upper classes (business owners, landowners, factory owners, and so on). He sent his private army, the storm troopers, to fight communist gangs.

Hitler in power

By July 1932, the Nazis were the most popular political party. So the President of Germany (the highest political position) asked Hitler to become Chancellor – even though he didn't particularly like him. The role of Chancellor was Germany's second highest political position. Hitler accepted the position on 30 January 1933. Just over a year later the President (Paul von Hindenburg) died and Hitler took over his job as well. Hitler decided on the simple title of **Führer** – the leader.

Key Words   Führer

▶ **SOURCE D**
A poster from 1932 urging Germans to vote for Hitler. The words translate to 'Our last hope: Hitler'.

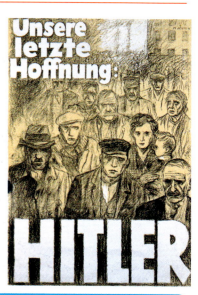

Over to You

1 Look at **Source B**.
   a What is Hitler doing?
   b Why do you think he did this?

2 Look at chart **C**. In your own words, explain what it shows.

3 Look at **Source D**.
   a Who was this poster designed to appeal to?
   b What does this poster tell us about the tactics used by the Nazis to increase their popularity?

Causation

1 Make notes on how each of the following helped the Nazis to become more popular:
   a Hitler's abilities as a speaker
   b the Great Depression
   c unhappiness with the current politicians
   d fear of communism
   e the organisation of the Nazi Party.

2 'The main reason for the increase in popularity of the Nazis was Hitler's talents as a public speaker.' How far do you agree with this statement? Explain your answer.

4.5A What was life like in Nazi Germany?

On 17 August 1934, shortly after the death of Germany's President Paul von Hindenburg, Hitler visited a large group of shipbuilders in Hamburg, northern Germany. He told them that he alone was now the supreme leader of Germany and that he wished to devote his whole life to one task: 'making Germany free, healthy and happy once more'. So what did he do? What changes did he make? To what extent were Germans 'free, healthy and happy' under Hitler's rule?

Objectives

- Assess how life changed for Germans under Nazi rule.
- Explain how the Nazis justified the way they ruled.

Work and bread

Over six million Germans were out of work when Hitler came to power. In his election campaigns, he had promised the voters 'work and bread' if he became leader. The Nazis set up a number of schemes, programmes and organisations to get people back to work and keep the party popular.

First was the National Labour Service, set up in 1935, which gave young men aged between 18 and 25 jobs in the countryside such as digging ditches and planting trees. They wore uniforms and lived in camps, and were given free meals and a small wage. The Nazis also provided work building roads, schools, hospitals and railways… and in making the army bigger and building tanks, fighter planes and battleships. The impact of all this was dramatic – and unemployment figures began to drop rapidly.

However, the Nazis used other methods to reduce unemployment. For example, women who gave up work to have a family were not counted in official figures. Also, the Nazis actually created jobs by sacking people. For example, many Jews were fired from their jobs, and were replaced by unemployed non-Jews. The Nazis then didn't count these newly-unemployed Jews in their figures.

Fact ✓

There were also cheap holidays, theatre trips and football match tickets if workers met production targets. These were organised by the 'Strength through Joy' programme. However, an organisation called the Labour Front controlled German workers strictly – for example, trade unions were banned, and wages were set by the Nazis.

▼ **SOURCE A** Recruits to the National Labour Service, pictured at a camp in 1942, holding spades.

▶ **SOURCE B** A 1938 poster advertising the 'people's car' or 'Volkswagen'. Built by Ferdinand Porsche (who went on to design sports cars), it was based on a sketch by Hitler himself. Hitler introduced a savings scheme to help millions of ordinary Germans save up for this practical, reliable, affordable car. However, not one ordinary German got their car; the money was used to build weapons instead.

The treatment of women

In Hitler's eyes, a woman's most important job was to have children – lots of them. Women were encouraged to stay at home and be good wives and mothers, and getting qualifications and a professional job were frowned upon. Loans were given to newly married couples – the equivalent of a year's wages – to encourage them to have children. Every year, on 12 August (the birthday of Hitler's mother), the Motherhood Medal was awarded to women who had the most children.

▼ **SOURCE C** A Nazi poster from 1937 showing a woman's role in life – to have babies, be a partner for her man and go to church. Hitler thought the ideal woman should concentrate on the 'three Ks' – Kinder, Kirche and Küche (children, church and cooking).

Fact ✓

The birth rate in Nazi Germany increased – around 970,000 babies were born in 1933, rising to 1,413,000 by 1939.

▼ **SOURCE D** Adapted from a 1934 speech by Joseph Goebbels, a leading Nazi.

'Women have the job of being beautiful and bringing children into the world. The female bird prepares herself for her mate and hatches her eggs for him. In exchange, the mate takes care of gathering the food and stands guard to keep away the enemy.'

Getting the message across

Hitler was determined to control how people thought. The Nazis controlled all newspapers, films, radio, plays, cinema and books – and made sure they put across Nazi ideas. One of Hitler's most trusted supporters, Joseph Goebbels, was put in charge of propaganda and censorship. He placed loud speakers on the streets so that people could hear Hitler's speeches while shopping, and ordered all books written by Jewish or communist authors to be destroyed. He banned jazz because it was played mainly by black American musicians, and had a war film destroyed because it showed a drunk German sailor. The death penalty was even introduced for telling an anti-Hitler joke.

Over to You ▫▪▪

1 Look at **Source C**. Why do you think the Nazis approved of this poster?

2 How did Hitler create jobs?

3 What effect do you think the creation of lots of jobs had on his popularity?

4 a Why do you think Hitler put someone in charge of propaganda and censorship?

   b Why do you think he gave the job to one of his most trusted friends?

Change

1 In what ways did the Nazis change the lives of workers in Nazi Germany?

Nazi racism

Like many people across Europe at the time, Hitler believed that humans were divided into races and some races were superior to others. Hitler said that Germans belonged to a 'master race' he called **Aryans** – and were the rightful rulers of Europe. He felt the superior races (like the Germans) needed to remain 'pure' and not mix with other races. He said that Germans had the right to dominate 'inferior' races, such as Jews, Roma and Sinti (sometimes known as 'Gypsies') and Slavs (such as the many peoples of Eastern Europe).

People who were disabled or had learning difficulties were also targets because Hitler thought they damaged the 'purity' of the German race. He thought these people should be dealt with so their illnesses and disabilities could not be passed on to their children. Around 400,000 men and women from families with **hereditary** illnesses were made to have operations to **sterilise** them; and thousands of people with learning difficulties were killed.

The Nazis and sport

Sport, health and physical fitness were important to the Nazis, so success in sport was used to promote Nazi ideas. The Olympic Games were held in Berlin in 1936, so the Nazis used this as an opportunity to show the world what they saw as the superiority of Nazi Germany. During this period, posters and newspapers showing racism against Jews were taken out of circulation. The Games were wildly popular and, to Hitler's great joy, the German Olympic squad came top of the medals table. This, Hitler claimed, showed how talented and strong the German race was and how it was superior to other 'inferior' races. World-respected film-maker and Nazi supporter Leni Riefenstahl filmed the entire Games – the first time TV cameras had been used in this way. The Germans also used the Games as a chance to show the brilliance of German technology – the most advanced 'photo-finish' equipment was in use and the main stadium contained the largest stop-clock ever made.

▼ **SOURCE E** A Nazi poster from the 1930s that attempts to justify the idea of killing people with hereditary illnesses and diseases. It reads: '60,000 Reichsmark is what this person suffering from a hereditary defect costs the community during his lifetime. Fellow Germans, that is your money too.'

▼ **SOURCE F** The England football team at football match in 1938 in Berlin, Germany, giving a Nazi salute before the match.

Meanwhile...

Judith Kerr fled Germany with her Jewish family in 1933. She later became a famous children's book writer and wrote about their escape in her book *When Hitler Stole Pink Rabbit*.

Pre-war Jewish life

In countries such as Britain and Germany, many Jews were **assimilated** into the country in which they lived. In fact, the vast majority of Jews in Germany at this time saw themselves first as Germans. Just like any other people, they felt their identity was made up of all sorts of things – their families, careers, interests, and much more. However, when the Nazis gained power, Jews were simply defined by the fact that they were Jews.

Nazi terror

Hitler was determined to stay in power, so his secret police, the dreaded **Gestapo**, hunted down anyone who might be against him. They could arrest and imprison people without trial, and set up a web of informers to report anyone who wasn't a loyal Nazi. Children were encouraged to report on their parents or teachers if they spoke out against the Führer. By 1935, every block of flats or housing estate had a 'local ruler' who listened for negative comments. By 1939, there were well over 100,000 people in prison for 'anti-Hitler crimes'.

Fact ✓

Once Hitler was in power, he moved quickly to gain complete control. He managed to get the Reichstag (the German Parliament) to give him the power to make his own laws. Soon after, he banned all other political parties.

▼ **SOURCE G** An incident reported in the Rhineland area of Germany, July 1938.

'In a German café, a 64-year-old woman remarked to someone sitting near to her: "Mussolini [leader of Italy] has more political sense in one of his boots than Hitler has in his brain." The remark was overheard and five minutes later the woman was arrested by the Gestapo who had been alerted by telephone.'

▼ **SOURCE H** Based on a news article in the *Daily Express*, a British newspaper, in November 1936. It was written by David Lloyd George, a respected and popular politician, who had been Britain's Prime Minister between 1916 and 1922.

'I have just returned from a visit to Germany... I have now seen the famous German leader and something of the great changes he has made... Whatever one may think of his methods – and they are certainly not those of a parliamentary country – there can be no doubt that he has achieved a marvellous transformation in the spirit of the people, in their attitude towards each other and in their social and economic outlook... One man has accomplished this miracle. He is a born leader of men.'

Fact

Hitler didn't run Germany on his own. He needed help – lots of it. Hitler himself was lazy, got up late and rarely read through official documents. He left much of the work to his loyal 'inner circle' of followers who worked on the details of his grand plans and put them into practice. Martin Bormann, Joseph Goebbels, Hermann Goering, Reinhard Heydrich, Heinrich Himmler and Joachim von Ribbentrop were some of his main officers.

Over to You

1 Write definitions for the following words:
   • hereditary
   • sterilise

2 Why do you think that Hitler was so pleased with:
   a the Olympic Games of 1936
   b the visit of the England football team in 1938?

3 Look at **Source E**. Why do you think the Nazis ordered posters like this to be produced?

4 Read **Source G**.
   a What was the Gestapo?
   b What does this source tell you about the role of ordinary Germans within the police state?

Source Analysis

1 Read **Source H**. In your own words, explain how you think Lloyd George felt about Hitler.

2 What do you think Lloyd George might have been shown on his visit to Germany that made him believe that a 'marvellous transformation' had taken place?

3 What things in Germany do you think Lloyd George *wasn't* shown on his visit?

4 What do you think Lloyd George meant when he wrote that Hitler's methods of ruling Germany were 'certainly not those of a parliamentary country'?

5 How useful is **Source H** to a historian studying attitudes to Germany of some politicians at this time?

Growing up in Nazi Germany

Hitler wanted young people to be loyal to him and the Nazi Party. He realised that in future he may have to call on them to fight and perhaps die for him. He needed young men who were 'as fast as a greyhound, as tough as leather and as hard as steel'. He wanted strong, practical girls too, so they could grow up to be the wives and mothers of a future generation of soldiers. To help achieve their aims, the Nazis changed Germany's school system (see **I**, **J** and **K**).

Outside school, young people had to belong to a Nazi youth organisation from the age of ten, though some participated from the age of six. Boys and girls were in separate groups and spent a few evenings a week and several weekends a year learning new skills and being taught how to show their loyalty to Hitler. Boys tended to learn military skills (model making, shooting practice and hiking), while girls learned mainly about cookery, housework and motherhood.

However, not all young Germans liked what they saw of the Nazi way of life and some refused to join up. Some formed their own gangs – which were harshly dealt with if discovered by the Nazis.

▼ **I** A typical day's timetable at a mixed school in Berlin, 1936. **Eugenics** is the study of how to influence or 'improve' the mental and physical characteristics of the human race.

	Lesson 1	Lesson 2	Lesson 3	Lunch	Lesson 4	Lesson 5	Lesson 6
Boys	German	History/ Geography	Eugenics/ Nazi Theory	Sport and music clubs	Physics and Chemistry	PE: boxing, football and marching	Maths
Girls	German	History/ Geography	Eugenics/ Nazi Theory		Biology/ health and sex education	Cookery	Maths

▼ **SOURCE J** Many school textbooks were rewritten to get across the Nazi message. This question is translated and adapted from a Nazi textbook.

Question 46:
The Jews are aliens in Germany. In 1933 there were 66,060,000 people living in Germany. Of this total, 499,862 were Jews. What is the percentage of aliens in Germany?

Fact ✓

Teachers had to belong to the German Nazi Teachers' League and were made to teach Nazi ideas in lessons – or lose their jobs. To make sure teachers knew exactly what to teach, they had to go on compulsory training sessions in the school holidays, run by the Nazis.

▼ **SOURCE K** A picture from a German school textbook, 1935. In these books, Jewish people were always portrayed as evil, or doing nasty or illegal things.

▼ **INTERPRETATION L** Hilma Geffen speaking on 15 February 1985. Born in Berlin in 1925, she grew up in a small town with her family – they were the only Jewish family living there.

'And the change came in 1933. Not very drastic, but nevertheless there was a change in attitude, in my attitude and behaviour toward me by the children and by the teachers and by our neighbours. We had very good relations with our neighbours.

...it started by the neighbours telling us not to come to their house anymore. They were afraid... and so when we met in the street we either just nodded to each other or pretended we didn't know each other at all... suddenly in school we were required to say "Heil Hitler". Instead of "good morning" the teacher said "Heil Hitler". And it was very awkward for me to say anything. Mostly I didn't say anything.'

▼ **SOURCE M** Hitler pictured with Hitler Youth members. As teenagers, boys were required to join Hitler Youth, and girls joined the League of German Maidens (seen in the background of this photo).

▼ **INTERPRETATION N** In this extract from his book *Through Hell for Hitler* (1970), Henry Metelmann refers to his experiences as a member of the Hitler Youth in the 1930s.

'At the time, it was smashing. When we went on our marches the police stopped the traffic and passers-by had to give the Nazi salute. We were poor and suddenly had fine uniforms. I'd never been on holiday; now they were taking us to camp by lakes and mountains.

I am ashamed to say now that, to us, Hitler was the greatest human being in the world. At rallies we couldn't hear what he was saying – but we all screamed anyway. When war came I was so excited. I thought, "Now, I can show the Führer what I'm made of."'

Key Words   eugenics

Over to You

1 Why do you think Hitler and the Nazis put so much effort into organising young people's lives?

2 Look at **I**.
   a Why do you think boys and girls were taught different things?
   b What is 'eugenics' and why do you think the Nazis put this on school timetables?

3 Look at **Source J**. Why do you think questions like this appeared in German textbooks?

4 Look at **Source K**. Why do you think the Jewish people in the picture have been drawn this way?

5 Look at **Interpretation L**. Describe how Hilma Geffen's life changed when Hitler came to power.

Interpretation Analysis

1 Read **Interpretation N**. How did Henry's life change when he joined the Hitler Youth?

2 Do you think this interpretation explains why Hitler and the Nazi Party were so popular with young people in Germany?

4.6A Why was there another world war?

Adolf Hitler was determined to make Germany a strong and powerful country again. He had fought for the defeated German army in the First World War and, like millions of Germans, was humiliated by the agreement Germany had to sign at the end of the fighting (see **A**). So did Hitler stick to the terms of the treaty once he was in power? What happened as a result?

Objectives

- Examine the build up to the outbreak of war in 1939.
- Assess the views of modern historians relating to the outbreak of war.

▼ **A** A summary of the Treaty of Versailles, 1919: Germany had to accept the treaty's terms and sign it.

- Germany must accept the blame for starting the war.
- Germany must pay for the war. The money will go to the winning nations, mainly Britain and France.
- Germany should only have a small army (100,000 men), a small navy (six battleships) and no submarines, air force or tanks.
- Germany must hand over large areas of its land to the winning nations. Some of the land will be used to make new countries such as Poland and Czechoslovakia.
- Germany must never unite with Austria again.
- No German soldiers can go into the Rhineland, a German region close to France.

Hitler's aims

Hitler had three main aims in his quest to make Germany a strong and powerful country once more:

- Firstly, he wanted to do everything in his power to get back all the land Germany had lost after the war. He felt he would have to build up his army, navy and air force to do this, even though this meant breaking the rules of the Treaty of Versailles. Hitler was determined to ignore the treaty and carry on regardless.

- Secondly, he wanted to join together anyone who spoke German into one big country, called the 'Greater German Reich' ('Reich' is similar in meaning to the English word 'empire').

- Finally, he wanted to make Germany bigger by taking land from other, weaker countries. He believed that true Germans were such a great and powerful race that they needed the extra living space ('lebensraum') to reach their full potential. He believed this living space should mainly be in Eastern Europe.

▼ **SOURCE B** From a speech given by Hitler in November 1923. In it, he talks of his hatred for the German politicians who signed the Treaty of Versailles (the 'November Criminals' as he calls them) and how he hopes to rebuild Germany.

'Now I am going to carry out the promise I made five years ago... to neither rest nor sleep until the November Criminals have been hurled to the ground, until on the ruins of the pitiful Germany of today has risen a Germany of power and greatness.'

Making Germany stronger

Three days after becoming leader of Germany, Hitler told his military chiefs to start building up the armed forces – a process called **rearmament** – in secret. By 1935, Hitler had thousands of planes, dozens more battleships than he was allowed, and around 500,000 soldiers. In late 1935, Hitler even told the world about his increased forces, but no one did anything, for fear of starting another war. Some countries felt that the Germans should be allowed to build up their military if they wanted to. After all, they were only protecting themselves, weren't they?

More rule-breaking

In 1936, Hitler broke the treaty's terms again by sending his soldiers into the Rhineland area of Germany. Remember – his soldiers were not allowed anywhere near France. Once again, no country stopped him – after all, he wasn't invading another country, just moving his soldiers around within his own, some thought (see **D**).

Yet Hitler's aggressive moves worried some politicians. Britain's Winston Churchill, for example, made many speeches in Parliament about the need to stand up to Hitler. But Churchill was not Prime Minister at this time; he was just an ordinary MP… and many people ignored his warnings. But Hitler's actions were starting to make world news. What would be his next move?

Key Words rearmament

▼ **SOURCE D** Adapted from British politician Lord Lothian's reaction to German troops marching into the Rhineland in March 1936.

'After all, the Germans are only going into their own back garden.'

Over to You

1 Summarise the ways Hitler hoped to make Germany a strong and powerful country once more.

2 **a** What was the Treaty of Versailles?

   b Write an account of how Hitler broke the terms of the Treaty of Versailles between 1933 and 1936.

3 Why did the leaders of some countries refuse to stand up to Hitler at this time? Use **Source D** to help you.

▼ **SOURCE C** A German postcard published in 1934. Germany, shown in orange, is seen surrounded by the armed forces of other countries in Europe.

Source Analysis

1 Look at **Source C**. How is Germany portrayed?

2 Do you think this postcard helps explain why Hitler wanted his army in the Rhineland?

3 How useful is this postcard to a historian studying German attitudes towards rearmament in the 1930s?

Invasion of Austria

In March 1938, German troops marched into Austria, the country of Hitler's birth. Once again, Hitler had broken the terms of the Treaty of Versailles. Once again, no country stopped him. And many Austrians actually wanted to be part of Germany.

Unstoppable?

By 1938, it seemed as if Hitler was unstoppable. His armed forces were getting stronger and he was demanding more land. He next turned his attention to the Sudetenland, a small area of Czechoslovakia that contained many people who spoke German as their first language. In September 1938, Neville Chamberlain, the British Prime Minister, made several visits to Germany to discuss Hitler's demands. On 30 September, at a meeting in Munich, the British (and also the French) agreed to let Germany have the Sudetenland. The Czechoslovakian leaders were not even at the meeting (nor were the Russians), but went along with the more powerful countries' decision. The world breathed a sigh of relief because it seemed that this agreement (known as the Munich Agreement) meant that Hitler was satisfied, and it had prevented a war. In Britain, Chamberlain was considered a hero. He had even got Hitler to sign a piece of paper saying that Britain and Germany would never go to war with one another again.

Hitler the liar!

But all Hitler's promises not to invade any more areas were broken in March 1939 when his soldiers took over most of the rest of Czechoslovakia. It seemed that Hitler wasn't satisfied, and wanted more. The countries of Europe realised that he could never be trusted, and prepared for war. They wondered if they would be next to be invaded. Britain and France had had enough of letting Hitler get away with things (known as **appeasement**) and agreed to help Poland if Hitler invaded.

▼ **MAP E** A map of Europe in the 1930s, showing the areas that Germany invaded.

War approaches

Sure enough, Poland was next on Hitler's hit list. A large area of Germany had been given to Poland at the end of the First World War – and Hitler wanted it back. In summer 1939, Hitler prepared his army to invade Poland. He was convinced the British wouldn't go to war to defend Poland, and that France would never attack Germany without British support. Hitler's only real concern was the USSR. He thought it might feel threatened if he continued to push his soldiers in their direction, and so he made a deal with Stalin, the Soviet leader. The Nazi-Soviet Pact (as the deal was known) meant that Germany and the USSR would not go to war over Poland. A secret part of the deal agreed that the USSR could have part of Poland if they let the Germans invade it.

War breaks out

On 1 September 1939, German troops invaded Poland. Chamberlain decided that enough was enough. Two days later, on 3 September 1939, Britain – and France – declared war on Germany.

▼ **INTERPRETATION F** Adapted from an article written by historian Alan Bullock in 1967. Here, Bullock also refers to the German invasion of the USSR in 1941. This is a traditional view of the outbreak of war – that Hitler always wanted war, and went about making sure he achieved his aims.

'[Hitler insisted that] the future of the German people could... only be secured by the conquest of living space (Lebensraum) in Eastern Europe... Such Lebensraum could only be obtained at the expense of Russia and the states bordering on her and could only be won... by force... Hitler first set these views down in *Mein Kampf*... and repeated them on almost every occasion... [up to] 1945. Not only did he consistently hold and express these views over 20 years, but in 1941 he set to work to put them into practice... by attacking Russia.'

▼ **INTERPRETATION G** Adapted from a book written by historian A.J.P. Taylor in 1961. This view was very controversial when it first appeared – Taylor wrote that the war didn't break out because Hitler planned it to, but that he took advantage of opportunities given to him by foreign politicians.

'Hitler was gambling on some twist of fortune which would present him with success in foreign affairs, just as a miracle had made him Chancellor in 1933. There was here no concrete plan, no directive for German policy in 1937 and 1938. Or if there were a directive, it was to wait upon events... Hitler did not make plans - for world conquest or for anything else. He assumed that others would provide opportunities, and that he would seize them.'

Over to You .ıll

1 How did Hitler break the Treaty of Versailles in March 1938?

2 **a** Define 'appeasement'.

   b In what ways did Britain 'appease' Hitler?

   c Why do you think Prime Minister Chamberlain decided to appease Hitler, rather than stand up to him?

3 **a** Look at **Source H**. Who is the man in the cartoon? Where is he going?

   b Why do you think the cartoon is called 'Still Hope'?

4 **a** What was the Nazi-Soviet Pact?

   b How did the Nazi-Soviet Pact help Hitler's conquest of Poland?

Key Words appeasement

▶ **SOURCE H** A British cartoon published in a magazine in 1938 featuring Neville Chamberlain. The cartoon is called 'Still Hope'.

Interpretation Analysis

1 How does **Interpretation F** differ from **Interpretation G** about Hitler's role in the outbreak of the Second World War?

2 Which interpretation do you find more convincing about the outbreak of war? Explain your answer using **Interpretations F** and **G**. Hint: When asked which interpretation you find more convincing, you need to decide which one best fits with what you think. Based on what you think about the outbreak of the war, which opinion (Bullock's or Taylor's) do you agree with more?

Quick Knowledge Quiz

Choose the correct answer from the three options:

1 Which of the following terms most correctly describes a system of government in which people vote to choose their politicians?

   a dictatorship
   b democracy
   c divergent

2 Which two nineteenth-century thinkers are most closely associated with 'communism'?

   a Hitler and Goebbels
   b Hitler and Mussolini
   c Marx and Engels

3 Which country turned to a communist system in the years after a revolution in 1917?

   a USA
   b Germany
   c Russia/USSR

4 Which revolutionary group attempted a takeover of Germany in January 1919?

   a the Spartacists
   b the Nazis
   c the Fascists

5 Which fascist leader took control of Italy in 1922?

   a Franco
   b Hitler
   c Mussolini

6 What name is given to a period of rapid price increases, where money becomes practically worthless, such as the situation that took place in Germany in 1923?

   a revolution
   b hyperinflation
   c nepotism

7 When, and where, was Hitler born?

   a Austria in 1889
   b Germany in 1889
   c Austria in 1899

8 What was the name of Hitler's secret police force?

   a NKVD
   b Gestapo
   c MI5

9 Which word is used to describe the rebuilding of a country's armed forces?

   a rearmament
   b demilitarisation
   c renaissance

10 On what date did Britain declare war on Hitler's Germany?

   a 1 September 1939
   b 3 September 1939
   c 13 September 1939

This government is a joke!

I completely disagree with you – but I'd fight to the death to defend your right to say it!

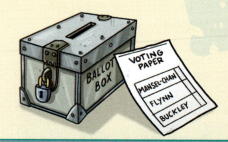

 **Literacy Focus**

Understanding interpretations

▼ **INTERPRETATION A** From an article titled 'Nazi aggression: planned or improvised?' by Hendrik Karsten Hogrefe, writing in The Historian Magazine, 2011.

A person who has extreme beliefs that may lead them to behave in unreasonable or violent ways.	A particular way of thinking about something.
The extra territory that Hitler believed Germany needed for its development.	Hitler went to prison for nearly a year in the mid-1920s when he attempted to take over Germany. In prison, he wrote a book about his ideas and beliefs called *Mein Kampf*.
Hitler's title as leader of Germany.	The book Hitler wrote in prison, published in 1925.
	A country's strategies and ideas when dealing with other countries.
	Someone who takes advantage of opportunities when they arise. They don't necessarily make detailed plans.
	Detailed plans.

'Since the 1960s, there have been two main schools of thought on Hitler and the outbreak of war. According to the 'fanatic' view, expressed by historians like Hugh Trevor-Roper, Hitler aimed consistently at expansion and war. His Lebensraum policy had been emphasised since the days of his imprisonment, and naturally struggle and war were seen to be vital to its success. Trevor-Roper believes Hitler had a clear vision that involved a master plan for war and he completely controlled the events that resulted in his attack on Poland in 1939. The evidence for this interpretation comes from *Mein Kampf* and, according to Trevor-Roper, the ideas expressed in *Mein Kampf* and the Zweite Buch – Hitler's secret book which was never published – are the keys to understanding German foreign policy after 1933. However, some historians suggest that these books only express broad aims that Hitler still held when he became Führer.

The 'opportunist' view has been expressed most controversially by A.J.P. Taylor. He argues that Hitler had no blueprint for aggression. Instead, he was an astute [clever] and cynical politician who took advantage of the mistakes and fears of other leaders and his apparent fanaticism was an act.'

1   Define 'Lebensraum'.

2   In your own words, explain the two main views in **Interpretation A** relating to Hitler and the outbreak of war.

3   Which two famous historians are linked to each view?

4   What do you think? Do you agree with one historian more than the other? Explain your view.

4 History skill: Causation

As you know, a **cause** is a reason why something happened. Most major historical events that you study will have a number of different causes.

Key Words

cause   consequence

Writing about the causes of an event can help historians explain why things happened.

Explaining the causes of an event

Here is one way to answer a question that asks you to explain the causes of, reasons for, or factors leading to an event.

1 **Plan:** Firstly, it is important to make sure you know about the event in the question. What do you already know about the causes/reasons/factors? Make a plan of the main causes/reasons/factors why the event happened.

2 **Check and add detail:** Organise the causes/reasons/factors and add dates and details.

3 **Write your answer:** When you are sure of the order of causes/reasons/factors, it's time to start writing your answer.

4 **Make links:** To improve your answer, try to link causes/reasons/factors together where possible. Did one of the factors lead to the other, for example? Explain how they are linked. This helps you to show that you know how the different causes/reasons/factors are connected and moves you beyond a collection of detailed facts.

TIP: For example, you know that the First World War had a number of different causes… and lots of **consequences** too!

TIP: Look at the two bullet points in the question and make notes on what you know about these. You must focus on both bullet points, so do each one in turn!

TIP: Remember also that the question may ask you to use information of your own. This means that you must also mention causes/reasons/factors that are different from those in the two bullet points.

TIP: Think about your introduction and structure your answer in a logical way.

TIP: Don't forget to add details, and bring in as much other information as you can. Remember to do this for both bullet points!

TIP: Make sure you check your spelling, punctuation and grammar. If you go on to study History at a higher level, extra marks are sometimes awarded for this.

Assessment: Causation

Your challenge is to answer a question that relates to the causes of one of the most famous events in twentieth-century history – the appointment of Adolf Hitler as Chancellor of Germany in January 1933:

> Explain why Hitler emerged as Chancellor of Germany by 1933.
>
> You may use the following in your answer:
> - strengths of Hitler
> - the Great Depression.
>
> You must also use information of your own. (20)

The steps and example sentence starters below will help you structure your answer.

1 **Plan:** Study the two bullet points. What do you already know about:
   - Hitler's strengths – what was it about Hitler himself that helped his rise to power?

   - the Great Depression – what was it? What was the impact on Germany? And how did it contribute to Hitler's appointment as Chancellor?

   - The question also asks you to 'use information of your own'. This doesn't mean you have to search for lots of brand new information; it simply means that you should also write about other reasons (as well as the two mentioned) for Hitler's rise to power.

> **TIP:** Look back at pages 90–91 to help you.

> **TIP:** Pages 90–91 don't just provide information about the strengths of Hitler and the Great Depression – these pages show other reasons for Hitler's rise to power. You must take these into consideration too.

2 **Check and add detail:** Organise your answer. Check that you have lots of detail. Can you add any dates to the events? Or add names and key terms? Think about an introduction too. Don't just start with something on Hitler's strengths; instead, try to 'set up' your answer.

3 **Write your answer:** Write about the events in the right order, including the detail you added in step 2. (15)

> **TIP:** To begin, introduce what you are going to write about.

In January 1933, Hitler…
One of the reasons that Hitler emerged as leader was…
Another reason for Hitler's emergence as Chancellor was…
However, there were other reasons why Hitler emerged as Chancellor in January 1933. For example…

> **TIP:** You *must* focus on both bullet points.

> **TIP:** Remember to use other information.

4 **Make links:** Try to connect the events together if possible. Did one thing lead to another? Was the consequence of one event the cause of another? (5)

> **TIP:** You might think that the failure of the Munich Putsch in 1923 meant that Hitler decided to organise the Nazi Party in a more structured way. Or that the impact of the Great Depression meant that more people were willing to listen to the extreme ideas Hitler spoke about so passionately and powerfully.

> **TIP:** One of the reasons you might focus on when looking at Hitler's emergence as leader of Germany was that he attracted votes from people who were unhappy with the current government. They viewed the current government as unable to deal with the country's problems – many of which were caused by the impact of the Great Depression. Here, an increase in votes for the Nazis (which helped Hitler to emerge as Chancellor) is linked to the Great Depression.

The Second World War lasted from 1939 to 1945 and is the largest global conflict the world has ever known. It was fought over six continents, and during six long years it is estimated that more than 50 million men, women and children were killed. So which countries fought – and where? What were the war's key events and turning points? And how did it end?

Mission Objectives

- Recall key terms such as 'Blitzkrieg' and 'Blitz'.
- Identify key turning points of the war.
- Outline the sequence of the main events of the Second World War.

Blitzkrieg

Germany invaded Poland on 1 September 1939 using a new method of fighting called **Blitzkrieg** ('lightning war' – see **A**). Blitzkrieg involved fast-moving columns of tanks supported by infantry soldiers and dive-bomber attacks. Parachutists were dropped behind enemy lines the night before to destroy Polish defensive positions and cut their telephone wires. By the end of September, the Polish armed forces had been defeated.

Britain and France had promised to protect Poland, but were too far away to stop the invasion. As a result, there was very little fighting for about six months after Poland was defeated. Instead, the British army crossed the English Channel to help its allies, France and Belgium, set up defensive positions along their borders.

Europe attacked

In the spring of 1940, Germany attacked France, Denmark, Norway, the Netherlands and Belgium. In just a few months, Hitler's armies occupied much of the centre of Europe, and there was little the defending armies could do. Thousands of British, French and Belgian troops escaped from Dunkirk to England in a fleet of yachts, paddle steamers, warships, and even rowing boats (see **B**).

▼ **A** The Blitzkrieg method of warfare.

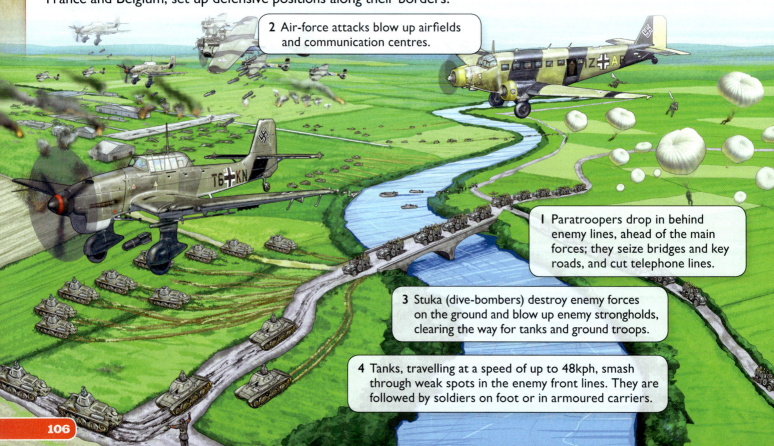

2 Air-force attacks blow up airfields and communication centres.

1 Paratroopers drop in behind enemy lines, ahead of the main forces; they seize bridges and key roads, and cut telephone lines.

3 Stuka (dive-bombers) destroy enemy forces on the ground and blow up enemy strongholds, clearing the way for tanks and ground troops.

4 Tanks, travelling at a speed of up to 48kph, smash through weak spots in the enemy front lines. They are followed by soldiers on foot or in armoured carriers.

▼ **SOURCE B** A painting of the evacuation of Dunkirk by Charles Cundall in 1940. He was an official war artist for Britain and was asked to make an official painting of events on the beaches. Cundall did not witness the evacuation personally, but relied on published accounts, photographs and eye-witness reports.

Key Words   Blitz   Blitzkrieg

▼ **SOURCE C** The wreckage of a double-decker bus that was blasted into a house during the Blitz, September 1940.

The Battle of Britain and the Blitz

As a result of the German attacks, by the end of 1940 Britain stood alone without any powerful European allies. Hitler wanted to complete his domination of Europe by invading Britain, so prepared an invasion force (code-named Operation Sealion). However, before he could transport his troops across the English Channel, he had to destroy Britain's air force. He could not risk his invading soldiers being attacked from the air. So, the Germans began a series of air raids on military air bases in southern England in the summer of 1940. The British air force fought back and, in August and September, the skies over Kent, Surrey, Sussex and Essex were a mass of aeroplanes as British Spitfires and Hurricanes fought against German Messerschmitts and Heinkels. This became know as the Battle of Britain.

However, the Germans lost this battle and Hitler abandoned his plans for invasion. Instead, he launched night bombing raids on major British cities, hoping to force Britain to surrender (see **C**). This period of intense bombing became known as the **Blitz**.

Fact ✓

During the Blitz, German bombers dropped around 20,000 tons of bombs on London and nearly 12,000 tons on other British cities such as Bristol, Plymouth, Coventry, Glasgow and Hull. They killed 61,000 civilians. Of every 26 houses in Britain in 1939, eight were damaged and one was destroyed by air raids.

Meanwhile...

In the late 1930s, Germany had signed a series of deals with both Italy and Japan. On 27 September 1940, Germany, Italy and Japan signed the Tripartite Pact. The three countries were now in an official alliance – and became known as the Axis Powers. Hungary, Romania, Bulgaria and Croatia later joined the Axis.

Over to You

1 a Describe the difference between 'Blitzkrieg' and 'Blitz'.

   b Why do you think Blitzkrieg was so effective?

2 In your opinion, by the end of 1940, how well was the war going for:

   a Germany   b Britain?

Source Analysis

Look at **Source B**.

1 What happened at Dunkirk in 1940?

2 How useful is this source to a historian studying the evacuation of Dunkirk?

More German victories

Despite the nightly onslaught by German bombers, the British held on. And, by 1941, Hitler had turned his attention towards his old hated enemy – the USSR. Despite the fact that Germany and the USSR had promised not to go to war with each other (agreed in the Nazi-Soviet Pact), Hitler still wanted to conquer the USSR. As early as 1924, in *Mein Kampf* (the book he wrote in prison), Hitler wrote that Germany must expand and take over Russian land.

Germany attacked the USSR in June 1941 (the attack was code-named Operation Barbarossa). The Russians were pushed back and back until, in October, Hitler was only 95km from the capital city, Moscow. As winter started to set in, it seemed that the German army was unstoppable.

Japan enters the war

Then, at the end of 1941, the Japanese entered the war. In an attempt to knock out America's navy in one go (and give it control of the rich lands in the Far East), Japan launched a surprise attack on the great US naval base of Pearl Harbor in Hawaii. Thousands of American soldiers were killed and dozens of US fighter planes and warships were destroyed, so the USA declared war on Japan and its allies (Italy and Germany). Japan won victory after victory against America. Japanese troops seized the British colonies of Hong Kong, Malaya and Burma, too, as well as the French colony of Indo-China.

By early 1942, the war seemed lost for Britain, the USSR and America. The Germans were almost in Moscow and had nearly pushed the British out of Africa. In the east, Japan was pushing back American forces and was close to invading India and Australia. Then, within a few months, three major battles changed the course of the war.

Key turning points

- **The Battle of Midway (June 1942)**: In the Pacific Ocean, the Japanese were beaten by US forces in the great air and sea battle at Midway Island. The Japanese advance was stopped and gradually the Americans began to drive them back, island by island. This area of conflict is sometimes called the Pacific War.

- **The Battle of Stalingrad (July 1942–February 1943)** (see **F**): In the USSR, after four months of very fierce fighting in the city of Stalingrad, a large proportion of the German army surrendered. Gradually, Soviet forces (the USSR's forces) began to push the German army out of the USSR and back towards Germany. This was the first time the Germans had retreated in large numbers. At the same time, British and American bombers began air raids on Germany.

- **El Alamein (October–November 1942)**: In Egypt (in North Africa), at El Alamein, British troops defeated the Germans. With help from the USA, the British drove the Germans out of North Africa and invaded Italy. British war leader Winston Churchill called El Alamein 'the turning point of the war'.

▼ **MAP D** A map showing Hitler's conquests up to early 1941.

Fact ✓

Fighting against the Axis Powers were the Allies, including Britain, France, Canada, Australia, New Zealand, India, the Soviet Union, China and the USA.

▶ **SOURCE E** A French cartoon from 1943 showing Adolf Hitler and Hermann Goering (a leading Nazi) changing course after the heavy defeats in the USSR, including the Battle of Stalingrad. The devil is behind them and the return route to Berlin is littered with the graves of German soldiers. A caption (not shown) reads: 'It is too cold! Let's go this way!'

Meanwhile...

In April 1941, the Germans helped their Italian allies invade Greece and Yugoslavia. They had invaded some parts of Africa where the British were based too.

Over to You

1 Look at **Map D**. Hitler was determined that Germany would become 'the master of all Europe'. How close was Germany to this aim by early 1941?

2 When and why did the USA enter the war?

3 **a** What do you think is meant by the term 'turning point'?

   b Why do you think the battles of Midway, Stalingrad and El Alamein are known as 'turning points'?

▼ **SOURCE F** Russian soldiers fighting in 1943 during the Battle of Stalingrad.

Source Analysis

Look at **Source E**.

1 Who is pictured in the cartoon?

2 What point do you think the cartoonist was making about the German military situation in the USSR?

3 How useful is this source to a historian studying the German military campaign in the USSR?

Italy surrenders

By the end of 1943, the British and American invasion of Italy was in full swing. As Italian forces surrendered, their leader, Benito Mussolini, was captured and shot.

In Britain, an invasion of France that aimed to push German forces back towards Germany was planned. The invasion date was set for June 1944.

D-Day

On D-Day (6 June 1944) British, American and other Allied troops landed on beaches in Normandy, north-west France. Despite brutal fighting on the beaches and in the French countryside, the Allies were able to advance and the Germans were gradually pushed back. In July, Hitler's opponents in Germany tried to assassinate him and in December a German attempt to retake some of the land they had lost failed.

Fact ✓

At Bletchley Park in Buckinghamshire, a group of scientists and mathematicians (including the brilliant Alan Turing), built an early type of computer that could decode encrypted enemy orders. It is estimated that this work saved thousands of lives and helped win the war.

Germany surrenders

By April 1945, British and US forces were moving quickly towards Berlin (Germany's capital). Along the way, they were freeing villages, towns and countries from German occupation. In the east, the Russian armies were advancing towards Berlin too. The German army was being beaten in battle after battle and food supplies in major German towns were running short.

Hitler and his closest followers retreated to a special underground bunker under Berlin's streets and, on 30 April, Hitler killed himself. Within days, Germany surrendered and the war was over... in Europe.

Nuclear bombs

Victory in Europe meant that more Allied troops could be sent to fight the Japanese. However, before the troops arrived, the US President made the decision to drop two nuclear bombs on the Japanese cities of Hiroshima and Nagasaki. The Japanese, rather than face the complete destruction of their islands if more were dropped, surrendered on 14 August. The Second World War was over.

▼ **SOURCE G** American troops arriving on Normandy beaches (north-west France) as reinforcements during the D-Day landings.

▼ **SOURCE H** A nuclear bomb test explosion on 25 July 1946 (you can see some of the old warships used to test the blast). The bomb dropped on Hiroshima was the equivalent of 20,000 tons of dynamite. When US President Harry S. Truman heard of the bombing, he said, 'This is the greatest thing in history.'

▼ **I** A chart showing Second World War deaths. Note the severe impact that the war had on civilians. The high numbers are a result of many factors including: the targeted bombing of large cities; the speed of modern warfare – which meant that many were caught up in fighting in cities before they could escape; and the systematic murder of many people (in the Holocaust, for example – see page 143).

Second World War deaths

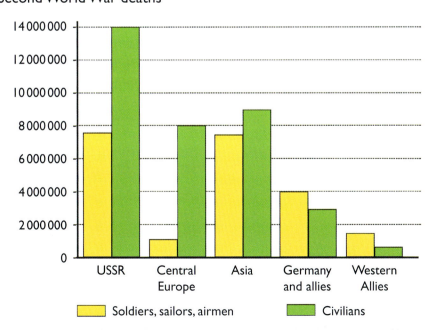

Over to You .ıll

1 Draw a timeline from 1939 to 1945. Add at least ten key battles, events or interesting facts.

2 Look at these three headings:
 • 'Bad times for Britain'
 • 'Things are changing'
 • 'Victory'
 a Add the headings to your timeline in the places you think they fit best. It is OK for the headings to cover a number of months or even years.
 b Explain why you have put each heading in the place you have chosen.

3 You have been given the job of choosing an image for the front of a new school textbook about the Second World War. You can choose either one or two images, but you can only choose from ones that appear on pages 106–111 of this book. Which image(s) will you choose? Explain your decision.

Causation

1 Explain two of the following:
 • the importance of America joining the war for Germany's eventual defeat in the war
 • the importance of the British victory at El Alamein for Germany's eventual defeat in the war
 • the importance of Blitzkrieg tactics for Germany's initial success in the war.

5.2A How should we remember Dunkirk?

When war officially began in September 1939, British troops crossed the English Channel and advanced into France to help the French prepare for a German attack. But by the end of May 1940, nearly half a million British, French and Belgian soldiers had become trapped between the sea and the advancing Germans (see **A**). How had they become trapped? What happened to them? And how have different people viewed this event?

Mission Objectives

- Identify reasons why the Dunkirk evacuations could be considered both a success and a failure.
- Examine different opinions about the Dunkirk evacuation.

When German troops finally invaded France (and Belgium, Luxembourg and the Netherlands) in May 1940, they quickly pushed the Allied troops back towards the Channel, trapping them at the coast. At that moment, it looked as if all was lost for the Allies. Hitler was close to wiping out the entire British army (and thousands of French and Belgian troops) before the war had really got under way.

Operation Dynamo

At the last moment, the British government organised a huge rescue operation known as Operation Dynamo. The plan was to evacuate the troops to Britain using warships. A request was made to ordinary citizens to help the evacuation using their own small boats, paddle steamers, fishing boats, yachts, and even rowing boats. Between 26 May and 4 June over 800 boats rescued around 200,000 British and 140,000 French and Belgian troops from the beaches of Dunkirk.

▼ **MAP A** The German advance of 1940.

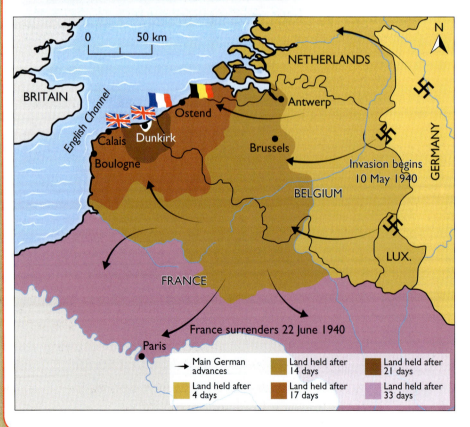

Fact ✓

At the height of the German advance towards Dunkirk, Hitler suddenly ordered the German army to stop. Many historians today think that he did this because he was unhappy with one of his generals who had ordered the attacks. By stopping the advance, Hitler was showing the general that he was in charge. The advance soon resumed, but Hitler's order gave the Allied troops more time to get off the beaches.

Reporting Dunkirk

The events at Dunkirk can be viewed in different ways. What happened has sometimes been seen as a great triumph, or even a miracle. But it has also been viewed as a disaster. How did these different viewpoints come about? Firstly, study the sources on these pages – they show how the evacuation was reported at the time.

▼ **SOURCE B** A newspaper headline about the Dunkirk evacuation, 5 June 1940.

▼ **SOURCE C** At this time, millions of people went to the cinema each week – and a short news report would accompany the main film. This report is from 6 June 1940. Films of British warships and small boats rescuing soldiers from the beaches were shown, accompanied by military music.

'More cheering evidence of the success of this amazing military exploit is the presence in Britain of large numbers of French soldiers. They are showered with hospitality... Enjoying an unexpected seaside holiday, they [lie] in the sun, awaiting orders to return to France. The story of that epic withdrawal will live in history as a glorious example of discipline [among the troops]... Every kind of small craft – destroyers, paddle steamers, yachts, motor boats, rowing boats – has sped here to the burning ruins of Dunkirk to bring off the gallant British and French troops.'

▼ **SOURCE D** From a speech Winston Churchill (Britain's Prime Minister) gave to Parliament on 4 June 1940, the day the last Allied soldier arrived home.

'Dunkirk was a miracle of deliverance, achieved by valour, by perseverance, by perfect discipline, by faultless service, by resource, by skill. The enemy was hurled back by the retreating British and French troops. He was so roughly handled that he did not hurry their departure seriously. We must be very careful not to assign to this deliverance [evacuation] the attributes of a victory. Wars are not won by evacuations, but there was a victory inside this evacuation and we must rejoice.'

▼ **SOURCE E** From a book published by three British journalists in July 1940.

'That night a miracle was born. This land of Britain is rich in heroes. She had brave, daring men in her Navy and Air Force, as well as in her Army. She had heroes in jerseys and sweaters and old rubber boots in all the fishing ports of Britain.'

▼ **SOURCE F** A British cartoon, published in the *Evening Standard* newspaper on 18 June 1940 after the evacuation. At this time, Britain felt very much 'alone' against Nazi Germany because of Hitler's dominance of much of Europe.

"VERY WELL, ALONE"

Over to You

1 a How did ordinary civilians help out during the evacuation of Dunkirk?

   b Why were British newspapers so keen to report how ordinary civilians had helped out?

2 After studying **Sources B** to **F**, which word best describes the events at Dunkirk from a British point of view – 'victory' or 'disaster'? Or would you choose another word or phrase to describe it? Give reasons for your answer.

3 Read **Source D**. In what way is Churchill's opinion of Dunkirk different from some of the other sources on these pages?

Source Analysis

1 Look at **Source F**. What point is the cartoonist trying to make about British attitudes?

2 How useful is this cartoon to a historian studying the British reaction to the Dunkirk evacuations?

The other story

The British government was keen to portray the evacuation of Dunkirk as some sort of victory or miracle. Look through these other sources and interpretations and investigate some alternative viewpoints.

▼ **SOURCE G** From the German magazine *Der Adler*, 5 June 1940.

'For us Germans the word "Dunkirchen" will stand for all time for victory in the greatest battle of total destruction in history. But, for the British and French who were there, it will remind them for the rest of their lives of a defeat that was heavier than any army had ever suffered before.'

▼ **SOURCE H** A British soldier produced an anonymous account of what it was like waiting on the beaches at Dunkirk in 1940.

'There was no singing, and very little talk. Everyone was far too exhausted to waste breath. A group of dead and dying soldiers on the path in front of us quickened our desire to get away. Stepping over the bodies we marched down the slope on the dark beach. Dunkirk was now a lurid study in red and black; flames, smoke, and the night itself all mingling together to compose a frightful panorama of death and destruction.'

▼ **SOURCE I** Some people in parts of France supported the Germans. This poster was created by a Nazi supporter who claims the British deliberately left 40,000 French soldiers behind at Dunkirk. In fact, the British did take out some of their own troops before they told the French army about the evacuation, so the French held back the Germans while the British were loaded onto ships. The poster says: '1940 – Dunkirk. The English prevent the last of the French soldiers, who had just protected their retreat, from boarding the boats.'

1940. DUNKERQUE. LES ANGLAIS S'OPPOSENT A L'EMBARQUEMENT DES DERNIERS FRANÇAIS QUI VENAIENT DE PROTEGER LEUR RETRAITE

Fact ✔

A large force of around 1,800 soldiers from the Indian Army played a vital role in the evacuation by using their animals (including 2,700 mules) to transport supplies, weapons and ammunition over ground that British trucks couldn't navigate.

▼ **INTERPRETATION J**
From *Global War*, a GCSE History textbook written by Josh Brooman, published in 1990.

'The evacuation of the British army from Dunkirk was a great defeat. Nearly 70,000 men were killed, wounded or taken prisoner. The survivors left 2,500 big guns, 90,000 rifles and 64,000 vehicles behind them. They also abandoned 150,000 of their French allies to become prisoners of the Germans.'

▼ **INTERPRETATION K**
British historian Clive Ponting in his 1990 book *1940: Myth and Reality*.

'One of the myths of Dunkirk is that the troops were evacuated from the beaches by an armada of small boats manned by volunteers from all over England. In fact two-thirds of those evacuated were lifted directly on to Royal Navy ships from the east of Dunkirk harbour.'

▼ **INTERPRETATION L**
A BBC news reporter commenting in a television news broadcast on the 60th anniversary of Dunkirk in 2000.

'Dunkirk was a military disaster – and took the British public by surprise… but almost at once, victory was being plucked from defeat and the newspapers began to create the Dunkirk myth… The government encouraged this myth to flourish – and allowed nothing to be published which might damage morale… Dunkirk was a military defeat but a propaganda victory.'

▼ **SOURCE M** A photograph of the Dunkirk beaches after the evacuation in 1940.

Over to You

1 a Read **Source G**. How does this German magazine report the Dunkirk evacuation?

b Do you agree? Was Dunkirk a German 'victory'?

2 Compare the sources on page 113 with the sources and interpretations on these pages.

a What are the main differences?

b Why do you think that these differences exist?

3 a Why do you think that, at the time, Dunkirk was mainly reported as a victory?

b Do you think that the British government was right to report Dunkirk as a victory?

c Is it possible for an event (such as Dunkirk) to be both a victory and a disaster? Explain your answer carefully.

Interpretation Analysis

1 Read **Interpretation L**. Summarise what is being said in this interpretation.

2 How convincing is **Interpretation L** about what happened at Dunkirk in May and June 1940?

Towards the end of 1940, posters like the one in **Source A** began to appear all over Britain. They marked an important event in the war and celebrated a victory for Britain. So why were these posters published? Why were the pilots smiling? And why did 'so many' people have to be thankful to 'so few'?

Mission Objectives

- Examine Operation Sealion.
- Assess why Hitler wasn't able to invade Britain in September 1940.

Nazi Europe

By July 1940, Hitler was close to becoming the 'Master of Europe'. He was friendly with, or his armies had successfully invaded, most European countries (see **B**). Britain and the USSR were two of the more powerful nations that might be able to stop him… but Britain was now firmly in Hitler's sights and he was hoping to invade in September 1940.

▼ **MAP B** Hitler's conquests up to September 1940.

▼ **SOURCE A** A poster which first appeared in 1940. It was inspired by a quote from a speech made by Winston Churchill on 20 August 1940.

"NEVER WAS SO MUCH OWED BY SO MANY TO SO FEW"
THE PRIME MINISTER

Hitler on top

In July 1940, serious planning began for a German invasion of Britain. Code-named Operation Sealion, the aim was to get German soldiers onto British soil by the end of August. On 16 July, Hitler signed top secret plans to begin the preparations for the invasion of Britain (see **C**).

Operation Sealion in action

For Operation Sealion to have any chance of success, Hitler knew he had to destroy Britain's Royal Air Force (**RAF**). He believed that if the **Luftwaffe** (German air force) could win control of the skies, it would be far easier for German ships to transport soldiers over the English Channel to begin the land invasion of Britain. If the RAF was destroyed, British planes could not attack Germany's troop ships.

Fact ✓

There were several female pilots too. While the women did not fight in combat, they delivered new, repaired and damaged aircraft between factories and airfields.

▼ **SOURCE C** An adapted summary of Hitler's invasion plans, July 1940.

GERMAN GOVERNMENT
TOP SECRET DIRECTIVE NO. 16
16 JULY 1940
FROM: ADOLF HITLER

TOP SECRET

Since Britain, in spite of its hopeless military situation, shows no signs of being ready to come to an understanding, I have decided to prepare a landing operation against Britain.

The aim of this operation will be to eliminate the British homeland as their base for the war against Germany and, if necessary, to occupy it completely.

I therefore order as follows:

(i) Troops will launch a surprise attack from Ramsgate to the area west of the Isle of Wight.

(ii) a) The British Air Force must be so reduced morally and physically that it is unable to deliver any significant attack against the German crossing.

b) The British Navy must be attacked by air and torpedo assaults.

(iii) I will be in overall command, but will assign roles to commanders in the army, navy and air force.

Throughout the summer of 1940, German and British pilots fought each other in the Battle of Britain high above southern England. From the start, the odds were stacked against the British:

- The Germans had 824 fighter planes and 1017 bombers. Britain only had about 600 fighter planes to fend them off.

- It took five minutes for German planes to cross the Channel from France. However, it took 15 minutes for British planes to take off and reach the invading planes after they were spotted.

- Many British pilots were part-timers and had not received the same level of training as the Germans. Germany trained 800 new pilots a month, while the British trained just 200.

▼ **SOURCE D** RAF pilots 'scrambling' to get to their planes to intercept approaching enemy aircraft.

Key Words   Luftwaffe   RAF

Slight delays

Hitler had initially wanted an invasion to take place by the end of August, but poor weather conditions meant this would be impossible. So a new target was set – Britain would be invaded along the south coast by mid-September. Troops would then move towards London and other major cities with the goal of controlling the whole country by Christmas. Now Hitler simply needed to defeat Britain's air force!

War in the air

Throughout the summer of 1940, the fate of the entire British nation rested on the shoulders of a handful of men. The outcome of the Battle of Britain not only depended on the bravery and skill of the pilots, but on the performance of the machines they flew. See pages 118–119 that fought in the skies above England.

Fact ✓

In total, over 3000 pilots fought against the Germans in the Battle of Britain. Over 2000 were from Britain but they were joined by New Zealanders (102), Poles (141), Canadians (90), Czechs (86), South Africans (21), Americans (7), and many more.

Over to You

1 Why might some people call Hitler the 'Master of Europe' by July 1940? Use **Map B** to help you.

2 a What was Operation Sealion?

b Do you think Hitler had good reason to believe that the destruction of Britain's air force and an invasion of Britain were possible? Give reasons for your answer.

5.3B Who were 'the Few'?

The main planes of the RAF in the Battle of Britain

HAWKER HURRICANE

Max Speed: 528kph

Weapons: Eight machine guns mounted on wings

Crew: Pilot only

Recognition: A short, sturdy plane with a wooden body (fuselage) that could turn sharply and take a lot of damage before the pilot had to 'bail out'. The Hurricane was the most common RAF fighter and shot down more German aircraft than the Spitfire.

SUPERMARINE SPITFIRE

Max Speed: 583kph

Weapons: Eight machine guns mounted on wings

Crew: Pilot only

Recognition: Sleek and beautiful, the Spitfire is one of the most famous planes in the world. It was fast, handled extremely well, and was more than a match for the German fighters.

The main planes of the Luftwaffe in the Battle of Britain

MESSERSCHMITT BF 109

Max Speed: 575kph

Weapons: Two machine guns mounted on the engine and two cannons on the wings

Crew: Pilot only

Recognition: This fast, shark-like plane had square-tipped wings and a bright yellow nose. It was the most deadly and feared of all the German aircraft.

MESSERSCHMITT BF 110

Max Speed: 562kph

Weapons: Four machine guns and two cannons in the nose, one rear-firing machine gun in cockpit

Crew: Pilot and gunner

Recognition: Heavily armed and able to fly long distances, this twin-engined plane was slow and clumsy to turn and was an easy target for the RAF fighters.

HEINKEL HE III

Max Speed: 398kph

Weapons: Three machine guns in the nose, top and belly; 2000kg of bombs

Crew: Pilot, gunner and bomb-aimer

Recognition: The most common German bomber, the Heinkel was slow, lightly armed and had large sections of glass over the cockpit. This allowed the pilot to see clearly – but offered no protection from a hail of bullets. When they did get past the RAF, they inflicted heavy damage on British airfields, towns and cities.

Fact ✓

After the Polish armed forces had been defeated in September 1939, most of the surviving Polish armed forces recruits left the country. Many Polish pilots were welcomed into the British Royal Air Force and took part in the Battle of Britain in 1940.

Battle of Britain

By the end of August, the RAF was only days away from defeat. Its airfields were badly damaged and it didn't have enough pilots. However, the Germans were encountering big problems too. Brand-new **radar** technology meant that the British could detect enemy planes before they reached Britain. A system of 51 radar stations directed British fighters to the Germans in a matter of minutes, leaving them enough fuel to attack the German planes time and time again. In fact, it soon became clear that the Germans were losing more planes than the British. More importantly, the Germans were only making about 150 new planes a month while the British were producing over 550!

Victory or defeat?

At 2:00pm on 15 September, Prime Minister Winston Churchill asked his air force commander what British fighter planes were available other than the ones in the air. 'None,' came the reply. However, on that same day, Germany lost 60 aircraft to Britain's 25. Two days later Hitler postponed Operation Sealion 'until further notice'. He had failed to defeat the RAF by mid-September, so decided to cancel his invasion plans. Instead, he started to target London in huge night-time bombing raids in an attempt to force Britain to surrender. This was known as the 'Blitz'.

The RAF pilots who fought in the Battle of Britain became known as the 'Few', after Churchill honoured their victory with a speech in which he said, 'Never in the field of human conflict was so much owed by so many to so few.'

▼ **E** Fighters and bombers lost by the Luftwaffe in the Battle of Britain.

Key Words　radar

▶ **SOURCE F**
A British 50p coin issued in 2015.

Over to You

1 a Draw a simple bar chart displaying the top speeds of the planes involved in the Battle of Britain.

b Which plane would you choose to fly into combat? Give reasons for your answer.

c Why do you think the Spitfire is better known than the Hurricane? Remember, the Hurricane shot down more German planes.

2 What is shown in **Source F**?

3 a Explain what you think Churchill meant when he said, 'Never in the field of human conflict was so much owed by so many to so few.'

b Write instructions for a design company to produce a poster or a coin to thank the 'Few'. Briefly describe what it should look like and why. Your explanation to the designer should include who the 'Few' were, what they did, and why it is important that we thank them for it. Look at **Source A** on page 116 for inspiration.

4 Look at chart **E**. Which set of figures do you think is most accurate and why?

Causation

1 Which of the following was the more important reason for Britain's victory in the Battle of Britain:
- the British developed radar technology
- Hitler did not meet his deadline and called off his attack?

Explain your answer with reference to both reasons.

Date	Official British figures	Official German figures	Figures agreed after the war
8–23 August	755	213	403
24 August–6 September	643	243	378
7–30 September	846	243	435
TOTAL	2244	699	1216

5.4 Soldiers of Empire

Meet a very brave person (see **A**), Ulric Cross. He was a navigator on a British bomber plane during the Second World War, and was awarded two of Britain's top bravery medals. Like millions of others, he joined up to fight for Britain even though he wasn't born in Britain, and had never even been to Britain! So why did men from India, Canada, Australia and the West Indies risk their lives to fight for Britain?

Mission Objectives

- Examine which countries helped Britain fight during the Second World War.
- Identify the contribution of these 'soldiers of Empire', and the countries that sent them.

▼ **SOURCE A** Cross was born in Trinidad in 1917. He was one of 250 Trinidadians who joined the RAF when war broke out. He flew over 80 bombing missions, 20 of them over Germany. His plane landed seven times without its wheels because they had been shot away or wouldn't lower.

Fact ✓

Noor Inayat Khan was a wartime British secret agent of Indian descent who was the first female radio operator sent into Nazi-occupied France. She was arrested and eventually executed by the Gestapo.

Contribution from the British Empire

The contribution of British Empire nations during the Second World War was huge. It is important to note that some of these places (such as Australia and Canada) were now 'self-governing', so they were not as tied to Britain as before. However, they were still strongly linked to Britain.

Not just about the soldiers

Nations did not just contribute to the war effort with soldiers, sailors and aircrew. India, for example, served as a training base and provided vast quantities of food to Britain. African countries supplied vital raw materials such as rubber, tin, palm oil, steel and cotton. Canada built thousands of tanks, ships and aircraft, while West Indian men and women volunteered to fill jobs in Britain where there was a shortage of workers, such as in factories and on farms. Most Empire countries even gave money to Britain to help it fight the war.

▼ **INTERPRETATION B** Adapted from a 2019 article by historian David Olusoga. In the article, he refers to **Source F** on page 113.

'The idea that Britain single-handedly defeated Nazism ignores the thousands of soldiers from the empire and fuels the dangerous idea that the British won the war by themselves… The way the war is now remembered is the idea that between 1940 and 1941 Britain "stood alone". The myth of national isolation is strong because it is one of the central pillars of British superiority, a delusion that exists as people forget the truth… In a cartoon appearing in the *Evening Standard* on 18 June 1940, a British soldier is shown standing by the coast. Rough seas hammer against the rocks and the bombers of the Luftwaffe thunder overhead. With a rifle in one hand, the soldier raises his fist at the enemy aircraft. "Very Well, Alone" reads the caption… Stirring stuff but Britain was not alone in June 1940. Indeed, over the six years of the war, Britain was only really alone for a matter of hours.'

▼ **MAP C** The contribution of British Empire soldiers to the war.

Canada: Just over one million Canadians fought against Italy and Germany in Europe and Japan in the Pacific region. Canadian troops played a key role in the D-Day landings of 1944. Canadian sailors fought to protect ships carrying vital supplies across the Atlantic Ocean. In total, more than 45,000 Canadians lost their lives, and 55,000 were wounded.

India: Two and a half million Indians fought in the war – the largest volunteer army in history. They fought in Europe, as well as in Sudan against the Italians, in Libya against the Germans and in Burma against the Japanese (among others). Around 90,000 people lost their lives while serving with the Indian forces. Indian soldiers, sailors and aircrew received over 4000 medals – including 31 Victoria Crosses, Britain's highest bravery medal.

Australia: Almost one million Australians served in the war. They fought against Germany and Italy in Europe, the Mediterranean and North Africa, as well as against Japan in Southeast Asia. Australia came under direct attack too, as Japanese aircraft bombed towns in northern Australia, and Japanese submarines attacked Sydney Harbour. Over 27,000 Australians lost their lives and over 20,000 were wounded.

New Zealand: Around 160,000 New Zealanders (about 9 per cent of the population) fought on Britain's side in many of the key campaigns in Europe and the Pacific region. Around 12,000 New Zealanders died.

West Indies: About 16,000 West Indians volunteered to serve. Around 6000 served with the RAF as ground staff, fighter pilots, bomb aimers and machine-gunners. Along with Ulric Cross (see A) around 90 West Indians won medals for bravery or leadership skills.

Africa: British colonies in West Africa (Gambia, Sierra Leone, the Gold Coast (now Ghana) and Nigeria) served as military bases. Thousands of people from British East Africa (Kenya, Uganda, Tanganyika and Zanzibar) joined the armed forces, as well as 60,000 from northern and southern Rhodesia (now Zambia and Zimbabwe). Many served as support troops in military hospitals, airfields and naval bases.

South Africa: Over 330,000 South Africans fought for Britain, and over 11,000 were killed. South African troops fought in North Africa, East Africa and Madagascar – and the air force made an important contribution in East Africa, North Africa, Sicily, Italy and the Balkans.

▼ **SOURCE D** This poster was issued in Britain in 1941, at a time when Britain seemed to stand alone against Nazi-occupied Europe. Its aim was to reassure people that they had allies around the world in the British Empire.

TOGETHER

Over to You

1 Complete the sentences with accurate terms:

   a Around 90 _____ were awarded to West Indians in Britain's air force for _____.

   b Japanese aircraft bombed towns in northwestern Australia, and Japanese _____ attacked _____.

   c Indian troops won over 30 _____ during the war, the highest bravery medal awarded by _____.

2 Look at **Source D**. Write a sentence or two explaining:

   a what the poster shows

   b what the point of the poster is

   c why you think it was published at that particular time.

3 Look at **Map C**. Describe the contribution of countries linked to the British Empire during the Second World War.

Interpretation Analysis

1 How convincing is **Interpretation B** about the contribution of soldiers of Empire to the British war effort?

5.5A Evacuation

During the First World War, some of Britain's cities had been bombed by the German air force and over 1000 people had been killed. Between the First and Second World Wars, great advances had been made in aircraft technology. As a result, many believed that Britain was once more going to be targeted from the air – this time on a much bigger scale. The government decided to move over one million people away from the danger areas. This was known as **evacuation** and it changed the lives of many people forever. So where were people evacuated from? Where were they moved to? And what did this mean for the people of Britain?

Mission Objectives

- Define the word 'evacuation' and explain why it took place.
- Assess the experiences of evacuees and their hosts.

Leaving towns and cities

For four days in September 1939 the government took over Britain's transport system. All of the buses and trains were used to move groups of people away from the places most likely to be bombed – mainly large towns and cities full of factories – and into the countryside where they would be safer (see **A**) Parents were not forced to evacuate their children, but it was strongly encouraged by the government. On one leaflet it read: 'The scheme is entirely a voluntary one, but clearly the children will be much safer and happier away from the big cities where the dangers will be greatest.'

Armed with a suitcase, a gas mask and a name tag tied to their coats, thousands of children left their familiar city surroundings for a completely new experience in the countryside (see **B**). Some would love their new life… but many others would hate every second of it!

▼ **SOURCE B** A helper at London's Paddington Station fixing a label onto a child being evacuated. The label contained details such as name, home address, date of birth and school attended.

▼ **A** Numbers of people evacuated by the British government in September 1939.

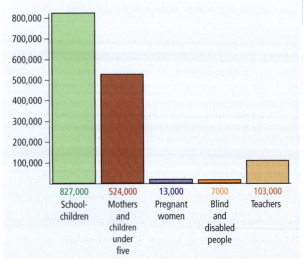

| 827,000 School-children | 524,000 Mothers and children under five | 13,000 Pregnant women | 7000 Blind and disabled people | 103,000 Teachers |

Finding a new home

None of the children knew where they were going and nothing prepared them for the experiences they would go through when they reached their countryside reception areas. There were two main methods of finding a new home or 'foster family'.

Method 1

Choose a child: children were lined up and local people would choose the ones they wanted. The smarter, cleaner girls tended to be chosen first… and the dirtier, scruffy little boys would often be left until last.

Method 2

Hunt for a home: evacuated children (or evacuees as they were called) were sometimes led around the town or village and taken door-to-door. Homeowners were asked if they would foster a child for a while.

Meanwhile… 1939

In 1939, Indian independence leader Mohandas Gandhi (see page 178) wrote to Adolf Hitler and asked, 'Is it too much to ask you to make an effort for peace?'

Fact

Britain wasn't the only country that evacuated people. France moved thousands away from its border with Germany. And Germany did the same.

▼ **INTERPRETATION C** A working-class evacuee recalls what happened when she and her younger brother arrived in the countryside.

'Villagers stood around watching us as we got out of the bus and went into the school. What followed was like an auction. Villagers came in to choose children. "Mr and Mrs Jones would like a nice little boy." Nobody wanted the awkward combination of a girl of 11 and such a small boy, from whom I had promised my mother never to be separated. We were left until the very last. The room was almost empty. I sat on my rucksack and cried.'

Key Words   evacuation

▼ **INTERPRETATION D** An example of a family who had to hunt for a home. From an interview with evacuee Anita Bowers in 1983, in *Keep Smiling Through* by Caroline Lang (1989). The term 'coloured people' was a way of describing people of colour at the time, but it is considered to be a racist label today.

'They unloaded us on the corner of the street; we thought it was all arranged, but it wasn't. The billeting officer [the person in charge of housing the children] walked along knocking on doors and asking if they'd take a family. We were the last to be picked. You couldn't blame them; they didn't have any coloured people there in those days.'

Over to You

1 **a** What is meant by the word 'evacuation'?

   b Look at the groups of people evacuated first by the government in September 1939 (chart **A**). Do you think the government was right? Which groups would you have moved first? Give reasons for your choices.

2 Look at **Source B**. Think about what you know about evacuation, and what you can infer from the image.

   a Why do you think the boy has a label tied to his coat?

   b What do you think is in his suitcase?

   c Who do you think the woman is?

   d Why is there a line of children behind him? And why is he out of line?

   e How do you think he feels?

   Compare your answers with the rest of the class.

3 Suppose you were evacuated now. You can take just ten of your things with you. Write a list of what you would take, giving reasons for each.

Interpretation Analysis

Read **Interpretations C** and **D**.

1 Describe the two different methods used to find these two young families a new home.

2 The two interpretations give different views on the reasons why each had difficulty finding a new home. What is the main difference between the views?

A better life?

Evacuation wasn't easy for anyone – evacuees or hosts. Some children settled down happily and loved their new lives in their new homes and schools – others hated country life and were homesick. The hosts had to put up with a lot, too. Some of the children arrived badly clothed, very thin and covered in lice and nits. Some of the 'rougher' evacuees shocked their foster families by swearing and being naughty. One young evacuee in Northallerton, Yorkshire, spent a whole day blocking up the local stream – later that night it was found that he'd flooded six houses and the local church! The following sources and interpretations outline some of these experiences.

▼ **INTERPRETATION E** Adapted from *The World is a Wedding*, the 1963 autobiography of Bernard Kops. In 1939, he was a thirteen-year-old boy from London who was evacuated to a village in Buckinghamshire with his sister.

'Rosie whispered. She whispered for days. Everything was so clean. We were given face cloths and toothbrushes. We'd never cleaned our teeth up till then. And hot water came from the tap and there was an indoor toilet. And carpets. And clean sheets. This was all very odd and rather scary.'

▼ **SOURCE F** Adapted from a diary entry by Muriel Green, November 1939.

'The village people objected to the evacuees mainly because of the dirtiness of their habits and clothes. Also because of their drinking and bad language. You don't often hear women swear in the village or for them to enter the local pub. But the villagers used to watch the evacuees come out of the pubs with horror.'

▼ **INTERPRETATION G** Kate Eggleston recalling her experiences of the war in a 1989 book.

'As a small child I can remember the evacuees coming. We were horrible to them. It's one of my most shameful memories, how nasty we were. We didn't want them to come, and we all ganged up on them in the playground. We were all in a big circle and the poor evacuees were herded together in the middle, and we were glaring at them and saying, "You made us squash up in our classrooms, you've done this, you're done that." I can remember them now, looking frightened to death. They were poor little kids from the east end of London, they weren't tough at all, they were poor little thin, puny things.'

▼ **SOURCE H** A report from a couple in Northampton, 1939.

'We are a couple living alone. We've always wanted children, and it's been our life's sorrow that they've been denied us. Now our home is alive for the first time. We've a boy and a girl, eight and six. They're not model children, but they'd not be natural if they were. They scream and race about the place, and yesterday the little girl was sick on the carpet. But that's what we've always wanted. Thank God for our little evacuees.'

▼ **SOURCE I** The countryside was a whole new world to many inner-city children. This group are nervously looking at a tame fox, November 1940.

A safe return?

After a few months in the British countryside, many children returned to their lives in the city. The enemy bombers hadn't arrived as expected, and by March 1940 nearly one million children had gone home. However, later that year the mass bombing of British cities (the 'Blitz') began and many children, but not all, went back to the country again.

Fact ✓

Many city children had never seen a farm animal before. They were shocked to see what cows, chickens and sheep looked like. In October 1939 the BBC broadcast this description of a farm animal written by a young evacuee – guess what animal he's describing.

'It has six sides... at the back it has a tail on which hangs a brush. With this it sends flies away so they do not fall into the milk. The head is for growing horns and so that the mouth can be somewhere... the mouth is to moo with. Under the animal hangs the milk... when people milk, the milk comes and there is never an end to the supply. How the animal does it I have not realised... one can smell it far away. This is the reason for fresh air in the country...'

In case you weren't sure, the boy is describing a cow!

Over to You .ıll

1 Read **Interpretation E**. You can infer a lot about Bernard and Rosie's lives before they were evacuated.

   a Write down at least three things you can infer.

   b How had their lives changed?

2 a Make a list of positive and negative experiences of evacuation. Make sure you write down the source or interpretation where you got your information from.

   b Who do you think enjoyed evacuation more – the evacuated children or their new families? Try to give reasons for your answer.

3 Imagine you are a child in one of the sources or interpretations you have been reading. Write a short letter (no more than 150 words) home about your new life. Use your imagination to build up a picture of your new surroundings for your family back home. Compare your letter with other people's letters in your class. Can they guess which source or interpretation you based your letter on?

Fact ✓

When some of the evacuated children finally returned home after the war, they found their homes had been bombed and their parents were missing. Some parents had even abandoned their children on purpose. About 40,000 children remained 'unclaimed' after the war.

▼ **SOURCE J** A British government poster issued in 1940.

Meanwhile... 1939

A different kind of evacuation took place in Europe. *Kindertransport* (German for 'children's transport') was the name of the mission that helped around 10,000 (mainly Jewish) children escape to the UK from Nazi-controlled Europe in the months before the outbreak of war.

Source Analysis

Look at **Source J**.

1 Who is standing next to the tree?

2 What is he doing – and why?

3 What is the message of the poster?

4 How useful is this source to a historian studying the British government's evacuation policy during the Second World War?

5.6 The home front

The Second World War did not just involve soldiers, sailors and airmen. The armed forces may have been the ones who went off to fight the enemy on foreign soil, but the people left at home had their part to play too, and were greatly affected by the conflict. So what impact did the war have on people back in Britain?

Mission Objectives

- Recall key terms and concepts such as rationing, Home Guard and total war.
- Identify ways in which the Second World War affected ordinary citizens.

In late 1940 German bombers began to bomb Britain's major cities. This was known as the 'Blitz'. Swansea, Cardiff, Bristol, Southampton, Plymouth, Birmingham, Coventry, Liverpool, Glasgow, Manchester, Sunderland, Aberdeen, Sheffield and many other cities were targeted. London suffered the heaviest bombing – for one 11-week period, London was bombed every night except one! By the end of May 1941, over 30,000 civilians had been killed in the raids and 87,000 were seriously injured. In London alone, over a million homes were destroyed or damaged.

In May 1940, the government urged all men aged between 17 and 65 who weren't in the army to join what became known as the 'Home Guard'. These men worked part-time in their local area to prepare it for attack. Many of the men in the Home Guard were not permitted to join the regular army because their jobs were necessary to the war effort – farm workers, teachers and railway workers, for example. Others were too old to join up or had health problems. They weren't paid and to begin with they didn't have any weapons… so some made their own!

When the war began, everyone expected to be bombed from the air – so civilians prepared for it. Millions of people built their own bomb shelters in their back gardens.

The Germans tried to cut off supplies of food and other goods by sinking the ships that brought the supplies to Britain. So, in 1940, the government introduced rationing. This meant that every person was entitled to a fixed weekly amount of fuel, clothing and certain types of food. The government also encouraged people to grow their own food in their back gardens or allotments. The slogan for the campaign was 'Dig for Victory'.

DIG for Victory
GROW YOUR OWN VEGETABLES

Fact ✓

Members of the Home Guard were meant to be male – but women served in some units as cooks, messengers and telephone operators.

Air Raid Precaution (ARP) wardens had the job of patrolling the streets at night to make sure that no light was visible. They also helped out if there was an air raid, directing people to shelters, giving first aid and assisting the emergency services. There were 1.4 million ARP wardens, many of them part-time volunteers who also had full-time jobs during the day.

People put up thick blackout curtains to prevent any glimmer of light from escaping. 'Blackouts' made it more difficult for enemy bombers to locate their targets. Street lights were switched off or dimmed too, and cars were fitted with masked headlights. Windows were taped to stop glass from shattering everywhere if a bomb exploded nearby.

The government had the power to move people to any job it felt necessary to help win the war. Millions of women worked in weapons factories, on farms, and in military bases. Single women were forced to work but married women weren't. However, many decided to work anyway, as well as looking after their families.

When war broke out, the government evacuated schoolchildren (and their teachers), pregnant women, blind and disabled people, and women with children under five. They were moved from the large industrial towns and cities to safer countryside areas.

The government issued millions of gas masks to civilians as a precaution against gas bombs.

KEEP CLEAR UNEXPLODED BOMB

Earlier on..

1914–1918

In 1915, a Women's Land Army was created so women (known as Land Girls) could work in farming, replacing men called up to fight. In 1939, the organisation was revived under the same name and by 1944 it had over 80,000 members.

Fact ✓

When a country uses all its resources to try to win, and the war involves all its people in some way, the conflict is often called a 'total war'. The term became well known in connection with the Second World War because it was used by leading Nazi Joseph Goebbels in a 1943 speech in Berlin.

Change ⭐

1 Explain two ways in which the home front in Britain in the First World War (see pages 50–51) and the home front in Britain in the Second World War were similar.

2 Explain two ways in which the home front in Britain in the First World War (see pages 50–51) and the home front in Britain in the Second World War were different.

Over to You

1 In your own words, define 'total war'.

2 Prepare a short talk, or design a poster, aimed at primary school students. It should explain what life was like in Britain during the Second World War. Include details about:
- the Blitz
- air raid precautions
- evacuation
- changing roles of women
- the Home Guard
- rationing
- the Dig for Victory campaign.

3 List the three biggest changes to civilian life during the war.

5.7 How did the Second World War change health and medicine?

There were important advances made in health and medicine during the First World War (see pages 44–45). It was a similar situation in the Second World War. There were millions of wounded soldiers, so doctors, surgeons and scientists worked hard to develop new medicines and techniques to help them. They also tried to develop some of the advances that had been made in the earlier part of the century. So what was the impact of the Second World War on health and medicine?

Blood transfusions

Injured soldiers can lose a lot of blood – and it sometimes needs to be replaced. This is called a 'blood transfusion'. Advances in storing blood in the years after the First World War meant blood could be kept fresh (and useable) for longer. Large blood banks were developed in the USA and Britain in the years leading up to the Second World War, much of it donated by civilians. These blood banks were widely used in the war and helped save many lives. In 1946, the British government set up the National Blood Transfusion Service.

▼ **SOURCE A** A blood donor poster from the 1940s.

IF HE SHOULD FALL   IS YOUR BLOOD THERE TO SAVE HIM?

THE ARMY BLOOD TRANSFUSION SERVICE NEEDS
BLOOD DONORS

Plastic surgery

A doctor from New Zealand, Archibald McIndoe (cousin of Harold Gillies – see page 45), developed new ways to deal with the terrible burns that many pilots suffered when their aircraft were on fire. He used drugs in new ways to prevent and control infections. His work on reconstructing damaged faces and hands was respected all over the world.

▶ **SOURCE B** A soldier, wounded in the Second World War, after treatment by Archibald McIndoe.

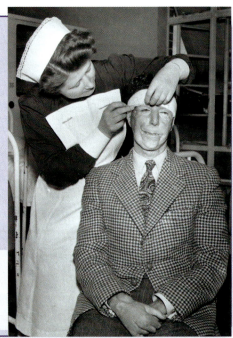

Earlier on...

FIRST WORLD WAR

In the First World War, Harold Gillies (the cousin of Archibald McIndoe) worked out a way of taking a healthy piece of skin and attaching it to an injured place on a patient's body, known as a skin graft. His work led to the development of what we now call 'plastic surgery' – and his cousin developed this work in the Second World War.

Heart surgery

Many soldiers suffered injuries to their hearts – from gunfire and bombs – during the war, and needed life-saving surgery. American army surgeon Dwight Harken developed ways to cut into beating hearts and remove bullets and bits of shrapnel (fragments thrown out by explosions). His findings helped heart surgery develop further after the war.

Diet

Shortages of some foods during the war meant that the government encouraged people to grow their own food. This actually improved people's diet because the food they encouraged civilians to grow – fresh vegetables, for example – was very healthy.

▶ **SOURCE C** A poster for the 'Dig for Victory' campaign.

Hygiene and disease

In order to keep the nation 'fighting fit' the government produced posters that encouraged people to keep healthy. They warned against the dangers of poor hygiene. A national **immunisation** programme against diphtheria (a bacterial infection that killed many children) was launched too.

▶ **SOURCE D** A diphtheria immunisation poster.

The National Health Service (NHS)

During the war, politicians began to plan how healthcare could be better organised once the fighting was over. In 1942, a government worker named William Beveridge proposed a 'free National Health Service for all'. Just after the war ended, the government put his plans in place, and the NHS was born.

Drug development

Penicillin, the first **antibiotic**, was developed in the years leading up to the war. The British and US governments realised how important this new 'wonder drug' could be in dealing with infections in deep wounds. By 1944, enough penicillin had been produced to treat all the Allied forces in Europe.

Key Words   antibiotic

Poverty

During the war, over a million children were evacuated from towns and cities into the countryside. Many of the children were very poor and the better diets and cleaner air they enjoyed in the countryside improved their health. Evacuation highlighted the poverty that existed in Britain's towns and cities, and increased the government's commitment to improve things after the war.

▼ **INTERPRETATION E**
Adapted from a 2005 interview with a woman who had been evacuated from Birmingham to a village in Leicestershire during the war.

'The home was well cared for and comfortable. How different this was to my previous home life. At midday I went home from school to a cooked dinner and what a joy that was. I could smell what was cooking as I entered the back door into the kitchen. I couldn't get in quick enough especially on Wednesday when we had steak and kidney pie. When I returned home from school in the afternoon there was a plate of jam sandwiches and a slice of homemade cake and a glass of milk ready for me. I soon put on weight and was no longer the thin weedy child I had once been.'

Over to You

1 For each of the following, write one sentence to summarise developments made during the war:
- blood transfusions
- plastic surgery
- heart surgery

2 Of the advances, ideas and developments featured on these pages, find an example that you think:

a would not have happened if it wasn't for the war

b would have happened anyway, but happened more quickly because of the war.

5.8 Penicillin and the war

If you have been ill or badly injured, you may have been treated using an antibiotic. If you haven't, you will certainly know someone who has! An antibiotic is a type of drug that kills bacteria and clears infections. The best-known and most widely used antibiotic in the world is called penicillin. It was also the first antibiotic ever used to cure an infected patient. How was it discovered? Who was involved in its development? And in what way is it linked to the Second World War?

Mission Objectives

- Examine the development of penicillin.
- Assess the impact of penicillin.

The discovery

Penicillin is a natural substance – in fact, it is a type of mould (the sort of stuff that grows in an unwashed coffee cup or on a two-week old uneaten sandwich). Doctors in the 1800s first noticed that some moulds were able to kill germs – but they didn't realise how useful this might be.

The story of how penicillin became the best-known and most widely used antibiotic in the world is one that involves brilliant scientists, war, technology, government help… and a bit of luck. Read it carefully:

1 Scottish scientist Alexander Fleming was experimenting with a particularly nasty type of germ (called staphylococcus) that caused a lot of infections.

He left some of this germ in a dish while he went on holiday

2 After his holiday, he noticed that mould had grown in the dish, killing the germs around it.

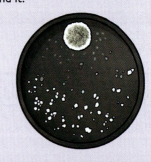

Upon investigation, Fleming found that this mould was penicillin, and he had discovered its germ-killing properties.

3 Fleming grew more of the mould and found it killed other germs too. But he didn't have the specialist help or money to continue experimenting with penicillin.

Instead, he wrote about his discovery in a medical magazine in 1929.

4 In the late 1930s, two scientists from Oxford University were making a list of all the substances that could kill germs.

Howard Florey (from Australia) and Ernst Chain (a German-born Jew who had come to Britain to escape the Nazis) read Fleming's article from 1929 on penicillin, and included it on their list.

5 When the Second World War began, the scientists got a small amount of money from the British government to do more research.

In May 1940, Florey and Chain began tests. Eight mice were injected with a germ called streptococcus. Four mice were given penicillin, and four weren't. The four mice injected with penicillin recovered, but the other four died. Chain called it a miracle!

6

In February 1941, they used penicillin to treat a policeman, named Albert Alexander, who had developed a severe face infection after scratching his face on a rose bush.

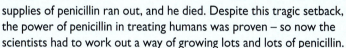

Alexander began to recover – but then supplies of penicillin ran out, and he died. Despite this tragic setback, the power of penicillin in treating humans was proven – so now the scientists had to work out a way of growing lots and lots of penicillin.

7

The Second World War was an important factor in the penicillin story. The growing number of wounded soldiers with nasty infections meant that more penicillin was needed – and quickly.

In June 1941, Florey went to America to meet with the US government. The Americans realised what an important drug penicillin could be and agreed to pay several large chemical companies to make millions of litres of it.

8

By the start of 1943, enough had been made to treat just 100 patients, but by 1944 there was enough to treat 40,000.

By the end of the war in 1945, enough penicillin was being produced to treat 250,000 people a month – and it has been estimated that penicillin saved the lives of 12 to 15 per cent of all the Allied soldiers.

Later on...

1945–TODAY

After the war, penicillin became available for use by ordinary citizens too. In total, it is estimated that penicillin has saved at least 200 million lives across the globe!

Fact ✓

The research team at Oxford University was not simply made up of Florey and Chain – they were joined by Dorothy Crowfoot Hodgkin, Arthur Gordon Sanders, Mary Ethel Florey (Howard's wife), Edward Penley Abraham, Norman Heatley and Margaret Jennings.

▼ **INTERPRETATION A** Adapted from an article on the website of the Wellcome Sanger Institute, which carries out medical research.

'From a contaminated dish in London to saving lives on the D-Day beaches of Normandy, penicillin has saved many millions of lives. Before antibiotics, even the smallest of cuts could be fatal; but that changed with the work of Alexander Fleming, Ernst Chain and Howard Florey... Antibiotics haven't just given us the ability to treat infections, they've also allowed for fundamental changes in modern medicine. Without antibiotics, routine surgery and many common treatments would all be incredibly risky procedures.'

Over to You ..ıll

1 What is an antibiotic?

2 Explain the part played in the penicillin story by: Alexander Fleming; Florey and Chain; Albert Alexander; the US government.

3 How was the discovery of penicillin speeded up by the Second World War?

4 Describe the work of Florey and Chain in developing penicillin in the 1930 and 1940s.

Significance

1 Read **Interpretation A**. According to this article, how significant was the work of Fleming, Florey and Chain in the history of medicine?

2 Explain the significance of Fleming's discovery of penicillin in 1928.

5.9A Why is Sir Arthur Harris such a controversial figure?

At about 9:00pm on 13 February 1945, 805 British bomber planes dropped 2690 tons of bombs on the German city of Dresden. Before long, an area of 28 square km was burning so ferociously that temperatures reached 1000 degrees Celsius. American bombers dropped more bombs on the city over the next two nights. The city blazed for seven days, during which time it is thought that around 25,000 civilians burned to death (though Nazi estimates at the time were as high as 250,000). But why was the city bombed on such a huge scale? Who ordered the bombing? Why was the decision to bomb Dresden so controversial?

Mission Objectives

- Explain the difference between precision bombing and area bombing.
- Formulate an opinion on why you think Dresden was bombed.

The statue

In 1992, a statue of a man in RAF uniform was unveiled in London. The statue was of Sir Arthur 'Bomber' Harris, the Head of Bomber Command (the part of the RAF that controlled its bomber forces from 1936 to 1968) and the man whose idea it was to bomb Dresden. Soon after the statue was unveiled, protesters threw paint at it, wrote graffiti over it and demanded its removal. What might have been the reasons behind their actions? Why is Sir Arthur Harris such a controversial figure? Was it wrong to bomb Dresden – or, as Sir Arthur Harris thought, was the raid necessary to shorten the war and save British lives?

Your task over the next four pages is to formulate an opinion. You must establish:

- why you think the raid happened in the first place
- why the raid caused so many deaths
- what you think the bombing of Dresden achieved.

You will then use your ideas and opinions to complete an extended piece of work.

▶ **SOURCE A** The vandalised statue of Sir Arthur Harris in London. Harris was the only war commander not to have a statue made of him immediately after the war.

▶ **SOURCE B** The devastated centre of the city of Dresden, 1945.

Why bomb Dresden?

Bomber planes changed the face of war between 1939 and 1945. American and British planes dropped nearly three million tons of bombs on 131 German cities. Up to half a million German civilians were killed, and around eight million were made homeless. German planes dropped bombs on British cities too – 40,000 people died in air raids on cities including London, Coventry, Glasgow and Hull.

When the war began, both sides had tried to use precision bombing to hit key targets, such as factories, ports, bridges, major roads and railway stations. It is sometimes called 'strategic bombing'. The idea was to destroy the enemy's ability to fight by making it impossible to manufacture weapons, build ships or move soldiers around. However, precision bombing didn't work as well as expected – bombs didn't always hit their targets and damage was often easily repaired – so area bombing was introduced instead. This devastating new type of attack meant that whole towns and cities were bombed in order to make sure that everything was destroyed… including the enemy's morale and will to fight.

In October 1944, a detailed report by the British on Dresden concluded that the city was an 'unattractive target'. In other words, there was no point in bombing it. However, in January 1945 British spies reported that thousands of German soldiers were collecting in Dresden before being sent off to fight. All of a sudden, Dresden had turned into a key bombing target – and this very likely influenced the decision to attack.

▼ **SOURCE C** Advice given to the British government in 1942 by a senior scientific adviser.

'Investigations seem to show that having your house destroyed is most damaging to morale... there seems little doubt that this will break the spirit of the [German] people.'

▼ **SOURCE D** Sir Arthur Harris, explaining why he ordered the bombing of Dresden, from his autobiography *Bomber Command* (1947).

'Dresden had become the main centre for the defence of Germany. A heavy air attack would disorganise this. It had never been bombed before. And, as a large centre of the war industry, it was very important.'

Key Words   area bombing   precision bombing

▼ **SOURCE E** Sir Arthur Harris talking to a US general in 1942.

'Destroy a factory and they rebuild it. If I kill all their workers it takes 21 years to provide new ones.'

▼ **SOURCE F** A British poster showing Lancaster bombers attacking munitions factories in Germany.

THE ATTACK BEGINS IN THE FACTORY

Over to You

1 What is the difference between precision bombing and area bombing?

2 What evidence is there so far that Dresden was targeted for military reasons?

3 What evidence is there so far that Dresden was *not* targeted for military reasons?

Source Analysis

1 Look at **Source F**. What does the poster show?

2 What was the purpose of **Source F**?

Depth Study

5.9B Why is Sir Arthur Harris such a controversial figure?

Why did so many die?

The planes dropped a mixture of incendiary and high explosive bombs. **Incendiary bombs** are specifically designed to start fires. Dresden, a very old city with many wooden-framed buildings, started to burn very quickly. The fact that the city was packed with people fleeing the Soviet army, which was advancing towards Germany, meant that any large fire was sure to kill thousands.

The bombs soon created a **firestorm**. The hot air that rose up from the burning buildings was replaced by cooler air rushing in from outside. Soon, hurricane-force winds of up to 193kph were fanning the flames and 'superheating' the fire.

The impact of the attack

There has been a great deal of debate about the bombing of Dresden over the years. Some argue that it contributed to the defeat of Germany, while others questioned whether it was necessary at all. The following sources and interpretations might help you form your own opinion.

▼ **SOURCE G** Adapted from a letter by Sir Arthur Harris to Sir Norman Bottomley (Harris's deputy at Bomber Command), March 1945.

'Attacks on cities... tend to shorten the war and so preserve the lives of allied soldiers... I do not personally regard the whole of the remaining cities of Germany as worth the bones of one British soldier.'

▼ **SOURCE H & I** The city of Dresden in 1944, before the bombing (below left) and in 1945, after the bombing (below right). At the time, the Nazis estimated that 250,000 people had been killed but many historians now agree that this figure was inflated.

▼ **INTERPRETATION I**
From a speech given by British historian Dr Noble Frankland in 1996. He served in the Royal Air Force from 1941 to 1945, as a navigator in Bomber Command.

'Most people were very pleased with Bomber Command during the war and until it was virtually won; then they turned round and said it wasn't a very nice way to wage war. This is the sort of issue that arises today, but people who indulge in that have simply failed to examine what the conditions of the Second World War actually were. It's all very well to say today that it was a great pity to kill all those civilians, but if minds are cast back to 1940 it all looks very different. Then Bomber Command's offensive was extremely popular and was a major factor in national morale and our ability to continue the war.'

▼ **INTERPRETATION J** Based on interviews with Albert Speer, a leading Nazi in charge of war production, who appeared in a 1973 documentary called *The World at War*.

'I know there is much argument over whether the bombing was good or bad, but the damage done reduced our production of tanks, ammunition and submarines by twenty or thirty per cent.'

▼ **SOURCE K** Adapted from the report of the British Bombing Survey Unit, set up at the end of the war to study the effects of area bombing on Germany.

'Many German towns were severely devastated by bombing, but the effect on the amount of weapons, tanks and fighter planes the Germans produced was small... the bombings didn't make the German people lose the will to fight either. The German people proved calmer and more determined than anticipated.'

▼ **INTERPRETATION L** From an online article written for the US air force by a military history writer. In the article, he mentions a British man named Victor Gregg who had been captured while fighting the Germans in the Netherlands in 1944, and sent to Dresden.

'It has been condemned as a war crime by many, including Allied prisoners of war who were there. "As the incendiaries fell, the phosphorus clung to the bodies of those below, turning them into human torches," Victor Gregg, a British paratrooper held in the city during the bombing, said 68 years later. "The screaming of those who were being burned alive was added to the cries of those not yet hit. There was no need for flares to lead the second wave of bombers to their target, as the whole city had become a gigantic torch. Dresden had no defences – no anti-aircraft guns, no searchlights, nothing."'

▼ **INTERPRETATION M** Dominic Selwood, a British historian and author, writing on the *Telegraph* website in February 2015.

'The key question remains whether the bombing of Dresden was militarily necessary – because by then the war was definitely over. Hitler was already hiding away in his bunker. The British and Americans were at the German border after winning D-Day the previous summer, while the Russians were well inside eastern Germany and racing towards Berlin.

Dresden was a civilian town without military significance. It had no role of any sort to play in the closing months of the war. So, what strategic purpose did burning its men, women, old people and children serve? Churchill himself later wrote that "the destruction of Dresden remains a serious query against the conduct of Allied bombing".'

Key Words

firestorm   incendiary bomb

Over to You

1 A television company is staging a debate on whether the statue of Sir Arthur Harris should be removed or not. Use the information from pages 132–135 (and any other information you can find) to produce an opening speech for the debate. You may choose to simply introduce the whole topic, and explain why the Dresden bombing is such a controversial topic. Or, you might decide to support Harris's actions or oppose them. Whether you are for or against, you should try to consider:

- whether Dresden was an acceptable target or not
- if the use of incendiary rather than explosive bombs tells us anything about the attack
- whether Harris was acting in Britain's best interests by trying to win the war – or if he was a war criminal guilty of killing innocent people
- what you think people might have felt about the bombing of German cities at the time
- if Harris was doing something that most British people supported
- whether, in a war, everyone who helps build weapons – including workers and their families – is a fair target
- if Harris can be criticised for killing Germans – after all, weren't they all part of Hitler's empire?
- whether the bombings actually achieved anything
- if the bombing helped Britain win the war.

5.10A Why is Winston Churchill on a £5 note?

Britain's Prime Minister during the Second World War, Winston Churchill, was chosen to feature on a new £5 note for 2016. The Bank of England, which decides on the historical figures who appear on the notes, said that Sir Winston Churchill was 'a truly great British leader' and a 'hero' whose 'energy, courage, wit and public service' should be an 'inspiration to us all'. But do you agree? Was he a great British leader? Do you think he should appear on a £5 note?

Mission Objectives

* Outline why Winston Churchill appears on a £5 note.
* Assess whether you think he was a 'truly great leader' or not.

What makes a good leader?

Before looking through these sources relating to Churchill, take a moment or two to think about the sort of qualities that make a good leader.

* List some words that would describe a good leader. Can you give examples of good leaders you know of?

* What are the most important qualities of good leaders? List your top three.

* Do you think leaders during wartime need any qualities that are different from the ones who lead in peacetime?

Who was Winston Churchill?

In the years before the Second World War broke out, the British government followed a policy called 'appeasement'. This meant that Britain (and France) allowed Hitler to get away with things (like building up his army or taking over other countries) in order to keep on friendly terms with him. It was hoped that Hitler would soon have all the land he wanted and so would eventually stop! Winston Churchill, who wasn't part of the government at this time, felt appeasement was wrong. He said that Britain must stand up to Hitler. So, when the idea of appeasement failed, and war finally broke out, it was clear that Britain needed a new leader. In May 1940, Winston Churchill became Britain's Prime Minister.

Winston Churchill (1874-1965)

Born:	30 November 1874 at Blenheim Palace, Oxfordshire, England
Education:	Harrow School and Royal Military Academy Sandhurst

Early career:
* Joined the army, fought in battles in India and Africa 1897–1898
* Worked as a war reporter during some of the Boer War (1899–1902)

Politics:
* 1900: elected as an MP
* 1910: became Home Secretary (in charge of law and order, and policing)
* 1911: put in charge of Royal Navy
* 1915: during First World War he planned an attack on Turkey that went badly wrong; many soldiers died and Churchill resigned
* 1924–1929: back in politics, became Chancellor of the Exchequer (in charge of the country's money and taxes), but his policies were not successful
* 1929–1940: remained an MP and said Britain should watch Hitler carefully, stand up to him, and get ready for a war; people took little notice of his warnings
* 1940–1945: First term as Prime Minister
* 1951–1955: Second term as Prime Minister

▼ **SOURCE A** Winston Churchill appeared on the first ever plastic British banknote in 2016.

Winston during wartime

The British government felt it was important for the new Prime Minister to be seen in a particular way during wartime. Look through **Sources B** to **F** carefully.

▶ **SOURCE B**
A poster produced during the Second World War, in 1940, that shows Churchill as a British bulldog.

▼ **SOURCE C** Extracts from some of Churchill's most famous wartime speeches.

'Never give in, never, never, never, never – in nothing great or small, large or petty... Never yield to force; never yield to the apparently overwhelming might of the enemy.'

'I have nothing to offer but blood, toil, tears and sweat. We have before us an ordeal of the most grievous kind. We have before us many, many long months of struggle and of suffering... You ask, what is our aim? I can answer in one word: it is victory, victory at all costs, victory in spite of all terror... for without victory there is no survival.'

'We shall go on to the end... We shall defend our island whatever the cost may be. We shall fight on the beaches, we shall fight on the landing grounds, we shall fight in the fields and in the streets, we shall fight in the hills; we shall never surrender.'

▶ **SOURCE D**
This 1940 poster shows Churchill leading troops from many Allied countries into battle.

▼ **SOURCE E** Winston Churchill inspecting bomb damage and rallying people in Birmingham in 1941.

▼ **SOURCE F** Adapted from an account by an assistant to Churchill.

'The ideas, the determination to push his ideas, provoking commanders to attack – these were all expressions of that blazing, explosive energy which helped steadily steer civilians and soldiers through so many setbacks and difficulties.'

Over to You

1 Complete the sentences with accurate terms.
   - Winston Churchill was born at _____ in 1874.
   - He worked as a _____ during the Boer War.
   - He became an MP in _____.
   - He was very critical of Hitler and became _____ in 1940.

2 Look at **Source B**. Why do you think Churchill is drawn in this way?

3 Look at **Sources C** and **D**. If you were an ordinary citizen who lived during the war, how might speeches and cartoons like these make you feel?

4 Look at **Source E**. Why do you think Churchill was keen to be photographed visiting bomb sites?

Knowledge and Understanding

1 Make a list of words you might use to describe the way Churchill was presented during the war.

2 Describe the role of Winston Churchill during the war.

5.10B Why is Winston Churchill on a £5 note?

Churchill: after the war

However, Churchill wasn't always viewed in such a positive way as in the sources you've studied on pages 136–137. Some cartoons at the time were critical of him (see **M**), and in the years after the war, some people questioned Churchill's leadership. For example, he has been heavily criticised for diverting vast quantities of food from India to Britain during the war, leading to widespread famine there which killed up to 3 million people. He has also been condemned for the way he brutally dealt with an uprising in Kenya during his second term as Prime Minister in the 1950s. Study the following sources and interpretations carefully.

▼ **SOURCE G** Adapted from the diary of Robert Menzies, the Australian Prime Minister, who visited Britain in 1941.

- 'No one disagrees with Winston, he is surrounded by people saying "yes" to him all the time. His colleagues fear him – the people have set him up as a God, and he is terrifically powerful.

- Winston is acting as the master planner of the war, without any qualifications, and without any strong, forceful leaders from the armed forces to help him.

- He loves war and spends hours with charts and maps. There isn't a proper policy for growing food. In brief, Churchill is a bad organiser.

- Winston should be leading the country, instead of touring bombed areas, which he has been doing all week. Let the King and Queen do this because they are better at it.'

▼ **SOURCE H** Adapted from the diary of Alan Brooke, a British army commander and one of Churchill's most important military advisers. In his diary Brooke writes that he felt it was important for him to remain close to Churchill to try to stop him making any major military mistakes.

'We had to consider this morning one of Winston's worst orders I have ever seen. I can only believe that he must have been quite tight [drunk] when he dictated it. My God! How little the world at large knows what his failings and defects are!'

▼ **SOURCE I** Leading US general Dwight D. Eisenhower (who later became US President), writing about Churchill in a book he wrote in 1948. Eisenhower also describes Churchill as someone who used his intelligence and humour to get his own way.

'An inspirational leader, typical of Britain's courage and determination. He was a man of extraordinarily strong beliefs and a master in argument and debate. Completely devoted to winning the war and being a responsible Prime Minister of Great Britain… I admired and liked him. He knew this perfectly well and never hesitated to use that knowledge in his effort to swing me to his own line of thought in any argument. Yet in spite of his strength of purpose, in those instances where we found our convictions in direct opposition, he never once lost his friendly attitude toward me.'

▼ **INTERPRETATION J** Adapted from the autobiography of politician Herbert Morrison, who knew Churchill, written in 1960.

'Churchill's ideas about the army annoyed some of the chiefs and generals. They said that if his ideas were adopted then the war might go badly. They may have been right, but I wonder if Churchill just said these things to get them thinking harder.'

▼ **INTERPRETATION K** Adapted from a 2019 interview with British historian Andrew Roberts who had recently published a biography of Winston Churchill.

'Churchill made blunder after blunder in his life. He got lots of things wrong. So, it's not as though we are faced with someone who never made a mistake. But as he himself told his wife, Clementine, "I should have made nothing if I'd not made mistakes." And so the interesting thing for me was the way in which he learnt from his mistakes – to an extraordinary degree. So this is the story of a man who made mistakes but learned from them.'

▼ **INTERPRETATION L** Written by Dr Anthony Storr, a psychiatrist. It is said that Storr is referring to Churchill's heavy drinking in this extract.

'In 1940, when all the odds were against Britain, a leader of sober judgement might well have concluded that we were finished... But only a man who had known and faced despair within himself could carry conviction at such a moment... Churchill was such a man: and it was because, all his life, he had conducted a battle with his own despair that he could convey to others that despair can be overcome.'

▼ **SOURCE M** A cartoon of Churchill published in 1953. At this time, some people thought Churchill should retire from politics. He hated the picture and was upset by it. He even said, 'There's malice [nastiness] in it. Look at my hands, I have beautiful hands... I shall have to retire if this sort of thing goes on.'

Fact ✓

Churchill was defeated in the 1945 general election, held shortly after the end of the war. He was viewed by many as a great war leader, but the public did not elect him to run the country in peacetime. He won the 1951 election, though, and became Prime Minister again for another four years.

Over to You .ıll

1 **a** Make a list of Churchill's strengths and weaknesses as a war leader. You should look back at the sources on pages 136–139 to help you. For each strength or weakness, write a short sentence about the source that you got your information from.

  b Can a strength also be a weakness? You might want to discuss your ideas with a partner.

2 When Churchill appeared on the new £5 note, he was described as a 'great British leader'. So, do you think he was a great leader? Did he deserve his place on a new note? Explain your views.

3 Why do you think views of people can change over time? Give reason for your answer.

Source Analysis

1 Look at **Source M**. How did Churchill react to this cartoon?

2 The cartoon is critical of Churchill. How do you know?

5.11A The journey to the 'Final Solution'

In January 1942, a group of leading Nazis gathered in the Wannsee district of Berlin. Hitler didn't attend, but had given clear instructions. Those who attended the Wannsee Conference (as the meeting became known) were informed of the plan to kill all the Jewish people left in Europe – an estimated 11 million people – by working them to death, using poison gas or shooting. This plan became known as the 'Final Solution'. No one at the table objected to the plan, they simply discussed how it would be carried out. But how had Jews been treated up to this point? Why did Hitler hate Jews so much? And how close did the Nazis come to achieving the destruction of Europe's Jews?

Mission Objectives

- Identify why Hitler and the Nazis persecuted Jewish people.
- Examine how the 'Final Solution' was organised.

The persecution of Jews

The unfair or cruel treatment of someone (or a group of people) over a long period because of their race, religion or political beliefs is known as **persecution**. The persecution of Jewish people is called **antisemitism** – and it has been common in Europe for many centuries. Among other things, Jewish people have been blamed for the death of Jesus Christ and the outbreak of the Black Death in the 1300s. Since the Middle Ages, Christian culture associated Jews with wealth and power – this false antisemitic belief was accepted widely around Europe. At one time or another, Jews have been persecuted in nearly all European countries and there are many nations today with a record of antisemitic violence in their history. In 1290, for example, King Edward I expelled all Jews from England, and they were banned from returning for over 350 years.

Persecution into the twentieth century

In the centuries after the Middle Ages, the persecution of Jewish communities continued in Europe. Jews were often treated as outsiders, and had few civil rights. In the late 1800s, a German writer named Wilhelm Marr wrote that he thought Jews would soon illegally take control of all of Germany's highest political positions. It was Marr who first used the term 'antisemitism'. In Russia at this time, false documents were published that told of a secret Jewish plot to take over the world. Although the documents were proven fakes, they were distributed worldwide. There were several massacres of Jews in Russia in the late 1880s and early 1900s.

By the turn of the twentieth century, antisemitic beliefs were widespread in many European countries, and Jews – who had no state of their own – were viewed with suspicion and mistrust. And when Hitler rose to power in the early 1930s, he made Jews the convenient **scapegoats** for Germany's problems. As leader of Germany he introduced laws and rules that made the lives of Jewish people very difficult (see **A** and **B**).

▼ **A** Examples of laws that were designed to make life more and more difficult for German Jews.

LAWS AGAINST JEWS, 1933–1939

- **April 1933:** All Jews banned from any sports clubs; all Jewish teachers sacked; all Jewish lawyers and judges sacked
- **September 1933:** 'Race studies' (Eugenics) introduced in German schools (see page 94)
- **January 1934:** All Jewish shops marked with a yellow Star of David – a symbol of the Jewish religion – or the word Juden (German for 'Jew'); soldiers stand outside shops turning people away
- **September 1935:** Jews not allowed to vote; marriages between Jews and non-Jews banned
- **January 1936:** No Jew allowed to own any electrical equipment (including cameras), bicycles, typewriters or music records; Jews banned from using swimming pools
- **July 1938:** Jewish doctors sacked
- **August 1938:** Male Jews must add the name 'Israel' and female Jews must add the name 'Sara' to their first names
- **November 1938:** Jewish children banned from German schools
- **December 1938:** Jewish and non-Jewish children forbidden to play together
- **April 1939:** Jews can be evicted from their homes for no reason
- **September 1939:** Jews no longer allowed out of their homes between 8:00pm and 6:00am

▼ **SOURCE B** A park bench in Berlin – the sign reads: 'Not for Jews'.

The impact of war

Many Jewish people had left Germany before the outbreak of the war, to escape the persecution and settle in nearby countries. However, they found themselves back under Nazi rule when Germany invaded these countries during the war. As the war went on, more Jews became trapped under Hitler's rule all over Europe – three million in Poland, up to three million in the Soviet Union and 1.3 million in France, the Netherlands, Belgium, Denmark, Norway and the Balkans. In some countries, from 1939, Jews were rounded up and forced to live in separate areas (called **ghettos**) in major cities, or sent to work in labour camps. It is estimated that around half a million Jews died in these ghettos of disease and starvation. Many also died in the labour camps.

Execution squads

Execution squads (called 'Einsatzgruppen') went out into the countryside to hunt down (and execute) as many Jewish people as they could find. Sometimes the local police were given the job of finding Jews and shooting them. Despite these measures, to many fanatical Nazis, including Hitler, the destruction of Europe's Jews was not happening quickly enough – and by the end of 1941 leading Nazis had begun working on plans for what they called 'a final solution to the Jewish question'.

▶ **INTERPRETATION C**

An interview that took place in the 1970s with Rivka Yoselevska, a Polish-Jewish survivor of a massacre in Poland by an execution squad during the war.

'Then he got ready to shoot me. We stood there facing the ditch. I turned my head. He asked, "Whom do I shoot first?" I didn't answer. He tore the child away from me. I heard her last cry and he shot her. Then he got ready to kill me, grabbed my hair and turned my head. I remained standing and heard a shot but I didn't move. He turned me around, loaded his pistol, so that I could see what he was doing. Then he again turned me around and shot me. I fell down. I felt nothing. At that moment I felt that something was weighing me down. I thought that I was dead, but that I could feel something even though I was dead. I couldn't believe that I was alive.'

The 'Final Solution'

At the Wannsee Conference, Nazi leaders discussed how to murder Europe's Jews – around 11 million people. This not only included Jews who lived in the areas of Europe controlled by Hitler, but also those in the UK, Switzerland, Ireland, Sweden, Spain and Portugal. Six large extermination camps (or 'death camps') were specially built for this purpose and soon Jews were being transported to them. At the largest of the camps, Auschwitz-Birkenau, Jews were joined by thousands of Roma and Sinti (sometimes known as 'Gypsies'), Poles and Soviets, political opponents and others. The other camps were designed specifically for the extermination of Jews.

Fighting back

The Nazis tried to destroy Jewish life and culture – but Jewish people fought back in several ways. For example, secret schools, theatres and places of worship were set up in some ghettos. Also, some Jews violently rebelled against what was happening to them. In 1943, in the Warsaw ghetto in Poland, Jews rebelled against the German soldiers there. It took 43 days for the Germans to finally regain control. They then arrested and executed all those involved and burned down the ghetto.

There were occasional rebellions in death camps. The best-known of all was in Treblinka in 1943. One of the prisoners managed to get into the weapons store where he handed out guns and grenades. After setting the camp on fire, 150 prisoners managed to escape, killing 15 guards in the process. However, the Nazis soon regained control and many escapees were killed.

The death camps

There were six main death camps – Auschwitz-Birkenau, Belzec, Chelmno, Majdanek, Sobibor and Treblinka (see **E**). Auschwitz-Birkenau was the largest and initially served as a detention centre for political prisoners. However, it grew into a network of camps where Jews and other 'enemies of the Nazi state' were either killed, or used as slave labour. The other camps did not have areas for slave labour – instead they were simply created to kill the Jews who arrived there.

Case study: Auschwitz-Birkenau

Auschwitz-Birkenau differed from the other death camps because it included a concentration camp and a slave labour camp, as well as large gas chambers for the killing of Jews. Upon arrival, Jews were sorted into two groups: those who looked over 15 years old and were strong and healthy were sent to one side; the old, the sick, pregnant women and women with young children were sent to another. The strong and healthy ones (usually about 10 per cent) were put to work helping to murder the others. Any refusals would result in an immediate death sentence. Those selected to die weren't informed of their fate. To prevent panic, they were told they were going to have a shower and were given soap and towels as they were marched into big chambers disguised as shower rooms. With as many as 2000 prisoners packed inside at any one time, the doors were sealed and poisonous gas was poured through the vents. In about 30 minutes, everyone was dead. The bodies were later burned.

Who knew?

Around six million Jews were killed by Hitler's Nazis, and around three million of these deaths took place in death camps. Thousands of people, not only loyal Nazis, helped with the 'Final Solution': ordinary people in Germany and from across the countries occupied by Germany were involved, such as railway workers who loaded Jewish people onto cattle trucks bound for the camps, office clerks, typists, telephone operators,

▼ **SOURCE D** A large group of Hungarian Jews arrive at Auschwitz-Birkenau in June 1944.

policemen and soldiers. 150 German companies used Auschwitz prisoners as slaves to build their goods. Other firms competed for the contracts to design and build the gas chambers and ovens in which people were murdered and burned. Also, many ordinary people, not only in Germany, knew what was going on too. Some people **collaborated** with the Germans to gain an advantage for themselves or their families.

For many years, there has been controversy over how much governments in other countries, such as the USA and Britain, knew about the death camps. Today, most historians agree that they knew what was happening, but decided against any action. In fact, when it was suggested to the Allied governments that they should bomb the death camps, the idea was rejected because they decided bomber planes should only be used to bomb German military targets, such as factories.

Key Words   collaboration   Holocaust

Fact ✓

The Nazis' attempt to wipe out the Jewish race is commonly known as the **Holocaust**. However, in recent years, some have objected to this word, as it means 'sacrifice'. They argue that this implies that Jews were 'offering themselves' in some way. The word 'genocide' is preferred by some, which means the deliberate extermination of an ethnic or religious group, or nation. Many Jews prefer the Hebrew term 'Shoah', meaning 'catastrophe'.

Over to You 📶

1 a Explain what the word 'Holocaust' means.

   b Why do you think some people don't approve of the word 'Holocaust' when describing what happened to Jews during the war?

2 Describe ways that Jews fought back and resisted what was happening to them.

3 Today, Auschwitz extermination camp is a museum. Many people were against turning it into a museum and wanted it to be pulled down.

   a Why do you think some people wanted Auschwitz destroyed?

   b Do you think we should forget a place like Auschwitz or not? Give reasons for your opinions.

▶ **MAP E** A map of Europe showing the main concentration and extermination camps. Concentration camps tended to be more like prisons where inmates were put to work in terrible conditions. They were often worked to death. The extermination camps' only purpose was to kill.

Change

1 Explain two ways in which Nazi persecution of Jews before the war was different from the persecution during the war.

N

BERLIN

🏠 Extermination camps
🏠 Concentration camps
— Transport routes (rail)

Number of Jews killed	
Poland	3,000,000
USSR	1,300,000
Hungary	450,000
Romania	300,000
Germany	210,000
Czechoslovakia	155,000
Netherlands	105,000
France	75,000

5.12 The war goes nuclear

At 7:55am on Sunday 7 December 1941 over 180 Japanese warplanes began a surprise attack on Pearl Harbor, a huge American navy base in Hawaii. Another wave of warplanes attacked around an hour later; 21 US warships were sunk or damaged and over 2000 Americans were killed. The next day, the USA (and its ally Britain) declared war on Japan. Three days later, Germany and Italy showed their support for Japan by declaring war on the USA. The Second World War had gone truly global. But why did Japan attack an American base? In what ways was the fighting different from that in Europe? And how did the dropping of nuclear bombs finally end the war?

Mission Objectives

- Explain how and why the USA joined the Second World War.
- Assess the immediate impact of the nuclear attack in 1945.

Japan's eastern empire

The USA and Japan had been rivals for many years. Both countries wanted influence and control over the rich lands of the Far East, which contain coal, oil, rubber, and copper. Japan itself has very few of these natural resources and had invaded other countries in the 1930s to get them. By attacking Pearl Harbor, the Japanese were hoping to destroy the massive US Pacific fleet – the only thing that might have stopped them taking all the land they wanted. The plan seemed to work – for a while at least. Japanese forces swept through the Far East, conquering Hong Kong, Malaya, the Philippines, Singapore, the Dutch East Indies and parts of New Guinea by May 1942 (see **A**).

The empire falls back

But Japan's advances did not last long. By the end of 1942, the USA (with the help of British Empire troops) had managed to stop the Japanese and was slowly taking back land in the Far East. In May 1945, the war in Europe came to an end when Nazi Germany was defeated – but the war with Japan still continued. However, Japan was on the verge of defeat – it had no allies, its navy was almost destroyed and the Japanese people were very short of food. The Japanese government had even started talking with the Russians (America's ally) about a possible end to the war. Despite this, the US President, Harry S. Truman, took the decision to use the most devastating weapon ever created – the nuclear bomb.

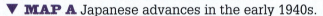

▼ **MAP A** Japanese advances in the early 1940s.

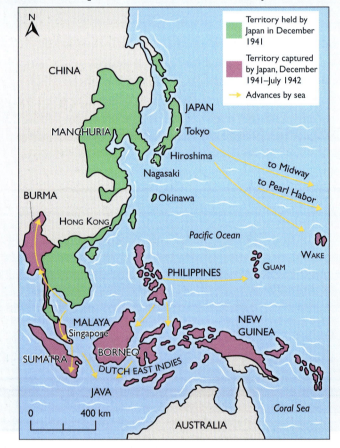

Final victory

On 6 August 1945, an American B-29 bomber dropped a single nuclear bomb on the Japanese city of Hiroshima. The bomb exploded 570 metres above the ground in an enormous blast many times brighter than the sun. Those closest to the explosion were evaporated in the 300,000 degree Celsius heat, leaving nothing but burnt shadows on the ground. Anyone within half a mile of the explosion was turned into smoking black ash within seconds.

The Americans estimated that 79,000 people were killed. The Japanese claimed 240,000 lost their lives. On 9 August, a second bomb was dropped on the port of Nagasaki. The Americans claimed 20,000 died in this blast – the Japanese claimed it was 50,000. A week later, Japan surrendered and the Second World War was over.

Why did America use the bomb?

Over the years, a number of different reasons have been put forward to explain why President Truman ordered the nuclear bombs to be dropped:

- To end the war quickly: Despite the fact that Japan was close to defeat, the bombs were dropped to force a quick surrender. Some US commanders believed that Japan would never surrender and that continuing the war for weeks or months would cause many more military and civilian deaths.

- To get revenge: Americans wanted revenge for the Japanese attack on Pearl Harbor in 1941. The Japanese had been cruel to some of the soldiers they had captured too.

- To justify the expense: The bombs cost a lot of money to develop (around £18 billion today) so the USA needed to show that the money had produced a useful and devastating weapon.

- To demonstrate power: The USA wanted to show the world (and particularly the USSR) how powerful and advanced it was.

▼ **INTERPRETATION C** Curtis Le May, a leading general in the US Air Force during the war, speaking in an interview for a TV series in the 1970s.

'Getting [the war] over with as quick as possible is the moral responsibility of everyone concerned. Now it's true that... if we just waited a little while it would be over because the Japanese were negotiating... but I believe that Truman made the proper decision to use [the bombs] because it probably hastened the negotiations and even if we just saved one day to me it would be worthwhile - you have to do it.'

▼ **SOURCE B** The devastated city of Hiroshima, August 1945.

▼ **INTERPRETATION C** The cloud of dust and debris which formed after the nuclear explosion in Nagasaki, 9 August 1945.

Later on... 1945–TODAY

As well as the immediate impact of the explosions, it soon became clear that people were suffering from radiation sickness as a result of exposure to such high levels of radiation. This can lead to burns, problems with the blood, and injury to many of the body's vital systems – even death. The Japanese use the word 'hibakusha' to describe a person who has become ill as a result of radiation sickness from the atomic bombs. The Japanese estimated that there were over 650,000 hibakusha.

Over to You

1 In 50 words or less, explain why Japan launched the attack on Pearl Harbor.

2 Read **Interpretation C**.
   a Write down five facts about the nuclear attacks on Japan in 1945.
   b Summarise the different reasons why the bombs might have been dropped.
   c Which of the reasons does Curtis Le May support? Explain your answer.

3 a Define:
   - radiation sickness
   - hibakusha
   b At the time, Americans denied that radiation sickness existed. Can you suggest why?

5.13 A United Nations

Towards the end of the Second World War, Britain, the USSR and the USA realised that they had to do something to prevent such a war happening again. They believed that if there was more cooperation between countries, they could work together to stop someone like Hitler before they got too powerful and started a war. They formed the United Nations (UN), which is still an important organisation today. So just how do countries get together and cooperate? How do they decide what action to take? And what decisions have they made that have improved the lives of people around the world?

Mission Objectives

- Explain what the United Nations is, and what it does.
- Examine how the UN is organised.

The UN Charter

When the UN was set up, a number of aims and rules were agreed. The 'Charter of the United Nations' says:

- the UN can't interfere in the way countries run themselves (elections, policing etc.)

- the UN should encourage cooperation at all times and promote **human rights** (see **A**)

- the UN should promote peace and can send 'peace keeping forces' to settle disputes in war-torn countries.

▼ **A** All countries must sign the Universal Declaration of Human Rights before being allowed to join the UN.

UNIVERSAL DECLARATION OF HUMAN RIGHTS

Rights include:

- All human beings are born free and equal.
- Everyone has the right to life, liberty and freedom from fear and violence.
- Everyone has the right to protection of the law without discrimination.
- Everyone has the right to a fair trial and will not be arrested without good reason.
- No one shall be a slave.
- No one shall be tortured or punished in a cruel, inhumane or degrading way.
- Everyone has the right to seek **asylum** from persecution in other countries.
- Adult men and women have the right to marry, regardless of their race or religion.

▼ **SOURCE B** The flag of the UN. Around the map of the world are two olive branches – a symbol of peace in Ancient Greece. The colour blue was selected because it is rarely used by countries on the uniforms or equipment of their armed forces.

The General Assembly

A sort of world Parliament, with each country having one vote. There were 51 member countries in 1945. By 2011, there were 193.

Educational, Scientific and Cultural Organization (UNESCO)

Gets countries to work together and share each other's scientific discoveries and ideas about education, literacy and communication. UNESCO also protects places of important historical interest (known as World Heritage Sites). From 1993 to 2004, for example, UNESCO worked to save Angkor in Cambodia, one of the most important archaeological sites in Southeast Asia.

Secretary-General

A key person who manages the UN and speaks on its behalf.

By 1960, 99 countries were members of the UN. This increased to 127 members by 1970, 154 by 1980 and 193 by 2011. There are currently over 1100 UNESCO World Heritage Sites across 167 countries, including the Pyramids of Giza in Egypt, the Great Wall of China, the ancient city of Petra in Jordan and Stonehenge in the UK.

Security Council

The five most powerful countries at the end of the Second World War (Britain, France, the USA, the USSR and China) formed the permanent Security Council. They are joined by ten other countries (temporary members) on a rotation basis. The Security Council meets when it looks like a dispute could turn into a war. They can stop countries attacking each other by:

- asking all UN members to stop trading with them until a shortage of supplies forces them to back away from war
- sending in soldiers – or peacekeepers – to prevent or contain the fighting.

Any decisions need a 'yes' from all five permanent members, and peacekeepers are sent from armies of several countries. In recent years, for example, UN forces have been keeping the peace on the border between Sudan and South Sudan.

Children's Fund (UNICEF)

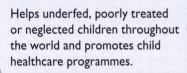

Helps underfed, poorly treated or neglected children throughout the world and promotes child healthcare programmes.

International Labour Organization (ILO)

Tries to protect workers all over the world by improving their conditions, pay, rights and insurance.

International Court of Justice

Based in the Netherlands. Fifteen judges, each from a different nation, settle legal disputes between countries before they lead to war.

World Health Organization (WHO)

Organises health campaigns, does research, runs clinics and vaccinates against infectious diseases. One of the WHO's greatest successes was the elimination of smallpox, one of history's biggest killers, through a large-scale vaccination programme.

There has been criticism of the UN in recent years. Some have argued that certain countries in the UN are given more power than others and that it is too costly to run. After the 2010 earthquake in Haiti, UN aid workers were blamed for spreading cholera throughout Haiti.

Over to You

1 Imagine you are representing your country at one of the first meetings of the UN. You are holding a press conference in your own country before you leave. What would be your answers to these questions?
   - Why is this new organisation necessary?
   - What is the Security Council and how can it stop one country attacking another?
   - Are all nations of the world in the UN?
   - How do all countries get a say in UN decisions?
   - Why do all countries have to sign the Universal Declaration of Human Rights before being allowed to join the UN?
   - People throughout the world are weak and vulnerable after the war – how will the UN help them?

2 Look at the Universal Declaration of Human Rights (**A**). Do you think that some rights are more important than others? Explain your answer carefully.

3 Look at the UN flag. Explain why you think the it was designed in this way.

Knowledge and Understanding

1 Describe the role of the United Nations in improving the world.

Quick Knowledge Quiz

Choose the correct answer from the three options:

1   What is the name for the method of attack, used by German forces in the Second World War, that involved fast-moving columns of tanks supported by infantry soldiers and dive-bomber attacks?

   a   Weltpolitik
   b   Blitzkrieg
   c   Gestapo

2   From which French beach were thousands of British, French and Belgian troops evacuated in May 1940?

   a   Dunkirk
   b   Normandy
   c   Calais

3   What was the code-name for Hitler's plan to invade Britain in 1940?

   a   Operation Barbarossa
   b   Operation England
   c   Operation Sealion

4   Which country provided two and a half million soldiers to fight as part of British Empire forces in the Second World War?

   a   Canada
   b   South Africa
   c   India

5   What was the name given to the night-time bombing raids against London and other British cities by Nazi Germany during 1940 and 1941?

   a   Blitzkrieg
   b   Oktoberfest
   c   the Blitz

6   Which well-known antibiotic was greatly developed during the Second World War?

   a   erythromycin
   b   penicillin
   c   bacteria

7   What was the name of the Head of Bomber Command who ordered the bombing of the German city of Dresden in February 1945?

   a   Arthur Harris
   b   Neville Chamberlain
   c   David Lloyd George

8   When did Winston Churchill become Britain's wartime Prime Minister?

   a   May 1940
   b   September 1939
   c   August 1945

9   The Japanese bombing of which naval base brought America into the war on Britain's side?

   a   Port Sunlight
   b   Pearl Harbor
   c   Cape Verde

10   Which part of the United Nations tries to help underfed, poorly treated or neglected children throughout the world?

   a   UNICEF
   b   UNESCO
   c   ILO

 **Literacy Focus**

Linking words

When writing historical narratives, it's really important that the story flows. It's vital to get things in chronological order, but it's also useful to be able to use a variety of connectives (joining words used to connect one part of text with another) to form longer sentences and improve the flow of your writing.

Original answer:

> ⊘ **TIP:** These two paragraphs are simply a collection of short, sharp sentences. Look at the paragraphs below to see how they have been improved.

> In 1928, a Scottish scientist named Alexander Fleming made a discovery. The discovery made large changes to medicine. He found that some mould had killed a particularly nasty type of germ. He had been experimenting with the germ. This germ was called staphylococcus. It caused infections.
>
> Fleming grew more of the mould. He found it killed other germs too. He found that the mould was penicillin. Fleming did not have the specialist help or money to continue experimenting with penicillin. He wrote about his discovery in a medical magazine in 1929.

Look at this answer with connectives added. You should be able to see that the flow of the paragraphs improves.

> In 1928, a Scottish scientist named Alexander Fleming made a discovery that resulted in large changes to medicine. He found that some mould had killed a particularly nasty type of germ that he had been experimenting with. This germ was called staphylococcus and could lead to infections.
>
> Fleming grew more of the mould and found it killed other germs too. He found that the mould was penicillin. However, Fleming did not have the specialist help or money to continue experimenting with penicillin. Instead, he wrote about his discovery in a medical magazine in 1929.

1 Now it's your turn. Add connectives to improve the flow of these paragraphs.

> In 1936, two scientists from Oxford University read Fleming's article on penicillin. They were called Howard Florey and Ernst Chain. Florey was from Australia. Chain was a German-born Jew who came to Britain to escape the Nazis. Just days after the Second World War began, they got a small amount of money from the British government. They began making small amounts of penicillin.

> In February 1941, they used penicillin to treat a policeman. The policeman was named Albert Alexander. He had developed a severe face infection. He had scratched his face on a rose bush. Alexander began to recover and his condition improved. Then supplies of penicillin ran out. He died. It proved the power of penicillin in treating humans.

Word bank: connectives

If you want to emphasise something:
- Most of all
- Above all
- Especially
- Notably
- In particular

If you want to add something:
- And
- In addition
- Furthermore
- Also
- As well as

If you want to give an example or illustrate a point:
- For instance
- For example
- These include
- Such as
- As revealed by

If you want to show cause or effect:
- As a result
- Because
- Therefore
- This led to
- Consequently

If you want to compare:
- Equally
- Similarly
- Likewise
- In the same way
- Compared to

If you want to contrast:
- In contrast
- On the other hand
- However
- Alternatively
- Whereas

If you want to put a sequence together:
- Firstly
- Secondly
- Finally
- Then
- Subsequently

Comparing interpretations

When analysing different interpretations, firstly work out what is being said, or what the message is, before comparing the different interpretations. Here is one way to compare two interpretations.

1 **What is the main difference?** For each interpretation, think about the **content** and try to understand what the person is saying and/or showing. Then, **compare** them: find the ways in which the content is different.

 TIP:
Think about:
- what the interpretations focus on
- what you know already about the topic
- the writers' backgrounds.
What do the captions tell you?

2 **Suggest why they give different views**. Is there a reason why the two people might have different opinions?

TIP: Which of these phrases fits best with your judgement?

strongly agree…

agree a little…

agree to a certain extent…

agree somewhat…

don't agree very much…

3 **Judge how far you agree.** How much (or to what extent) do you agree? Use information from both interpretations and your own knowledge to help you judge and explain your answer.

TIP: What do you know about the topic – in this case, about the life and influence of Winston Churchill? Look at your notes or pages 136–139 to help you. Also, remember that Churchill played a part in politics in the early part of the twentieth century too (see pages 12–13).

Assessment: Interpretation analysis

Your challenge now is to answer this question about analysing interpretations:

1 Interpretations **A** and **B** give different views about Winston Churchill. What is the main difference between the views?

2 Suggest one reason **Interpretations A** and **B** give different views about Churchill.

3 How far do you agree with **Interpretation A** about Winston Churchill? Explain your answer, using both interpretations and your own knowledge of the historical context. **(20)**

 TIP: In your answer, you should include details from both interpretations.

TIP: It is important to read the caption to find out more about the author. Think why Johnson might say positive things about Churchill.

▼ **INTERPRETATION A** Adapted from an article in the *Telegraph*, January 2015, by Boris Johnson. At the time, Johnson was the Conservative Mayor of London. He later became Prime Minister and leader of the Conservative Party – the same party that Churchill belonged to.

TIP: How does he describe Churchill? Is he being mainly positive – or not?

'His legacy is everywhere. He helped set up the modern welfare state, supporting unemployment insurance and other social protections in the years before the First World War. It was Churchill alone who made sure that Britain continued to fight during the Second World War. It was Churchill who brought America in. If Churchill had not been Prime Minister in 1940, there seems little doubt that Britain would have let Hitler have his way, plunging Europe into darkness. No other politician at the time had the guts to do what he did; and it is to him that the world owes thanks for the eventual victory over Nazism, and the 70 years of peace that have followed.'

Assessment: Interpretation analysis

▼ **INTERPRETATION B** Annette Mackin was a journalist for the *Socialist Worker*, a publication that supported equality and working-class ideals and would be described as 'left-wing'. 'Right-wing' is the opposite and is usually linked to ideas that support traditions and keeping things the way they are. When Mackin refers to Churchill's 'class' in this article (published in January 2015), she is talking about the fact that he comes from a very old, rich, land-owning family.

> **TIP:** Think why Mackin might have these opinions.

'Racist and brutal – and against social progress. That is the way we should remember Winston Churchill. But the ruling class are desperate for us to celebrate a myth. Leading the charge is Boris Johnson who recently published a biography of Churchill. David Cameron has spoken of how Churchill is his "favourite" prime minister. They argue that through the power of his speeches he inspired the people of Britain to rise up against the Nazi threat during the Second World War. This is a lie. Churchill was not an anti-Nazi hero, he wanted to defend his class. What motivated many people to fight was vastly different from what motivated Churchill. He wasn't against Hitler because he was a Nazi. It was because he threatened Britain.

The truth about Churchill's role in many atrocities is slowly emerging. During the Indian famine in 1943 it is now estimated that over five million people died. The famine was a product of the Second World War. Churchill refused to send emergency famine relief. Instead he said Indians were used to starving. His racism didn't stop there. He waged a war at home against the working class in Britain. In 1911 transport workers walked out on strike for better pay. In response, Churchill sent in the military to help rail bosses. They opened fire on ordinary people in Liverpool.'

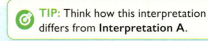

The steps and sentence starters below will help you structure your answer.

> **TIP:** Think how this interpretation differs from **Interpretation A**.

1 What is the main difference?

A main difference is that Interpretation A...	(2)
However, in Interpretation B...	(2)

> **TIP:** You can quote the interpretation if you like, but make sure you use your own words as well to explain.

2 Suggest why they give different views.

The writer of Interpretation A...	(2)
However, the writer of Interpretation B...	(2)

3 Judge how far you agree.

Interpretation A says that... I (agree/don't agree) with this opinion about Churchill because...	(3)
Interpretation B offers a different view of Churchill when it says...	(2)
Interpretation A also says that... I (agree/don't agree) with this opinion about Churchill because...	(3)
Interpretation B offers a different view of him when it says...	(2)
To conclude...	(2)

> **TIP:** What do you know from what you have studied about him? Does the interpretation back up what you know, or not? You are using your own knowledge here.

> **TIP:** This is where you sum up 'how far' you agree. Do you agree 'fully' or 'partly', for example? Explain why you think this.

6.1A NHS: why we don't pay to see a doctor

There is almost no one in Britain who isn't helped at some point by what is known as the **welfare state**. This is the name of the system by which the government aims to help those in need – mainly the old, the sick and the unemployed. It is sometimes called **social security**. It aims to make sure that nobody goes without food, shelter, clothing, medical care, education or any other basic need as a result of not being able to afford it. But why was the welfare state created and what has been its impact on people in the UK?

A caring country

Although many people in Britain take the things outlined in diagram **A** for granted today, it is not a system that has been in place for many years. From 1906, the government had introduced some help for the most vulnerable people in society, including free school meals for poorer children, free school medical check-ups and treatment, small pensions for the over 70s, and basic sick and unemployment pay. But it was only after the Second World War that the welfare state really took shape.

The impact of the Second World War

The war highlighted all sorts of problems that people in Britain were facing at that time. There had been shock at the filthy, under-fed, badly clothed children who had been evacuated to the countryside, for example. Wounded soldiers had needed free (and specialist) medical care and pregnant women and young children had needed extra food. People felt that, after the war, the sacrifices that people had made should mean that the future would be a lot better for them.

▼ **A** This diagram gives a basic outline of how the welfare state in Britain works.

Earlier on...   1906

The measures to help some of the most vulnerable people in society in the early part of the twentieth century were known as the Liberal Reforms (see pages 12–15). These reforms did not solve all the problems connected to poverty and ill-health – but they established that it was the responsibility of the government to look after people who could not look after themselves.

Even before the war was over, the government asked Sir William Beveridge to investigate ways that the country might help out the most vulnerable people once the war was over – the sick, the unemployed, low-paid workers and elderly people. His report (known as the Beveridge Report), published in 1942, said that people all over the country had a right to be free of the 'five giants' that could ruin their lives:

- Disease
- Want (need)
- Ignorance (poor education)
- Idleness (no job)
- Squalor (very poor living conditions)

The report suggested ways to improve things and said that the government should 'take charge of social security from the cradle [baby's bed] to the grave'. For example, Beveridge suggested that every worker in Britain should pay some money directly out of their wages to the government – and in return they would receive money if they were sick, were injured at work or lost their job. He suggested improved old age pensions, financial help for parents to bring up their children, and free medical care for all, paid for through taxes and National Insurance contributions. In a Britain where people hoped that life would be better once the war was over, the Beveridge Report became a surprise bestseller, selling over 100,000 copies its first month of publication.

▼ **SOURCE B** A letter from Vita Sackville-West, a novelist, poet and journalist, to her husband (a politician) in 1942. She is talking about the Beveridge Report.

'I am all for educating the people into being less awful, less limited, less silly, and for spending lots of money on (1) extending education; (2) better-paid teachers, but not for giving them everything for nothing, which they don't appreciate anyhow. Health, yes. Education, yes. Old age pensions, yes, I suppose so... But not this form of charity which will make people fold their arms and feel that they have no enterprise since everything will be provided for them. It is surely a psychological error.'

▶ **SOURCE C** A Labour Party election poster from 1945. As well as introducing the welfare state, the Labour Party also **nationalised** large industries including electricity, coal and the railways. This meant they came under the control of the government, not private companies.

SHE LABOURED FOR YOU.... NOW IT'S-
LABOUR FOR HER
LABOUR STANDS FOR DECENT PENSIONS

Key Words National Insurance
nationalise   social security   welfare state

▼ **INTERPRETATION D** From a 2004 interview by Aaron Wilkes, with Nottingham resident Frederick Rebman, remembering the introduction of the welfare state.

'We were sorry to see Churchill voted out, he was our war leader, but he never promised to give the new ideas a go. The Labour Party did, you see, and they publicised this in all the papers... servicemen [men in the army, navy and air force] like me expected so much after the war, perhaps Utopia [a perfect world], and the welfare state seemed to be a good start. I didn't mind the idea of paying a bit more of my salary to know that a doctor or dentist was there if I needed them.'

Over to You

1 In your own words, describe how the most vulnerable people in society were looked after before the Second World War.

2 a What was the Beveridge Report?

  b In your own words, explain what you think Beveridge meant when he said that the government should 'take charge of social security from the cradle to the grave'.

3 Read **Source B**. Why does the writer think the government should not carry out any changes based on the Beveridge Report?

4 Read **Interpretation D**. According to the person interviewed, why did the Labour Party win the election in 1945?

Knowledge and Understanding

1 Explain what is meant by the term 'welfare state'.

2 Describe two features of the welfare state.

The war ends

As the war ended, an election was held to decide who would run the country next. The Labour Party promised to follow Beveridge's advice, but the Conservative Party, led by Winston Churchill, refused to make such a promise. The Labour Party won the election easily – and Winston Churchill, the man who had led Britain during the war, was out of power!

The new Labour government, led by Clement Atlee, kept its promise – and put many of Beveridge's ideas into practice.

Rebuilding Britain

Some reforms had already taken place before the end of the war. In 1943, for example, the 'Ministry of Town and Country Planning' was set up that allowed councils to take over bomb-damaged areas and redevelop them. However, after the new government took over in 1945, a flurry of changes took place:

- A National Health Service (NHS) was set up to provide healthcare for everyone.

- A weekly family allowance payment was introduced to help with childcare costs.

- The very poor received financial help or 'benefits'.

- Pensions for the elderly and disabled were increased.

- The school leaving age was raised to 15 to give children a greater chance of a decent education for longer, and more schools were opened that catered for students of different abilities. The School Milk Act of 1946 even provided free milk (a third of a pint a day – about 190ml) to all schoolchildren.

- A number of new towns were built, providing people with both housing and jobs. Stevenage, in Hertfordshire, was the first to be built, with over 20 more created within ten years. By 1948, councils were building 280,000 homes each year that local people could rent (known as 'council houses').

The National Health Service

Perhaps the best-known of all changes that took place after the war was the introduction of the National Health Service (NHS). The aim was to provide healthcare for everyone and make all medical treatment – including that offered by doctors, hospitals, ambulances, dentists and opticians – free to all (see **E**).

▼ **SOURCE E** From a speech by Aneurin Bevan, the government official responsible for setting up the NHS, 1946. Here, he refers to the fact that, before the NHS, seeing a doctor would cost money – and women in particular would go without treatment for illness in order to save money for the family's other needs.

'A person should not be stopped from seeking medical assistance by the worry of doctors' bills... medical treatment should be made available to treat rich and poor alike, according to medical need and no other criteria. Worry about money in a time of sickness is a serious barrier to recovery... Records show that it is the mother in the average family who suffers most from the absence of a full health service. In trying to balance her budget she puts her own needs last.'

Problems faced by the NHS

Of course, all the services provided by the NHS cost money. All workers had to pay for it through taxes on the money they earned. Over the years, the cost of the NHS has increased dramatically (see **F**). In fact, the NHS itself did not stay free for long. Working people today have to pay for medicines and dental treatment, for example. However, anyone that needs vital services including some kinds of physiotherapy, cancer screening and treatment, surgery and clinical care is entitled to it under the NHS.

Fact

New towns built in the first few years after the war included Basildon, Bracknell, Crawley, Hatfield, Harlow, Hemel Hempstead, Stevenage and Welwyn Garden City (all around London) – as well as Peterlee and Washington in the North-East; Skelmersdale and Runcorn in the North-West; Corby, Telford and Redditch in the Midlands; Cwmbran and Newtown in Wales; and East Kilbride, Glenrothes, Cumbernauld, Livingston and Irvine in Scotland.

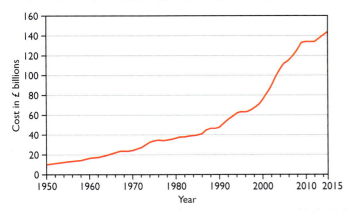

▼ **F** The cost of the NHS, 1948–2015

Healthcare in the news

You have probably heard or read a news story about the NHS. It is a huge organisation with some major problems. We hear of doctors and nurses being overworked, eventually leaving their jobs because of the stress. People talk of being on waiting lists for surgery for months, and some hospitals have been found to be unhygienic, overcrowded and badly run. The biggest problem, and the cause of many other problems, is a lack of money. Modern drugs and equipment can be very expensive. Better treatment and medicines mean that more people are living longer, so there are more elderly people than ever before, who tend to use the NHS more than younger people. There are also modern healthcare issues such as obesity and diabetes that are affecting a lot of people across the country.

▼ **INTERPRETATION G** Adapted from an article in the *Guardian* newspaper, July 2018, by Pamela Duncan and Juliette Jowit.

'Nothing inspires national pride quite like the National Health Service. More than two-thirds of people questioned in a recent survey said they considered the establishment of the institution, which turns 70 this week, to be Britain's greatest achievement.'

Fact ✔

Many doctors didn't want a National Health Service. They worried that they would lose their independence because they would be working for the government and couldn't charge what they wanted. The person in charge of setting up the NHS (Aneurin Bevan) won them over by promising them a good salary and allowing them to have 'private patients' too.

▼ **SOURCE H** Schoolchildren drinking free milk – a result of the School Milk Act of 1946.

Over to You 📶

1 Read **Source E**.
   a Who was Aneurin Bevan?
   b What point does he make about women?

2 a Why did some doctors object to the setting up of the NHS?
   b How did Bevan and the government get doctors to accept the NHS?

3 Why do you think the NHS is still a controversial topic today?

Change

1 Describe how vulnerable people in society were looked after before the Second World War.

2 Explain two ways in which the care of vulnerable people before the Second World War was different from the care of vulnerable people after the Second World War.

During the Second World War the USA and the USSR (and other nations, including Britain) fought together to defeat Nazi Germany and its allies. As the war came to a close, it became clear that the enormous differences between these two countries would be hard to ignore once the fighting ended. So what were these differences? Why had allies turned into enemies? How close did the USA and USSR get to fighting each other?

Objectives

- Define what was meant by 'Cold War'.

- Explain why the allies of the Second World War became enemies.

Different ways to run a country

By the end of the war, the USA and the USSR were the two most powerful countries in the world by far, and both became known as **superpowers**. They each had huge, skilled populations, large armed forces and vast reserves of raw materials such as coal, iron and oil.

However, although they were allies in the war, there were many differences between them. To begin with, the two countries organised themselves in entirely different ways – the USSR was communist, the USA was **capitalist** (see **A**).

Differences over the past

As well as having different political systems, tension between the USA and the USSR had been building up for a long time. At this time, the USA (and its main allies in Europe) were known as 'the West', while the USSR (and its allies) were referred to as 'the East'.

- Russia (as the USSR was then) had pulled out of the First World War in 1917 when ordinary Russians rebelled against their leaders during the Russian Revolution. Russia had been on Britain, France and America's side in the war – and their withdrawal left many thinking the Russians could not be trusted.

- After the Russian Revolution, the country was controlled by a communist government and became the USSR. The USA (and also Britain, France, Italy and others) had sent troops and supplies to help in the fight against the new communist government. The leader of the USSR during the Second World War, Joseph Stalin, had not forgotten this.

▼ **A** A diagram to show the basic differences in the way communist and capitalist countries are organised.

CAPITALISM	COMMUNISM

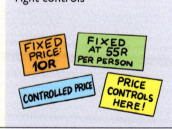

- Stalin ruled the USSR brutally, which many in the West did not like. He had also signed a peace deal (the Nazi-Soviet Pact) with Hitler just before the war started. This deal meant that Hitler could invade Poland without any interference from the USSR – but Britain and France had promised to protect Poland. It was the Nazi-Soviet Pact that eventually brought Britain and France into the war. Countries in the West had not forgotten this.

Differences over the future

What to do in war-ravaged Europe quickly caused disagreement. Britain and the USA wanted European countries – including Germany – to recover quickly so they could trade goods with them. Stalin wanted to keep Germany weak and create a 'buffer' of countries that he controlled between the USSR and Germany. Despite several attempts to reach agreement, Europe became divided in two by what Winston Churchill called an **Iron Curtain**. The countries to the west of the curtain were 'capitalist' and had close relationships with the USA. The countries to the east became 'communist' and were heavily influenced by the USSR (see **B**).

▼ **MAP B** How Europe was divided after the Second World War.

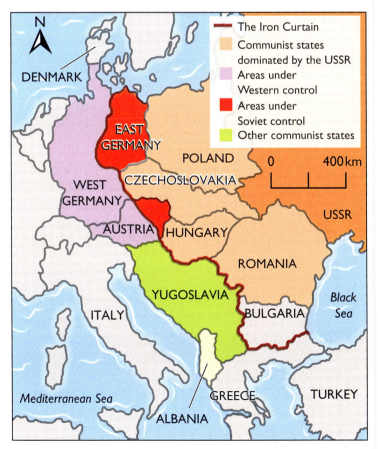

Key Words

capitalism   Iron Curtain
superpower

Money from the USA

In 1947, US President Harry S. Truman offered money to European countries to repair war damage, such as bombed cities. It was known as the 'Marshall Plan' when it was launched in 1948, because it was coordinated by US General George Marshall. Truman wanted a strong Europe to trade with, and also thought people would be less likely to support communism if they were well fed and had good jobs. In total, the USA gave around $17 billion to 16 countries – with Britain receiving the most, followed by France, Italy and West Germany. Stalin thought Marshall Aid was a US plot to get more support and influence in Europe, and banned countries in the East from taking the money. As a result, countries in Eastern Europe recovered more slowly than those in the West.

Over to You

1 In under 50 words, try to explain the differences between capitalism and communism.

2 a List different reasons why the wartime allies split up.

   b Which reason do you think was most important? Explain your answer.

3 a What was Marshall Aid?

   b Do you think Marshall Aid increased tension between the East and the West at this time? Explain your answer.

Knowledge and Understanding

1 Complete the sentences with accurate terms:

   a A country that is one of the most powerful on Earth is often called a _____.

   b The USA and its main allies were known as 'the West', while the USSR and its allies were referred to as _____.

   c The USA was a capitalist country while the USSR was _____.

   d The imaginary barrier between the communist countries in the East and countries in the West was called _____.

Germany is divided

At the end of the war, it was decided that Germany should be divided into four zones, each one controlled by one of the four major winning countries – the USA, Britain, France and the USSR. It was also decided that Berlin, Germany's capital, should be divided into four. Berlin was actually within the Soviet area of Germany… but was still divided between the USA, Britain, France and the USSR (see **C**).

Tension increases

In March 1948, France, Britain and the USA discussed plans to unite their three zones of Germany into a single zone (later called West Germany). They would later do the same with their zones in Berlin. This angered the USSR because it wasn't told about the plans. In June 1948, the USSR cut off all road and rail links between the Allied area of Berlin (West Berlin) and West Germany. The plan was to force France, Britain and the USA to withdraw from their areas in Berlin because they wouldn't be able to survive without food and fuel. This was known as the Berlin Blockade. Soviet leader Stalin hoped that this would result in West Berlin coming completely under his control.

▼ **MAP C** A map to illustrate how both Germany and the city of Berlin were divided into four at the end of the war.

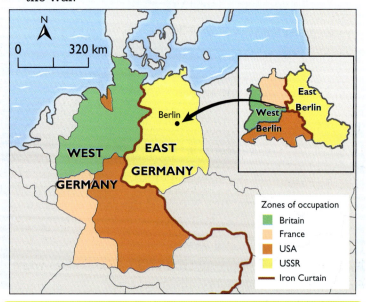

Fact ✔

At this time, the USSR is sometimes known as Soviet Russia… or Russia. And people from the USSR are sometimes called Soviets, or Russians.

▼ **SOURCE D** An American cartoon from 1948. The USSR is shown as a bear.

Tough decision

The allies knew that they couldn't leave two million West Berliners to starve. Troops could deliver supplies over land but this would mean marching into the Soviet zone and directly confronting Soviet soldiers. That could have meant war. The solution they chose was to supply West Berlin by air and hope that the Russians would not shoot down any aircraft flying over their territory.

The Berlin Airlift

The Americans and British organised a round-the-clock airlift of essential supplies such as food, fuel and medicine. A cargo plane left an airfield in West Germany every 30 seconds, and in 11 months a total of 275,000 flights delivered an average of 4000 tons of supplies every day. Stalin clearly expected the West to give up and hand over the city but, when he realised that this wouldn't happen, he ended the blockade and reopened the roads in early May 1949.

Results of the crisis

The West saw the USSR's backdown as a victory. On 23 May, the USA, Britain and France announced that their zones would officially join together to form the Federal Republic of Germany, known as West Germany. In October, the Soviet zone became the German Democratic Republic, known as East Germany. There were now two Germanys, and inside East Germany Berlin was also split in two: West Berlin and East Berlin.

► **SOURCE E** A plane containing supplies of food, fuel and medicine arrives in Berlin during the airlift, watched by German children.

Military rivalry

The division between East and West was increased when two rival defence organisations were set up. The North Atlantic Treaty Organization (NATO) was a military alliance linking 12 major Western powers – including the USA, Britain, France, Italy and Canada – together. West Germany joined in 1955. Immediately afterwards, the USSR responded with its own military alliance of Eastern European communist states. The Warsaw Pact, as this was known, linked the USSR with East Germany, Poland, Czechoslovakia, Hungary, Romania, Albania and Bulgaria.

Later on...   1961

Through the night of 13 August 1961, communist East Germany built a huge wall along the border between East and West Berlin. It was designed to stop East Germans fleeing to the West. The wall stood as a symbol of the Cold War until November 1989 when the border between East and West Berlin was opened and the destruction of the wall began.

A 'cold war'

Despite the tension and hostility between the USA and the USSR, no actual fighting took place between American and Russian troops – which is why it became known as the **Cold War**. If the two sides had sent their armies into battle, it would have become a 'hot war' – just like all the others in history.

Nuclear tension

In 1949, the Soviet Union successfully tested its first nuclear bomb. Now both East and West had nuclear weapons. Both sides were terrified that the other would soon have more of these horrific weapons than them, so they quickly began making lots of nuclear weapons. They hoped that by having so many, they would put the other side off launching an attack, as it would mean the certain destruction of both countries – and possibly the world! This theory became known as Mutually Assured Destruction – or MAD for short.

Over to You

1 How was Germany divided after the war?

2 Describe the difference between the Berlin Blockade and the Berlin Airlift.

3 Define NATO and the Warsaw Pact.

4 Explain how the Cold War got its name.

5 a In no more than 50 words, explain the theory of Mutually Assured Destruction.

  b What are the dangers of MAD?

Source Analysis

1 Look at **Source D**. Describe the cartoon.

2 How useful is this source to a historian studying American attitudes to the situation in Berlin after the war?

In March 1947, President Truman made a speech in which he said that America would offer money and military help to countries that were in danger of being taken over by communism. That way, America would 'contain' communism and stop it spreading from country to country. This attitude towards the worldwide spread of communism became known as the 'Truman Doctrine'. How did the Soviets respond to this? How did the Americans actually try to 'contain' communism? How close did the USA and USSR come to all-out war?

Objectives

- Define the 'Truman Doctrine'.
- Examine ways in which the USA tried to 'contain' communism.
- Identify where Cold War conflicts took place around the world.

▼ **SOURCE A** Part of a government speech made by Truman in March 1947. Here, Truman argued that the world was becoming divided into capitalist countries, which he said were free, and communist countries, which were not.

'Nearly every nation must choose between alternative ways of life – the choice is often not a free one. One way of life is based on the will of the majority, free elections, and freedom of speech and religion. The second way of life is based upon the will of a minority forcing themselves upon the majority; it relies upon terror, a controlled press and radio, fixed elections and a lack of personal freedom. I believe the United States must support people who are trying to resist being enslaved by armed minorities or by outside pressures. I believe we must help people work out their own destiny in their own way.'

▼ **SOURCE B** President Truman pictured shaking hands with Britain's war leader, Winston Churchill, on a visit to Britain in 1950.

The Soviet response

Stalin, the leader of the USSR, responded to Truman's speech by setting up 'Cominform' in September 1947 – this was an organisation of all communist countries and groups. Cominform members would meet regularly in Moscow to make sure they were united and sharing the same ideas and policies.

Cold War hotspots

Soldiers from the two major Cold War nations – the USA and the USSR – never actually fought directly against each other in over 40 years of tension… but they came very close. Over the next few pages, study examples of when the Cold War turned hotter, and the USA and USSR came *very* close to conflict.

East versus West: The Korean War

A divided country

During the Second World War, Korea was controlled by Japan. After Japan's defeat, it left Korea, which was then split into two zones. The USSR occupied the north and the USA occupied the south (see **C**).

Tensions in Korea

The USSR set up a communist government in North Korea. The Americans set up a government friendly to themselves in South Korea. On 25 June 1950, the North Korean army invaded South Korea, with the aim of creating one united – and communist – Korea. The North Korean army had been provided with weapons and equipment from the USSR.

▼ **MAP C** The two Korean zones set up after the Second World War. It was decided to use the 38th parallel (line of latitude) of the Earth as a dividing point – mainly because it divided the country approximately in half. Seoul (Korea's capital) was just inside South Korea.

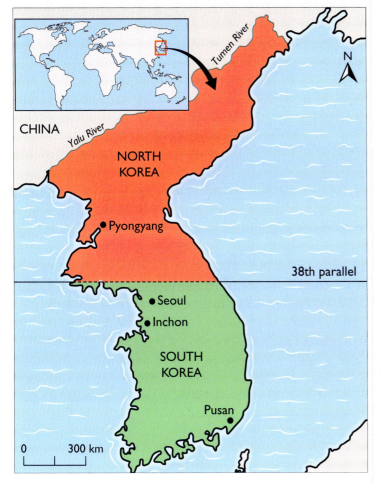

The Korean War

The North Koreans quickly captured the South Korean capital, Seoul. The South Korean army, supported by US troops who were stationed there, were pushed back very quickly. The North Koreans captured most of South Korea – and for a time it looked as if the whole of Korea would become a communist country.

The American response

President Truman – determined to stop the spread of communism – persuaded the United Nations (see pages 146–147) to defend South Korea. In September 1950, a United Nations army landed in South Korea and started to push the North Koreans back. In total, 16 countries sent troops to fight (including Britain, Thailand, Australia, France and Colombia) – but the USA provided by far the most. The man in charge of the UN troops was also American (General MacArthur), and he took orders from Truman – not the UN.

China gets involved

The UN troops gradually pushed the North Korean army back out of South Korea and into North Korea. By October 1950, they had captured most of North Korea and were close to the Chinese border. China, which had become communist in 1949, felt threatened by this and launched a massive invasion of Korea that forced the UN forces right back again.

With America strongly supporting UN forces on one side and the USSR and China supporting the other, the two sides were fairly evenly matched. By 1953, they had reached stalemate and both sides were roughly at the same original border – the 38th parallel. In July 1953, a ceasefire was agreed. North Korea remained communist while South Korea stayed capitalist.

Meanwhile... 1950s–1960s

Whenever Eastern European countries under Soviet influence showed signs of wanting to break free of Soviet control, Soviet troops would march in to end any rebellions and restore order. This happened in Hungary in 1956 and Czechoslovakia (now Czech Republic or Czechia) in 1968.

Over to You

1 Explain what is meant by 'containing' communism.

2 Explain how Korea was divided after the Second World War.

3 Put the following events in the correct chronological order:
  • China becomes a communist country
  • A United Nations army lands in Korea
  • North Korean army invades South Korea
  • Korea is divided after the Second World War
  • A ceasefire is arranged
  • China joins the war on the side of North Korea

4 Why did China get involved in the Korean War?

Source Analysis

1 Read **Source A**. Which political system does Truman describe first?

2 Why, according to Truman, should people fear the 'second way of life'?

3 How useful is this source to a historian studying US attitudes towards communism?

East versus West: The Cuban Missile Crisis

Perhaps the closest that the USA and the USSR ever came to a full-scale war was in October 1962. For 13 days, the world faced the very real possibility of a Third World War. So why did this terrible situation occur? Exactly how close was a nuclear attack? And how did this crisis come to an end?

Communist Cuba

Cuba is a Caribbean island lying 150km off the south-eastern American coast. In 1959, a communist named Fidel Castro and his followers had seized control of Cuba. The USA was still following a policy of 'containing' communism – and was alarmed at having a communist country so close. As a result, US President John F. Kennedy ordered a top secret invasion of Cuba in an attempt to get rid of the communists. This invasion, in April 1961, was a total flop and a great embarrassment for the US President. Castro remained in power – and the incident pushed Cuba into a closer relationship with the communist USSR.

Missiles in Cuba

Nikita Khrushchev, leader of the USSR, promised to help defend Cuba from attack by supplying it with nuclear weapons. So, in the summer of 1962, the USSR began transporting nuclear missiles to Cuba and building missile launch bases there. However, on 14 October 1962, a US spy plane flying over Cuba spotted these bases, which were now in easy range of most major US cities – New York, Washington, Boston, Miami and Chicago.

The Cuban Missile Crisis

US spy planes spotted more missiles being transported from the USSR to Cuba by sea – so the USA sent warships to stop the missiles reaching their destination. For a few days, it seemed to many that this would result in all-out war (see D and E).

▼ **INTERPRETATION D** Robert McNamara, one of President Kennedy's advisers, speaking in a meeting in Moscow in 1987 about the crisis in 1962.

'It was a beautiful autumn evening, the height of the crisis, and I went up into the open air to look and to smell it, because I thought it was the last Sunday I would ever see.'

▼ **INTERPRETATION E**
Fyodor Burlatsky, one of Khrushchev's advisers, speaking at the same meeting in 1987 about the crisis in 1962.

'I phoned my wife and told her to drop everything and to get out of Moscow. I thought the bombers were on the way.'

Crisis over

As the world held its breath, the leaders of the USA and USSR – Kennedy and Khrushchev – negotiated with each other. Finally, after nearly two weeks of tension, an agreement was reached. America promised not to invade Cuba and agreed to remove some of its own missile bases that were near the USSR – and the USSR agreed to turn its ships around. The world breathed a huge sigh of relief when the news was announced.

▼ **SOURCE F** US citizens in New York taking part in a protest during the Cuban Missile Crisis.

▼ **MAP G** The distances that short-range and long-range missiles could reach from Cuba.

▼ **SOURCE H** Nuclear missiles on the Soviet ship *Kasimov*, heading for Cuba during the crisis, September 1962.

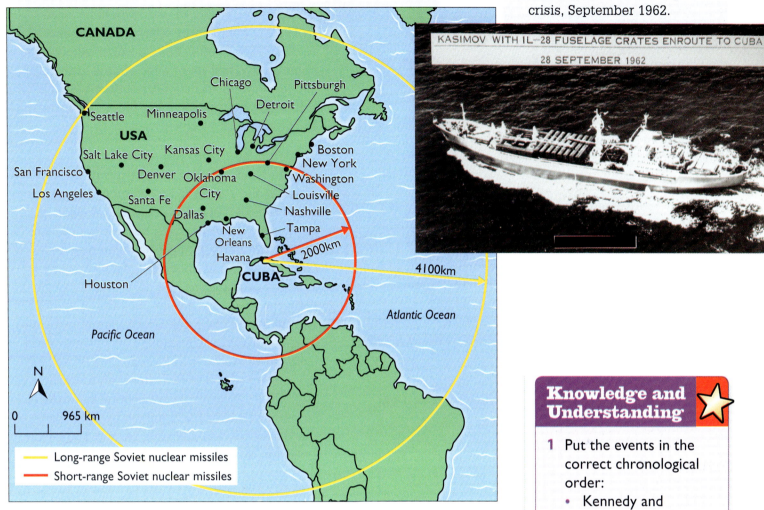

Over to You

1 Complete the sentences with accurate terms:
   a Cuba is a Caribbean island around 150km off the coast of _____ .
   b Fidel Castro and his followers seized control of Cuba in _____ .
   c The US President during the Cuban Missile Crisis was _____ .
   d The USSR was led by _____ .

2 Why was America so concerned about the construction of missile bases in Cuba? Refer to **Map G** in your answer.

3 a Read **Interpretations D** and **E**. Briefly summarise what each interpretation says.
   b How useful are these interpretations in telling us how close the world came to nuclear war?

4 In your opinion, did the Cuban Missile Crisis have any 'winners'? Explain your answer.

Knowledge and Understanding

1 Put the events in the correct chronological order:
   • Kennedy and Khrushchev begin negotiations
   • US invasion of Cuba fails
   • US spy planes spot more missiles being transported from the USSR to Cuba by sea
   • Fidel Castro takes control of Cuba
   • Agreement is reached between the USSR and the USA
   • The USSR begins to transport nuclear missiles to Cuba

2 Write an account of how the events of October 1962 became an international crisis.

East versus West: The Vietnam War

Another well-known example of Cold War conflict between the USA and the USSR is the Vietnam War. Although the two countries did not *directly* go to war, they each supported a different side. Like the war in Korea (see pages 160–161), American soldiers also fought in this conflict. So what started the conflict in Vietnam? Why did America become involved? What happened in the Vietnam War?

The French in Vietnam

In the late 1800s, the country that is now Vietnam was taken over by France. It was part of an area of land in Southeast Asia known as French Indochina. During the Second World War, the Japanese took control of this land. After Japan's defeat in 1945, the French tried to take back Vietnam – but fighting broke out because Vietnamese communists (called the Vietminh) were prepared to fight the French so they could be free of French control. The Vietminh were led by a soldier named Ho Chi Minh.

Vietnam is divided

In 1954, the French were defeated in Vietnam by Ho Chi Minh's forces. At a conference in Geneva, it was decided that Vietnam should be split in two, roughly halfway down the country. North Vietnam would be ruled by Ho Chi Minh. South Vietnam would be ruled by Ngo Dinh Diem – a leader who hated communism, had spent a lot of time in the USA and knew many leading US politicians well. Hanoi became the capital of North Vietnam and Saigon of South Vietnam.

The Americans get involved

Ho Chi Minh was angry about this division of Vietnam and supported a communist group called the Vietcong, who began a rebellion in the South. The Americans became concerned that South Vietnam might be taken over by communists – and once again decided to try to 'contain' communism (see page 160). To begin with, the USA sent money, military equipment and advisers to help the South Vietnamese – but by the mid-1960s, US soldiers and airmen were fighting the Vietcong in Vietnam in a brutal and devastating war. By 1965, there were nearly 200,000 American soldiers fighting in Vietnam, increasing to over half a million by 1968. By then, the USA was spending around $30 billion a year on the war.

The war escalates

The Vietcong were supplied with weapons and supplies by their fellow communist states – China and the USSR – along a supply route through thick jungle forest known as the Ho Chi Minh Trail (see J). The Vietcong attacked US troops and supply lines in surprise, hit-and-run raids known as guerrilla attacks. In 1965, the USA began bombing communist North Vietnam, and later in the war it bombed the nearby countries of Cambodia and Laos because the Vietcong were using them as a base and supply route and parts of the Ho Chi Minh Trail ran through them.

Protest in the USA

Many people in the West were so horrified by the devastation caused by the US military that large-scale protests began, particularly in America itself. On 15 November 1969, the largest anti-war protest in US history took place in Washington DC, with around 500,000 people gathering to hear speeches and to sing songs about ending the war.

▼ **SOURCE I** Ho Chi Minh, pictured in 1959 (on the left) with two leading politicians from the USSR. The one on the right is Leonid Brezhnev, who later became the leader of the USSR between 1964 and 1982.

▼ **MAP J** The locations of US bombing raids in Cambodia, Laos and Vietnam, 1969–1972. The map also shows the Ho Chi Minh Trail.

- Ho Chi Minh Trail
- One US bombing raid

0   150 km

The end of the war

When Richard Nixon became President in 1969, he hoped to end US involvement in the war. Over a period of several years, the number of US troops in the region was gradually reduced and in March 1973, the final US troops were removed from Vietnam. In December 1974, communist North Vietnam attacked South Vietnam. Without US support, South Vietnam was quickly beaten and surrendered in April 1975. After 30 years of struggle in Vietnam, the conflict was finally over. The USA had failed to prevent the spread of communism into South Vietnam, and Vietnam was now a unified communist country.

Fact ✓

US President Dwight D. Eisenhower (president from 1953 to 1961) used the term 'domino theory' to describe his fears over the spread of communism. He thought that if South Vietnam was taken over by communists, other countries in the region would become communist too – like a row of falling dominoes.

Key Words   guerrilla attack

▼ **SOURCE K** US troops jump from a helicopter during a 1968 operation in the Vietnam War.

Over to You .ıll

1 Write a sentence to explain the following:
   a Ho Chi Minh
   b Ngo Dinh Diem
   c Ho Chi Minh Trail

2 Explain the difference between the Vietminh and the Vietcong.

3 In what way was the USSR involved in the Vietnam War?

Consequence

1 Look back over pages 160–165 and write a sentence or two to summarise what happened in each of the following places during the Cold War:
   • North and South Korea
   • Cuba
   • Vietnam

2 'The USA was successful in containing communism.' How far do you agree with this statement? Explain your answer. You may use the following in your answer:
   • The Korean War
   • The Cuban Missile Crisis

   You must also use information of your own.

Cold War rivalry

There were many great technological and scientific developments and discoveries in the decades after the Second World War. One of the greatest advances was in space exploration. The USA and the USSR became great rivals in space exploration and competed in a frantic **space race** to explore space and be the first to put a human on the moon. So who won the space race? Why was there a space race in the first place? How else did the USA and USSR compete?

Objectives

- Recall key events in the space race.
- Examine how space, chess and sport were related to the Cold War.

The USSR takes the lead

In October 1957, the Soviets successful launched the first satellite, Sputnik 1, into orbit. American scientists had been working on achieving the same thing, so it was a huge victory for the USSR and communism. While the USA scrambled to catch up, the USSR sent up another rocket in November 1957, this time containing a dog (named Laika). Then in 1961, the Soviet cosmonaut Yuri Gagarin became the first man in space – and two years later Valentina Tereshkova (also from the USSR) became the first woman in space. By the mid-1960s, it seemed that the Soviets had won the space race... but not for long!

Walking on the moon

In 1962, US President John F. Kennedy responded by setting what many thought was an impossible target – to land a human on the moon and return them safely to earth, by 1970. On 20 July 1969, American Neil Armstrong (closely followed by Buzz Aldrin) became the first human to walk on the moon. Millions watched the event live on television. Superpower rivalry in the Cold War had led to one of the greatest scientific and technological moments of the century.

Why was there a space race?

The USSR and the USA both wanted to show that their countries and their system of government were better than the other. However, there was another side to the space race. Long-distance nuclear missiles had been developed by both countries – and they needed to leave the Earth's atmosphere and travel through space in order to reach their target. One reason why the two sides were so keen to develop space technology was to enable them to create bigger, more powerful nuclear weapons that could totally destroy their opponents.

▼ **SOURCE A** Laika, the first animal to go up into space and orbit the Earth, November 1957.

Other 'battlefields'

The game of chess even came to symbolise the struggle between the USSR and the USA. Chess had been extremely popular in the USSR for many years, and Soviet chess players were some of the very best in the world. In 1972, a 29-year-old American named Bobby Fischer reached the World Chess Championship final.

▼ **INTERPRETATION B** Adapted from a 2016 interview with Garry Kasparov. He was from the USSR, and was World Chess Champion from 1985 to 1993.

'It wasn't so much about chess, it was more about politics. In the Soviet Union, chess was very important and was used to demonstrate the intellectual superiority of the Soviet communist system over the West. That's why the Spassky defeat was treated by people on both sides of the Atlantic as a crushing moment in the midst of the Cold War.'

Fischer beat the reigning Russian world champion, Boris Spassky. This ended 24 years of Soviet domination of the Championships – and was a powerful victory for the USA. However, in 1975, a Soviet player won back the title (by default – Fischer refused to play after a disagreement about match rules), and players from the USSR remained world champions until the end of the Cold War.

▼ **SOURCE C** The famous Fischer/Spassky chess match in 1972. Fischer is on the right.

Olympic rivalry

The 1952 Olympic Games in Helsinki was the first time that the two superpowers went head-to-head in the sporting arena. America won this first battle, winning 40 gold medals to the USSR's 22. Both sides then invested huge sums of money developing their athletes and tactics.

▶ **SOURCE D**
American pride was dented in the 1972 Olympics when the Soviets (in red) beat the US team (in white) in the final. The game ended in controversy, and the defeated Americans refused to accept their silver medals. No US basketball team had ever lost an Olympic match up to this point.

Key Words   space race

The USSR eventually won the 'battle of the Olympics' – winning a total of 400 gold medals to America's 373 during the course of the Cold War (1952–1988). Many in the West believed that the Soviets gave their athletes performance-enhancing drugs to ensure victory.

When the Olympics were held in Moscow in 1980, the USA refused to allow its athletes to attend, in protest against the Soviet invasion of Afghanistan. When the games were held in Los Angeles four years later, athletes from the USSR and other communist states refused to attend.

The Cold War thaws

Towards the end of the 1980s, the USSR began to struggle to afford its huge army and massive stock of nuclear weapons. The Soviet people were very poor and started to demand an improved quality of life. One by one, the communist countries of Eastern Europe won their freedom from Soviet control. In 1991, the USSR itself started to split up into different states that began to rule themselves. By 1993, the people of Russia (one of the newly independent states) had free speech and free elections. The Cold War had come to an end.

Over to You

1 Describe the role played by the following in the space race:
   a Yuri Gagarin
   b Neil Armstrong
   c Valentina Tereshkova
   d Laika

2 a Make a list of reasons why the superpowers entered the space race.
   b Which do you think is the most important reason, and why?

3 Read **Interpretation B**.
   a Who were Bobby Fischer and Boris Spassky?
   b What point does Kasparov make about the importance of the chess game?

4 The Olympic Games were once described as 'war minus the shooting'. How might this comment relate to the Cold War?

A United Europe

During the first half of the twentieth century, Western Europe was devastated by two world wars. During the second half of the twentieth century, Europe witnessed peace, increased wealth and close cooperation. So why did Europe become a more peaceful place? Just how closely do the countries of Europe cooperate? And which countries are members of the European Union?

Objectives

- Explain why the countries of Europe cooperated more and more in the second half of the twentieth century.
- Outline which countries belong to the European Union and investigate when they joined.

Europe in ruins

Wars between European nations – particularly between Germany, France and Britain – had been raging on and off for centuries. At the end of the Second World War, the leaders of Europe saw that things had to change and were determined to avoid another large-scale war. They felt that future peace was far more likely if they put aside differences in language, culture and history and worked together. Rather than compete as rivals, they could work together to increase wealth and ensure peace. This vision of a united Europe – that is as closely linked together as the 50 states of the United States of America – has gradually evolved over the decades. Today, hundreds of millions of Europeans now share the same currency, vote in European elections and live under similar laws and regulations. So how did this happen?

▼ **SOURCE A** A German poster for the ECSC in 1952. The slogan means: 'Day of the Free Europe. First step: coal and steel'.

The evolution of the European Union

Britain officially recognised the **Republic of Ireland** as an independent country. Northern Ireland remained part of the United Kingdom.

The **Treaty of Rome** was signed, joining the group together as the European Economic Community (EEC). The countries also agreed to cooperate with each other in producing nuclear power.

The **Common Agricultural Policy** (CAP) was launched, which meant that all farmers in the EEC were paid the same for their produce, such as wheat and milk. The main idea behind it was to make sure that Europeans always had enough food to eat, and to ensure a fair standard of living for those people involved in the farming industry.

1957

1960s

1962

1968

1973

1951

1949

1979

Many countries gained their independence from the British Empire and it became clear to Britain that the EEC was becoming an economic success.

The EEC began to trade with other countries as a single group – the biggest trading organisation in the world.

By this time the success of the EEC had attracted other countries and it expanded to include three more members: **Britain, Denmark and Ireland**.

The European Parliament was elected by EEC citizens. At first it could just advise, but now it can pass laws that apply in all member countries.

Six countries (**France, West Germany, Italy, Belgium, the Netherlands and Luxembourg**) signed a treaty to join their coal and steel industries together to form the **European Coal and Steel Community** (ECSC). That way, they could never build up their armies on their own, and without the other countries finding out.

Fact ✓

The Common Agricultural Policy actually led to too much food being produced at times. Tonnes of extra butter and milk (known as 'butter mountains' and 'milk lakes') had to be kept in large warehouses and containers across the EEC. It was often sold to less economically developed countries.

▼ **SOURCE B** A secret cold store in North London where chunks of the EEC butter mountain were stored, 1987.

Key Words   currency   Euro   foreign affairs   single market

Fact ✓

Britain didn't join either the ECSC or the EEC to begin with. At this time Britain still had strong ties with the remaining countries (and former countries) in the British Empire. Britain was also closely linked with the USA.

Over to You ▁▃▅

1 Explain why many Europeans wanted to increase the cooperation between countries in the 1950s.

2 Why do you think Britain decided not to join the ECSC or EEC in the beginning?

3 Why do you think Britain eventually joined?

4 a Look at **Source A**. Describe the poster.

   b Why do you think the poster was designed in this way?

Twelve member countries adopted new **Euro** notes and coins as their currency, and 300 million Europeans now carried the same coins and notes in their pockets.

Two more countries joined (**Romania and Bulgaria**), raising the number to 27 and the population within the EU to 492.8 million. There were now 23 official languages in the EU.

The EU created a **single market**. This meant that goods, services, money and people could move freely between all 12 EU countries.

Three more members joined the EEC: **Greece (1981), Spain (1986)** and **Portugal (1986).**

Another three countries became members (**Austria, Sweden and Finland**) and the EU agreed to accept more members in the future.

Croatia joined the EU.

People in the UK voted to leave the EU.

The UK left the EU.

2002 **2004** **2007** **2013** **2016** **2020**
1980s **1990** **1992** **1993** **1995**

The **Maastricht Treaty** was signed, which renamed the community as the European Union (EU). All countries agreed to cooperate even further, in issues such as **foreign affairs** and security. For example, the EU can send help to the world's trouble spots, take part in peacekeeping efforts, or provide help to areas affected by war or famine. Member countries also work together on issues such as drug trafficking and anti-terror strategies.

Ten more countries joined the EU, together representing more than 100 million citizens.

Today, the EU has several main goals. Many are to do with the citizens living within the EU – protecting their freedom and security, respecting their cultures, and fighting discrimination. Other goals are concerned with the economy of the region, while at the same time protecting the environment and developing new technologies.

Later on... 2017

In 2017, the EU's law enforcement department helped to coordinate police officers and customs officers in Europe to seize precious goods such as coins, paintings, musical instruments and sculptures that had been stolen and illegally sold around the world. This was part of a larger global operation involving 81 countries. In total, over 41,000 items were recovered and 53 people were arrested.

▼ **SOURCE C** A European Parliament building in Strasbourg, France.

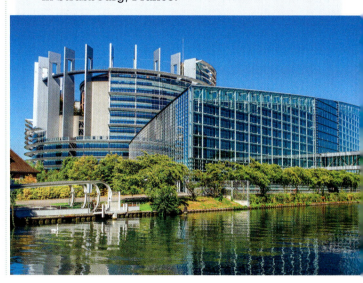

▼ **MAP D** The European Union has grown steadily since it was formed in 1951.

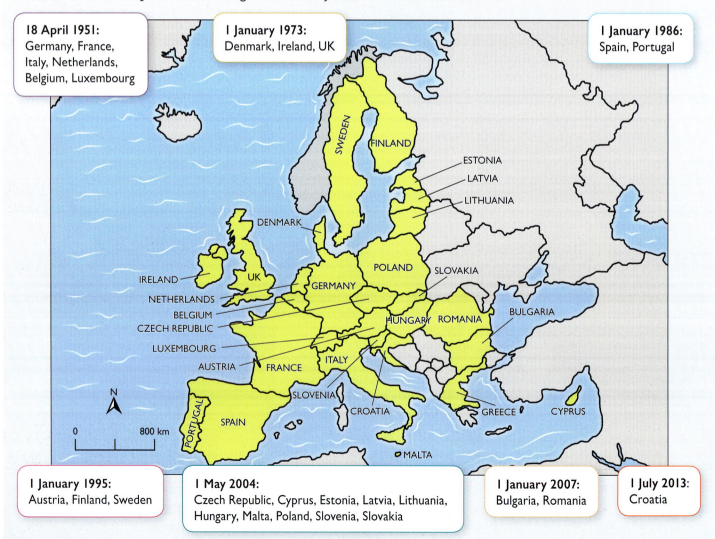

18 April 1951:
Germany, France, Italy, Netherlands, Belgium, Luxembourg

1 January 1973:
Denmark, Ireland, UK

1 January 1986:
Spain, Portugal

1 January 1995:
Austria, Finland, Sweden

1 May 2004:
Czech Republic, Cyprus, Estonia, Latvia, Lithuania, Hungary, Malta, Poland, Slovenia, Slovakia

1 January 2007:
Bulgaria, Romania

1 July 2013:
Croatia

A divided Britain

The British public has been divided over membership to the EU since it joined. In 1975, for example, 26 million people voted in a **referendum** that asked whether Britain should remain part of the EEC. The result was two to one in favour of staying in. Those in favour of Britain remaining part of the EU believe that the country benefits from the strong trade links and '**collective security**' of its membership. These people are known as 'Pro-Europeans'. However, those against it argue that Britain is unique and different from other European countries. They worry that Britain is losing its independence and identity and should be free to make all its own decisions. These people are called 'Eurosceptics'. In June 2016, another referendum was held in the UK to decide whether Britain should remain part of the EU. This time, 52 per cent voted to leave the EU (in a process that became known as 'Brexit') while 48 per cent voted to remain. Eventually, after nearly four years of debate, the UK finally left the EU on 31 January 2020.

▼ **SOURCE E** The voting slip used in the June 2016 EU referendum in the UK.

▼ **SOURCE F** The UK's decision to leave the EU was controversial and provoked heated debates. This demonstration in London in 2017 was attended by people who wanted the UK to remain in the EU.

Key Words

collective security
referendum

▼ **SOURCE G** A political cartoon by Patrick Chappatte that appeared in a US newspaper in June 2016. Chappette is a Lebanese-Swiss cartoonist who creates many political cartoons for several European and US newspapers.

Over to You

1 What do you think have been the three most important developments in the evolution of the EU? Explain your choices.

2 What different beliefs are held by Pro-Europeans and Eurosceptics?

3 Look at **Source G**. What point is the cartoonist making about the British people who voted to leave the EU?

Knowledge and Understanding

1 Describe two features of the EU that have helped promote stability in Europe since the end of the Second World War.

⟳ Quick Knowledge Quiz

Choose the correct answer from the three options:

1 What name is given to the system by which the government aims to help those in need, particularly the old, the sick and the unemployed?

   a Beveridge Report
   b welfare state
   c Cold War

2 Which of the following was set up after the war to provide healthcare for everyone?

   a Ministry of Healthcare
   b National Health Service
   c Board of Health and Medicine

3 What was the term used to describe an imaginary barrier between the communist countries of the East and the capitalist countries of the West after the Second World War?

   a Iron Curtain
   b Eastern Barrier
   c Berlin Wall

4 What was the name of the military alliance of Eastern European communist states?

   a NATO
   b Warsaw Pact
   c Marshall Plan

5 The Korean War began in which year?

   a 1945
   b 1950
   c 1953

6 In 1962, the USSR began transporting nuclear missiles and building missile launch bases on which Caribbean island?

   a Jamaica
   b Dominican Republic
   c Cuba

7 As well as Vietnam, which neighbouring countries were bombed by the USA during the Vietnam War?

   a Cambodia and Laos
   b China and Japan
   c North and South Korea

8 On 20 July 1969, who became the first person to walk on the moon?

   a Buzz Aldrin
   b Neil Armstrong
   c Yuri Gagarin

9 In 1951, six countries (France, West Germany, Italy, Belgium, the Netherlands and Luxembourg) joined their iron and coal industries together. What was this union called?

   a ECSC
   b EU
   c EEC

10 In what year did people in the UK vote to leave the EU?

   a 2014
   b 2016
   c 2020

Literacy Focus

Check and correct

1   Look at the following five statements about events that took place during the Cold War. Each statement has one factual error and one spelling error. The order of events in the statements is all mixed up too.

Write out each statement in the correct chronological order, ensuring that you correct each spelling and factual error.

- Korea was divided in two after the Second World War. It was decided to use the equator of the Earth as a dividing point – mainly because it divided the country aproximately in half.

- A potential nuclear war was avoided over Cuba in 1962 after US President Truman and USSR leader Krushchev negotiated an agreement.

- In 1929, the Soviet Union successfully tested its first nuclear bomb. Now both East and West had nuclear wepons, and both sides quickly began to make more and more.

- Over a period of several years, the number of US troops fighting in Vietnam was gradualy reduced and, in March 1965, the final US troops were removed from Vietnam.

- At the end of the war, Germany was divided into three zones, each one controlled by a different one of the major winning countries – the USA, Britian, France and the USSR. It was also decided that Berlin, Germany's capital, should be divided into four.

Writing in detail

2   Look at the sentence below. It is a very basic answer to the question:

What was the impact of the Beveridge Report?

However, the answer does not contain many specific, factual details. Rewrite the paragraph to include more detail – adding names, dates, examples and facts where possible.

> What did the report say? For example, what were the 'five giants' he identified that could ruin people's lives?

> Who was 'Beveridge'? When did he write the report? And for what reasons?

> The Beveridge Report was a report that led to changes in the way people were looked after.

> What happened as a result of the report? The basic answer mentions 'changes to the way people were looked after', but gives no detail. You need to explain what changes took place. Look back at pages 152–155 to help you.

> What changes/reforms did the report suggest? You might want to mention the fact that he felt that the government should look after people 'from the cradle to the grave' here.

> You might also want to mention that there was a change of government after the war: the Labour Party promised to follow Beveridge's advice, but the Conservative Party, led by Winston Churchill, refused to make such a promise. The Labour Party won the election easily.

History skill: Causation

As you know, a cause is a reason why something happened. While most historical events have a number of different causes, there is often one cause that is more important than the others. Historians need to be able to justify *how much* they agree or disagree about the causes of an event. They might respond to a statement that contains a judgement, and argue which cause is the most important.

Responding to statements about causation

This chapter's assessment requires you to think about the causes of the increasing tension between East and West in the years after the end of the Second World War.

'The main reason for the increase in tension between East and West from 1945 to 1949 was the issue of Berlin.' How far do you agree with this statement? Explain your answer.

> **TIP:** Do you agree a little or a lot (or somewhere in between) with the statement? Think about the extent to which you agree that the problems over Berlin at the end of the war were the main cause in the increased tension. This means that you also need to think about other causes, and judge which one is the main cause.

The question asks you to respond to a statement about the causes of tension between East and West in the years after the end of the war. The steps below show one way to answer this type of question.

1 **Plan:** Study the statement. Do you agree or disagree with it? What do you know about the topic? What *other* causes led to the event?

> **TIP:** Look back at your notes or pages 156–159 of this book to remind yourself of the reasons why tension built up after the war.

2 **Judge:** You need to decide which cause you think was the most important. List the reasons for your choice.

> **TIP:** You may not think that one cause was more important than the others. But you can still answer the question – you can argue that several causes are equally important, as long as you can explain your reasons.

3 **Answer:** You are asked to respond to the statement, so make sure you answer the question. How far do you agree with the statement? Do you disagree, slightly agree, or strongly agree?

4 **Explain:** Add details/reasons to support your response and explain your view. Use your plan to help you add detail. Try to refer to other reasons when answering the question.

> **TIP:** Don't simply write about your choice only. Include other reasons and back them up with factual detail. You might even be able to link the causes.

> **TIP:** Write why your choice is the most important – and why you don't think the others are as important.

5 **Conclude:** Write a concluding sentence, stating your overall view.

Now, considering all these points, try putting this into practice!

Assessment: Causation

Your challenge is to answer this statement question about causation:

'The main reason for the increase in tension between East and West from 1945 to 1949 was the issue of Berlin.' How far do you agree with this statement? Explain your answer.   (20)

The steps and example sentence starters below will help you structure your answer.

1   **Plan:** Study the statement, which assumes that the issues in Berlin in the years after the war was the main cause of tension between East and West. Do you agree? What do you know about this?

2   **Judge:** Look at your mind-map. Which of the causes do you think was the most important source of tension? Try to explain why.

3   **Answer:** Now respond to the statement so you are **directly answering the question**. Remember that the question is asking you the extent to which you agree with the statement.

Make sure you back up your responses with facts and reasons.

4   **Explain and conclude:** Sometimes, causes can be linked together, so add any links you can find. For example, would Marshall Aid have been available if Truman had not announced his Truman Doctrine?

Finally, add some **details and reasons** to support and explain your view. Try to refer to other causes when answering the question.

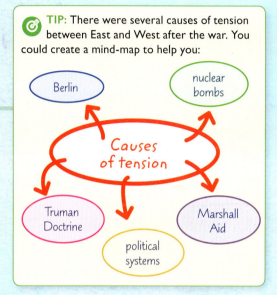

TIP: There were several causes of tension between East and West after the war. You could create a mind-map to help you:

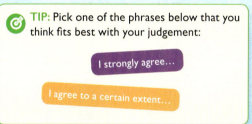

TIP: Pick one of the phrases below that you think fits best with your judgement:

I strongly agree…

I agree to a certain extent…

The Cold War was a period in history when…
The increase in tension between East and West after the end of the Second World War had several causes. The main cause was…   (5)
This was an important cause because…   (5)
Other causes, such as… and… , were less important because…   (5)
Overall, I (strongly agree/agree to a certain extent/disagree) with the statement because…   (5)

TIP: Remember to conclude your answer. Explain how far you agree with the statement.

The decline of the British Empire

From the 1600s onwards, Britain conquered foreign lands all over the world and claimed them as part of the British Empire. During Queen Victoria's reign (1837–1901) Britain ruled around 450 million people (approximately one quarter of the world's population) and the empire covered about one quarter of the world's total land area – the largest empire the world had ever known! But almost 50 years after the end of Victoria's reign, and after two world wars, the British Empire began to break apart. More and more countries wanted to rule themselves and cut ties with Britain. So how and why did this happen?

Objectives

- Recall how Britain gradually lost its empire.
- Examine the role played by the First and Second World Wars in the decline of the British Empire.

The impact of two world wars

Before the First World War, Britain was one of the richest countries in the world. However, after four years of fighting, the country's wealth was nearly all gone. In fact, Britain was now in debt because it had borrowed money, mainly from the USA. Also, during the war, Britain had not been trading with lots of other countries because it had been concentrating on trying to win the war. As a result, these other countries had found new nations to trade with, or had developed their own industries. The First World War changed Britain's status in the world – it was no longer the world's economic superpower!

However, in the years after the war, Britain *did* recover some of its strength – but it was then completely bankrupted by the Second World War. Britain was in more debt than ever before – and needed more huge loans from the USA to get back on its feet. This was also the time when the USA and the USSR became world superpowers, and Britain was no longer as important on the world stage.

◀ **SOURCE A** A 1902 map showing the extent of the British Empire. The Latin words mean 'Edward VII, by the Grace of God, King of all British people, Defender of the Faith, Emperor of India'. Note the different animals (common in several of the colonies) above the map. They are facing a lion, which represents Britain.

Leaving the empire

By the time the First World War started in 1914, several of Britain's colonies – such as Canada, Australia, New Zealand and South Africa – had been running their own affairs for several years. These countries, and others in the empire, had played an important role in Britain's victory in both world wars, supplying troops and materials. But by the end of the Second World War, many other British colonies were demanding the right to rule themselves. And Britain no longer had the military strength or the wealth to hold onto them. Also, many British people felt that rebuilding Britain after the war was far more of a priority than holding on to colonies in distant lands.

Why did some colonies demand to rule themselves?

There were several reasons why there were increasing demands for independence in some countries:

- The Africans and Indians who had fought for Britain felt they were fighting to defend freedom for Britain, but were getting increasingly frustrated that their own countries were not yet free. They thought it wasn't right that they should fight to stop the Germans occupying other countries, but not fight to stop Britain occupying theirs.

- As ideas about democracy, freedom and nationalism spread around the world in the 1800s, many people in the colonies began to demand independence. In India and other colonies, such as Jamaica, the demand for independence became a common feature.

- Researchers and historians were showing how important the cultures and achievements of Africa and Asia had been before the Europeans had taken over. Many people in the colonies were proud of their culture and wanted to revive their old traditions – and this could only be done if the British left. After the Second World War, the British Empire declined rapidly. One of the first colonies to gain independence after the war was India (see pages 178–179), followed by other colonies, including many in Africa (see pages 180–181).

A new perspective

In the years since becoming independent, many countries have taken steps to remove some of the reminders of their past as a British colony. For example, in 2015 in Cape Town, South Africa, a statue of Cecil Rhodes was removed. Rhodes (1853–1902) was a key figure in expanding Britain's empire, and many streets, schools and other buildings were named after him. After he died in 1902, statues of him were built in many colonies.

However, Rhodes had very strong ideas about Britain's superiority over other countries, and their people. He introduced laws that pushed people from their lands and increased taxes on their homes. He also made a huge amount of money from mining gold and diamonds in southern Africa.

▼ SOURCE B The statue of Cecil Rhodes being removed from the University of Cape Town, South Africa, 9 April 2015.

Over to You

1 Describe the size and scale of the British Empire at the end of Queen Victoria's reign.

2 What impact did the First World War have on the British Empire?

3 Why did some colonies begin to demand their independence from Britain?

4 Why do you think the statue in **Source B** is being removed?

Source Analysis

1 What does **Source A** show?

2 How useful is this source to a historian studying Britain's view of its own empire at the turn of the twentieth century?

Independence for India

After the Second World War, Britain lost its empire very quickly. It had taken centuries to build up, but took only decades to lose. One of the first nations to break away after the war was India – one of Britain's largest ever colonies. How did this happen?

Objectives

- Recall key events in the campaign for Indian independence.
- Assess factors that led to the partition of India in 1947.

Victoria and India

During the reign of Queen Victoria (1837–1901), Britain took direct control of India. The British ran many parts of everyday life, such as education, the army, railways, and law and order. Queen Victoria proudly called herself 'Empress of India', learned to speak and write Hindi and Urdu, and had Indian food on many of her dinner menus (see **A**).

British rule

There is little doubt that Britain changed India. The issue of British control and influence in India has always been controversial and has often been interpreted differently. Admirers of British rule have argued that India benefitted from British influence in some ways through the building of roads, schools, hospitals, factories and railways. Today however, the vast majority of experts agree that India suffered greatly during the era

▼ **SOURCE A** Queen Victoria pictured with her Indian secretary, Munshi Abdul Karim, at Balmoral Castle in Scotland, around 1900.

of the British Empire. British customs were forced on the people and local traditions, culture and religions tended to be ignored. Indian workers were exploited, the county's raw materials were taken back to Britain, and native lands were seized.

Towards independence

By 1900, many Indians started to believe that India should be free from British control. A political group called the Indian National Congress had been formed in 1885 to bring this about. It held meetings and organised demonstrations to further its cause, but the British ignored its demands.

In 1914–1918, many Indians fought alongside British soldiers in the First World War, and India gave Britain a huge amount of money, food and materials to help with the war effort. Nearly 64,000 Indian soldiers died in the war.

In 1919, after India's significant contributions in the First World War, the British made slight changes to the way India was governed. Law-making councils were set up all across India and over five million property-owning, educated Indians were given the vote. However, the British government in London still controlled taxation, the police, the law courts, the armed forces, education, and much more. While some Indians welcomed the changes as a step in the right direction, others were bitterly disappointed and there were many large demonstrations. One such demonstration, in the town of Amritsar, led to the deaths of 379 people when the local British commander ordered his men to fire into the crowd.

Gandhi

In the 1920s, the Indian independence movement gained more support under the leadership of Mohandas Gandhi, a Hindu and former lawyer. He led a series of non-violent protests against the British, such as refusing to buy British-made goods and pay taxes. He gained millions of supporters.

Eventually, in 1935, the Government of India Act gave Indians the right to control everything except the army. India, however, was still part of the British Empire and was still ruled by a **viceroy**. Many Indians, including Gandhi, continued to demand complete independence. By now, Muslims in India had formed their own independence group (the Muslim League). Their leader, Mohammed Ali Jinnah, called for a new country for Indian Muslims.

After the Second World War, it was clear that Britain would have to give India its independence, and Britain offered to do so in 1946. However, the Indian National Congress (which was not tied to any particular religion) and the Muslim League political parties became involved in a bitter struggle for power. The Muslim League wanted an independent Muslim State – Pakistan. Terrible violence broke out between Hindus, Sikhs, and Muslims. Hundreds of thousands were killed, and millions lost their homes.

Partition

Finally, Indian and British leaders agreed to **partition** (split) British India into two states – Hindu India and Muslim Pakistan. Pakistan became independent on 14 August 1947, and India the next day. Immediately, over seven million Muslims fled to Pakistan and around the same number of Hindus and Sikhs fled to India. Severe violence erupted at this time between the different religions and hundreds of thousands of people lost their lives. Tensions between the independent nations of India and Pakistan continue to this day.

▼ **MAP B** How India was divided in 1947. Areas where more than half the people were Muslim became Pakistan, while areas where over half were Hindu became independent India. It has been estimated that over 14 million fled to the 'other side' in 1947. Thousands from both religions were murdered in the process.

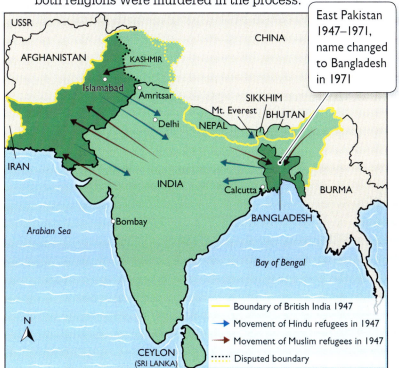

East Pakistan 1947–1971, name changed to Bangladesh in 1971

▼ **SOURCE C** From a leaflet written in 1907 by Indians in Bengal, in east India, who wanted the British out.

'Can these thieves really be our rulers? These thieves... import a huge number of goods made in their own country and sell them in our markets, stealing our wealth and taking life from our people. Can those who steal the harvest of our fields and doom us to hunger, fever and plague really be our rulers? Can foreigners really be our rulers?'

▶ **SOURCE D** Gandhi on a visit to Britain in 1931. He came to discuss a possible end to British control of India.

Over to You

1 How do we know that Queen Victoria was proud and pleased about Britain's connection to India?

2 a How did India contribute to the First World War?

   b What changes were made to the way India was governed after the war?

   c Why were some Indians happy with these changes, while others were disappointed?

3 a Read **Source C**. Who do you think the thieves were?

   b What point does the source make about British rule?

4 Why was India split into separate countries in 1947?

USSR
CHINA
AFGHANISTAN
KASHMIR
Islamabad
Amritsar
SIKKHIM
Mt. Everest
BHUTAN
Delhi
NEPAL
IRAN
INDIA
Calcutta
BURMA
Bombay
BANGLADESH
Arabian Sea
Bay of Bengal
N
CEYLON (SRI LANKA)

Boundary of British India 1947
Movement of Hindu refugees in 1947
Movement of Muslim refugees in 1947
Disputed boundary

Map A shows the huge continent of Africa – the colours indicate which European nation was in control of each particular area in 1901. Almost all of Africa was ruled by seven European nations – Britain, France, Germany, Spain, Portugal, Belgium and Italy. But why were these nations so keen to control Africa? How and when did this control end? What happened in some of Africa's independent nations?

Objectives

- Recall why so much of Africa had been colonised by 1901.
- Explain how African nations regained their independence during the twentieth century.

Dividing Africa

In the early 1900s, there only a few countries in Africa that were independent. Most had become colonies – between 1880 and 1900, over 80 per cent of Africa was taken over by European powers in a time known as 'the scramble for Africa'. This was a time of great rivalries between some of the major European nations, and having large colonies in Africa was a way to demonstrate power and influence. Also, European leaders thought that if they could take over vast areas of Africa they could sell goods to the people who lived there – and could also take (or steal) valuable raw materials such as rubber, cotton, copper, gold and diamonds. Britain, for example, gained control of 16 colonies in Africa, including Egypt, Sudan, Nigeria, British East Africa (Kenya, Uganda, Tanganyika and Zanzibar), Sierra Leone and South Africa.

Today, no country in Africa is a colony of a European power, and a modern map of the continent looks very different from a map from the early 1900s.

Controlling Africa

The vast majority of Africa was controlled by four main European powers in the early 1900s: Britain, France, Belgium and Portugal. While all of these countries stood mainly to gain wealth and power from their colonies, each of them viewed their colonies differently.

Britain saw itself as a 'mother country' that should not only protect its colonies, but help them develop. Cecil Rhodes, a British businessman and politician, said in 1877 that British people were 'the finest race in the world, and that the more of the world we inhabit the better it is for the human race'. Queen Victoria said that Britain should 'protect the poor natives and advance civilisation'. France felt it had a similar role to Britain, but also wanted to turn Africans into French people – including speaking and writing in French. Its colonies were tightly controlled from Paris and were treated as part of France. Belgium and Portugal ruled their colonies very harshly and were determined to hold onto them for as long as possible.

In general, though, all European powers exploited their colonies in some way. They took their raw materials and used local people as a cheap workforce. Little attempt was made to understand the wishes or needs of the locals themselves, so differences in race, language, culture and traditions were largely ignored, and the European nations grabbed what they could. Africans had no say in how their countries were ruled and European settlers banished Africans from the best land and took it for themselves.

▼ **SOURCE A** British politician Lord Rosebery in a speech made in 1893, during the 'scramble for Africa'. He became Prime Minister a year later.

'At present we are "pegging out claims for the future". We have to remember that it's part of our heritage to make sure that the world is shaped by us. It must be English-speaking. We have to look forward to the future of our race. We will fail in our duty if we fail to take our share of the world.'

Fact ✔

To prevent war between the European powers in Africa, their leaders held a conference in Berlin (Germany) during the winter of 1884 to decide which European nation could take which areas of land.

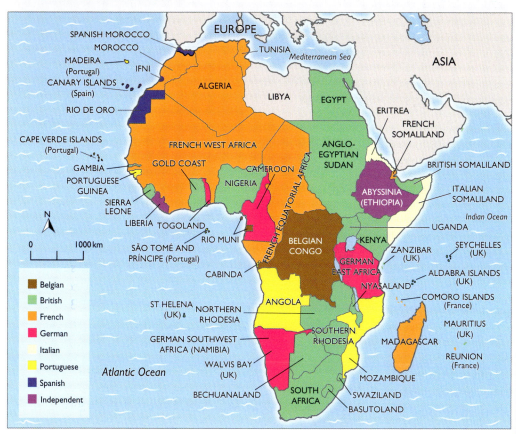

Legend:
- Belgian
- British
- French
- German
- Italian
- Portuguese
- Spanish
- Independent

African resistance

Many locals fought to defend their lands, but weapons such as machine guns gave European armies a big advantage over the Africans, who were mainly armed with spears and swords. Sometimes, African tribes scored major victories over European countries (such as in the Zulu War of 1879), but more often the European invaders wiped out the African forces and destroyed their traditional ways of life.

Over to You

1 In your own words, explain what is meant by the term 'scramble for Africa'.

2 Why do you think Britain was so keen to take part in the 'scramble'?

3 Describe how either the British, the French, the Belgians or the Portuguese ruled their colonies.

▼ **SOURCE C** A cartoon from 1911 showing an African man leaning asleep against a tree while several European countries plant flags labelled 'England', 'Portugal', 'Belgium', 'Turkey', 'Italy', 'Germany', 'Spain' and 'France' all around him.

Source Analysis

1 Read **Source A**. In your own words, describe the point that Lord Rosebery is making.

2 Look at **Source C**. In your own words, describe what is happening in the cartoon.

3 What point is the cartoonist trying to make?

4 How useful are **Sources A** and **C** to a historian studying attitudes to European expansion in Africa?

The impact of the Second World War

By the end of the war, some of Britain's colonies had been running their own affairs for years. Australia, for example, had been part of the British Empire since 1770, but by 1901 it had its own Parliament that made most of the key decisions about the country. New Zealand became a British colony in 1840, but had started to run its own affairs by 1907. In Africa, South Africa had been self-governing since 1910 and Egypt since 1922. More and more colonies were now demanding the right to govern themselves.

The war had weakened countries like Britain and France, which no longer had the strength or wealth to hold onto their colonies. In addition, many Africans had fought for Britain and France against Germany, defending freedom, while their own countries were not free. By the late 1940s, there were large independence movements in several African nations including Gold Coast (now Ghana), Nigeria, Rhodesia (now Zimbabwe) and Sierra Leone.

Indian example

When India gained its independence from Britain in 1947, many other countries started to demand their freedom too. The British decided to allow independence in colonies they felt were stable enough. They hoped that by freely granting independence, they were more likely to have a successful relationship with the newly formed countries. In 1957, the first British colony in Africa got its independence when the Gold Coast (as it was known under British rule) became Ghana. Chart **D** shows the speed at which independence then spread through Africa.

The transfer of power

After Ghana, several other British colonies in Africa quickly became independent. However, the switch to independence was not particularly peaceful. There were riots and severe violence in some places. Indeed, in 2013 the British government apologised for the way it had dealt with a rebel uprising in Kenya and agreed to pay compensation.

Since independence, nations such as Nigeria, Gambia and Kenya have been invited to join the Commonwealth, an organisation of independent, free countries with close cultural, trade and sporting links to Britain.

▼ **D** Some of the African nations that achieved independence in the 1960s and 1970s.

	Country	Ruler	Date of independence
	Ghana (formerly the Gold Coast)	Britain	1957
	Congo	France	1960
	Mauritania	France	1960
	Nigeria	Britain	1960
	Senegal	France	1960
	Algeria	France	1962
	Uganda	Britain	1962
	Kenya	Britain	1963
	Angola	Portugal	1975
	Mozambique	Portugal	1975
	Zimbabwe (formerly Rhodesia)	Britain	1980

▼ **SOURCE E** The Commonwealth Games, once known as the British Empire Games, is a sports competition held every four years in one of the former colonies of the British Empire. Athletes from former British colonies are invited to participate.

Meanwhile...

1940s–1970s

Some of the other European nations were reluctant to give up their African colonies. In Angola and Mozambique, for example, Portugal's determination to hang onto these colonies led to a long war between African and Portuguese soldiers. In Algeria, French forces fought to keep control from 1945, until independence was finally agreed in 1962.

A new Africa

For many newly independent nations, freedom produced its difficulties as well as its benefits. Some nations, like Morocco, Tunisia and Egypt, developed successful tourist industries, while others have made use of raw materials such as rubber, gold and diamonds. Many African nations have developed fast-paced modern economies with vibrant cities and culture. However, some countries have seen rivalries between tribes flare up into bloody civil wars. This happened in Nigeria in the 1960s, Uganda in the 1980s, and Sierra Leone, Rwanda and Somalia in the 1990s. Many nations have struggled to create their own systems of government, build up their own industry and trade, and cope with differences between groups of people. However, perhaps the greatest problem the newly independent nations have had to deal with is poverty. Of the 25 poorest countries in the world, 22 are in Africa… and despite recent investment in Africa the problems of poverty and long-term debt still remain.

▼ **SOURCE F** A jubilant crowd carries Julius Nyerere, Premier of Tanganyika (Tanzania), after being granted internal self-government. A few months later he was made president when the country was given independence.

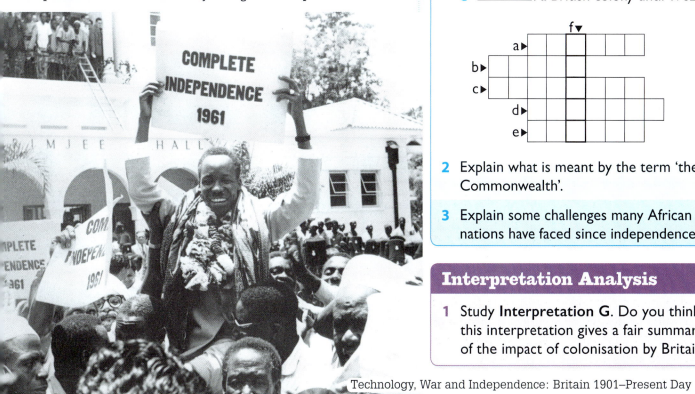

Key Words   Commonwealth

▼ **INTERPRETATION G** Adapted from an article by historian David Olusoga in the *Guardian* newspaper, 23 January 2016.

'The empire did bring economic developments and peace to some parts of the world, though many of those developments did not last and were mainly arranged to suit British interests. And it delivered war and devastation to other regions.'

Over to You

1 Copy out and complete the word grid below, using clues a–e. When you have correctly completed the grid, a word will be revealed (f). Write a sentence about the word in line f.
Clues:

a Portuguese colony, independent in 1975

b _____ Africa: self-governing since 1910

c Formerly Rhodesia

d Former French colony

e _____: a British colony until 1962

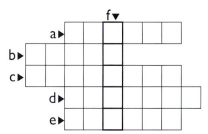

2 Explain what is meant by the term 'the Commonwealth'.

3 Explain some challenges many African nations have faced since independence.

Interpretation Analysis

1 Study **Interpretation G**. Do you think this interpretation gives a fair summary of the impact of colonisation by Britain?

Why did people migrate to Britain after the war?

Different groups and nationalities have been moving to Britain for hundreds of years. During the twentieth century, however, there was an increase in the number of people from all over the world deciding to make their homes in Britain. So why did people decide to move to Britain? How many came? And where did they come from?

Objectives

- Explain where Britain's immigrant population moved from.
- Examine the reasons why they migrated to Britain.

Why come to Britain?

There were several reasons why large groups of **immigrants** came to Britain after the Second World War. Some came as **refugees** from war-torn Europe. Their homes and livelihoods had been destroyed so many looked for a new life and new opportunities in Britain. Other migrants came from parts of the British Empire to find work and build a better life. The government encouraged and welcomed them because there was a shortage of workers after the war, and people were needed in mining, building, transport, healthcare and farming. The map outlines some of the main areas where immigrants came from in the years immediately after the war. It also shows where people have moved from in later years.

Ireland

Famine in Ireland and the search for work in the 1800s meant that there were already around 600,000 Irish immigrants living in Britain at the start of the twentieth century. After the Second World War a new period of immigration increased the number to around one million. By 2001, around six million people (ten per cent of the British population) had either Irish parents or grandparents.

Caribbean islands

Around 15,000 West Indians settled in Britain after the First World War. During the Second World War thousands more moved to Britain to help with the war effort, although most returned home when the war ended. From the late 1940s to 1970, more immigrants (around half a million) from colonies such as Jamaica, Barbados and Trinidad and Tobago were encouraged to come to Britain because of a shortage of workers.

Europe

By the start of the twentieth century, around 200,000 Jews from Eastern Europe had fled persecution and settled in Britain. In the 1930s, around 60,000 German Jews came to Britain when the Nazis rose to power. When fighting broke out in 1939, thousands of Poles sought safety in Britain too. When the war ended, around 114,000 of them decided not to return to Poland. By 1950, around 100,000 Hungarians, Ukrainians, Estonians, Latvians and Lithuanians who had fled from the USSR had also settled in Britain.

West Africa

The countries of British West Africa (now Gambia, Nigeria, Sierra Leone and Ghana) made a large contribution to the British effort in the Second World War. They provided soldiers, raw materials and air bases. After 1948, many West Africans moved to Britain to find jobs and get a better standard of education.

Over to You

1 **a** Make a list of reasons why different groups have moved to Britain. You might want to divide your list into 'push' and 'pull' factors: push factors are reasons why people are driven away (or pushed) from their own country, while 'pull factors' are reasons why people are attracted to life in Britain.

   b In your opinion, which was the most common reason why people came to Britain?

2 Can you make a link between immigration to Britain and the British Empire? Explain your answer.

Cyprus

Cyprus was very poor and unsettled in the years following the Second World War and many Cypriots came to start a new life in Britain. After Turkey invaded and divided the island in two in the 1970s, a further 70,000 Cypriots left to make their home in Britain.

Far East

People from the Far East began to move to Britain throughout the 1950s and 1960s. Most came from the poorer areas of the British colony of Hong Kong, and by 1961 there were around 30,000 people from the Far East living in Britain. In 1997, Hong Kong stopped being a British colony and became part of China. Around 50,000 people from Hong Kong were given British passports at this time.

Kenya and Uganda

Many Asians from Kenya and Uganda came to Britain in the 1960s and 1970s. They had moved to Africa from India and Pakistan when these nations were part of the British Empire – but now the newly independent Kenyan and Ugandan governments were driving them out. Around 44,000 Asians from Kenya and 26,000 from Uganda came to Britain at this time.

South Asia

When India gained independence from Britain in 1947, it split into different countries: India and Pakistan. This partition led to fighting and many thousands of people died as whole populations moved across the dividing lines. Some came to Britain to escape the violence and by 1955 around 10,000 people had moved to Britain, hoping to find work and better education.

Why should we remember the *Empire Windrush*?

On 22 June 1948, a ship named the *Empire Windrush* landed at Tilbury docks in London. On board were 492 passengers – mostly men – who had come to live in Britain. It was an event that would change British society forever. So what made these newcomers special, and why did they move to Britain? How were they treated? And how did they help to change life in Britain?

Objectives

- Define the term 'Windrush generation'.
- Outline the experiences and impacts of the 'Windrush generation'.

Moving to the 'mother country'

Many people from the Caribbean had contributed to Britain's effort in the Second World War. When the fighting ended most went back to their home countries, but life was very hard in the Caribbean. Jamaica had been devastated by a hurricane in 1944 and poverty and hardship were common. The Caribbean had not yet developed a tourist industry to provide jobs, and the price of sugar – the Caribbean's major export – was at an all-time low. Many West Indians had been taught in school that Britain was a kind of 'mother country' where they would always feel supported and welcome – so for many ambitious young people, it was clear that their future lay there.

Why Britain?

In 1948, Parliament passed the British Nationality Act. This meant that all the people of the Empire – now called the Commonwealth – had British citizenship, which meant they could have a British passport and migrate to Britain. Many had been brought up speaking English, named after British heroes and educated to love Britain. Also, Britain was very short of workers after the war. The NHS, London Transport, the British Hotels and Restaurants Association and the British Transport Commission all encouraged people from the Caribbean to move to Britain.

▶ **SOURCE A** The *Empire Windrush* arriving in London, 22 June 1948. The West Indian immigrants who arrived in Britain became known as the 'Windrush generation'. Between 1948 and 1970, nearly 500,000 people from the Caribbean settled in Britain.

Welcome, *Empire Windrush*?

The voyage made headlines in Britain before the ship had even docked. Many immigrants from Europe and Ireland had been entering Britain since the war had finished, but it was the arrival of this ship that caused alarm. Newspapers were full of stories of the 'colour problem' that was heading towards Britain's shores and some MPs demanded that the ship was turned around. Shortly after the *Empire Windrush* arrived, most immigrants had found jobs, and friends and relatives followed in search of work. Although at this time, immigrants made up a tiny proportion of the population, this event was the start of an immigration boom that was to change British society forever. In time, immigrants would also arrive from Africa, Asia and other places around the world – all helping to create a more **multicultural** Britain.

Later on... 2018

In late 2017, some of the 'Windrush generation' were told that they were in Britain illegally because they didn't have official paperwork (such as a UK passport). Some were sent back to the Caribbean. Others lost their jobs, or were stopped from having free medical care. This became known as the 'Windrush Scandal'. In August 2018, the British government admitted its mistakes and said that anyone who had left the UK would be helped to return.

The British experience

Not all Britons welcomed the new arrivals. Some were suspicious of people of another race and culture, while others feared they would lose their jobs to the immigrants. As a result, many West Indians faced hostility. Some found it hard to get good jobs (even though they were qualified engineers, doctors or scientists) and decent housing (see **B** and **E**). Some politicians with extreme anti-immigration views gained some support, but racist political parties remained fairly small. Yet, despite the discrimination, racial tension and obstacles such as low pay, many thousands of West Indians (and other immigrants) decided to settle in Britain. Some did go back to the West Indies, but most remained, determined to stay despite the difficulties.

▼ **INTERPRETATION B** John Richards, a passenger on the *Empire Windrush*, interviewed by the BBC in 1998.

'I knew a lot about Britain from schooldays, but it was a different picture when you came face-to-face with the facts. They tell you it is the "mother country", you're all welcome, you're all British. When you come here you realise you're a foreigner and that's all there is to it.'

▼ **INTERPRETATION C** Sam King, a passenger on the *Empire Windrush*, interviewed by the BBC in 1998. King had served in England in the RAF during the war, but went home in 1945. He returned on the *Empire Windrush* and went on to become the first black mayor of Southwark, London. He also co-founded the Notting Hill Carnival.

'The second day in England I was offered five jobs. If someone want to leave, let them leave, but I have been here during the War fighting Nazi Germany and I came back and help build Britain. People said that we would not stay longer than one year; we are here, and I and my people are here to stay.'

▼ **INTERPRETATION D** Adapted from an article written in 2018 for the British Library by Professor Linda McDowell, a human geographer at Oxford University.

'It is clear that these early post-war workers made a huge contribution to the British economy and economic growth, not only in the immediate post-war period but also across decades of continuous employment. As the demand for both skilled and unskilled labour continued to grow throughout the 1950s as the economy recovered, employers and managers in key sectors actively began to recruit in the Caribbean, rather than waiting for workers to arrive in the UK.'

▼ **SOURCE E** Many of the new arrivals settled in large industrial cities such as London or Birmingham. They faced prejudice and difficulty finding housing.

Over to You

1   List reasons why:
   a people may have wanted to leave the Caribbean at the end of the Second World War
   b people from the Caribbean may have chosen to move to Britain
   c people from the Caribbean believed they had a right to live in Britain in the 1940s and 1950s.

2   **a** What was the *Empire Windrush*?
   b Who were the 'Windrush generation'?
   c What was life like for them in the 1940s and 1950s?

Interpretation Analysis

1   Read **Interpretation B**. Summarise the experience of John Richards.

2   Read **Interpretation C**. Summarise the experience of Sam King.

3   How does **Interpretation B** differ from **Interpretation C** about experiences for immigrants to Britain at this time?

The first immigrants to Britain after the Second World War were often treated like outsiders, but over the years they became an important part of, and made large contributions to, British society and culture. Today, it is hard to imagine what life in Britain would be like without the influence of immigration. So how has immigration changed Britain?

Objectives

- Define the term 'multicultural Britain'.
- Describe the benefits of immigration to British society.

Cultural contribution

These pages outline how a variety of different people with different religions, languages and backgrounds in Britain has made an impact on the country.

▼ **SOURCE A** The Notting Hill Carnival in London is the second biggest street festival in the world. It was started in 1964 by the area's large Caribbean community to celebrate their culture. It is now a major event that attracts up to two million visitors from all backgrounds every year.

▶ **SOURCE B** In 2019, British singer-songwriter Stormzy (born Michael Ebenezer Kwadjo Omari Owuo Jr., and of Ghanaian descent) became the first black solo British headliner at Glastonbury music festival.

▼ **SOURCE C** The four British women representing Britain in the 4×400m relay race at the 2016 Olympic Games in Rio de Janeiro, Brazil: Christine Ohuruogu (parents born in Nigeria), Emily Diamond, Eilidh Doyle and Anyika Onuora (parents born in Nigeria). The team took home the bronze medal.

▼ **SOURCE D** England's cricket team has long included many players of different backgrounds. Here, Moeen Ali and Adil Rashid (both of Pakistani descent) celebrate taking a wicket in the 2019 World Cup with Jofra Archer (born in Barbados) and Ben Stokes (born in New Zealand).

Getting better

Many people see the National Health Service as one of Britain's greatest achievements. It gives everybody access to free healthcare. But this service may not have been possible without the help of immigrants. In 2008, of the 243,770 doctors who worked for the NHS, 91,360 trained abroad before moving to work in British hospitals. Thirteen per cent of nurses were born outside the UK and, for the last ten years, half of all the other vital NHS positions have been filled by people who qualified abroad.

Currently, around 150,000 of the 1.2 million NHS England employees were born abroad – around one in eight (12.5 per cent). These figures are for all NHS workers, but among doctors, the figure is higher: 37 per cent trained abroad before moving to work in British hospitals, with 20 per cent coming from Asia, mainly India and Pakistan.

A changing diet

Immigration has changed what many people in Britain eat and drink. Tea, one of Britain's favourite drinks, originated in China and was brought to Britain in the 1600s. Coffee (probably from Turkey) arrived around the same time. Coca-Cola (USA), Sprite and Fanta (both Germany) also have their origins abroad, while the first fish and chip shop was opened in 1860 in London by a Jewish immigrant. Both pizzas (from Italy) and kebabs (from Turkey) are some of Britain's bestselling 'fast foods'. Tesco, Britain's largest supermarket chain, was started by the son of a Polish Jewish immigrant.

In 1957, there were only 50 Chinese restaurants in the whole country. By 1970, there were over 4000, and now there is one in almost every town (and lots in every city!) in Britain. Curry (brought by immigrants from India, Pakistan and Bangladesh) has become even more popular, and now rivals the Sunday roast and fish and chips as Britain's 'national dish'. Chicken tikka masala is the country's bestselling ready meal and 'getting a takeaway' has become a weekly event for millions of Britons.

▼ **SOURCE E** Brick Lane in east London is one of many areas in Britain that has lots of Indian, Bangladeshi and Pakistani restaurants.

Fact ✓

Immigration has even influenced the English language. Look below at just a few everyday words that have been absorbed from other cultures:

- Arabic: sofa, alcohol, sugar
- Turkish: coffee, yoghurt
- Hindi: bangle, shampoo, pyjama

Fact ✓

Many of Britain's greatest Olympians have been either immigrants or the descendants of immigrants – Katarina Johnson-Thompson, Kelly Holmes, Christine Ohuruogu, Amir Khan and Mo Farah, for example.

Over to You ▁▃▅

1 Explain what you think is meant by the term 'multicultural Britain'.

2 Describe how immigration has affected British:
   a healthcare
   b diet
   c sport
   d music.

🔄 Quick Knowledge Quiz

Choose the correct answer from the three options:

1 During Queen Victoria's reign, the British Empire covered approximately how much of the world's total land area?

  a   one sixth
  b   one quarter
  c   half

2 What was the name of the political group, formed in 1885, that worked to free India from British control?

  a   Indian National Congress
  b   Free India Pact
  c   India for Indians

3 In what year was British India divided (partitioned) into two states?

  a   1937
  b   1947
  c   1957

4 What name was given to the time between 1880 and 1900 when over 80 per cent of Africa was taken over by European powers?

  a   scramble for Africa
  b   African takeover
  c   African revolt

5 The Gold Coast was the first British colony in Africa to get its independence after the Second World War. The Gold Coast now forms which country?

  a   Ghana
  b   Egypt
  c   South Africa

6 Which of the following was not a British colony in Africa?

  a   Nigeria
  b   South Africa
  c   Angola

7 What name is given to the international association consisting of the UK and the countries that were previously part of the British Empire?

  a   Commonwealth
  b   European Union
  c   United Nations

8 In what year did Hong Kong stop being a British colony and become part of China?

  a   1945
  b   1997
  c   2015

9 What was the name of the ship that famously brought nearly 500 West Indian immigrants to Britain in June 1948?

  a   *Titanic*
  b   *Mary Rose*
  c   *Empire Windrush*

10 Tea, one of Britain's favourite drinks, originated in which country?

  a   USA
  b   Germany
  c   China

 **Literacy Focus**

Note-taking

Note-taking is a vital skill. To do it successfully, you must pick out all the key words in a sentence. These are the words that are vital to the meaning (and your understanding). For example, in the sentence:

> From the 1600s onwards, Britain conquered foreign lands all over the world and claimed them as part of the British Empire. During Queen Victoria's reign (1837–1901) Britain ruled around 450 million people (approximately one quarter of the world's population) and the empire covered about one quarter of the world's total land area – the largest empire the world had ever known!

… the important words are: From 1600s Britain conquered foreign lands; claimed as part of Brit. Emp.; Q. Victoria's reign (1837–1901) Britain ruled around 450m people (quarter world's pop.); covered quarter of world's total land area – largest empire ever.

The original sentence was over 60 words long – but the shortened version is 35 words long and contains abbreviations. Note-taking like this will help your understanding of events – and provides you with a great revision exercise.

1   Write down the key words in the following paragraphs. These key words are your notes.

   a   The Africans and Indians who had fought for Britain felt they were fighting to defend freedom for Britain, but were getting increasingly frustrated that their own countries were not yet free. They thought it was wrong that they should fight to stop the Germans occupying other countries, but not fight to stop Britain occupying theirs.

   b   By 1900, many Indians started to believe that India should be free from British control. A political group called the Indian National Congress had been formed in 1885 to bring this about. It held meetings and organised demonstrations to further its cause, but the British ignored its demands.

   c   In the early 1900s, there were only a few countries in Africa that were independent. Most had become colonies – between 1880 and 1900, over 80 per cent of Africa was taken over by European powers in a time known as 'the scramble for Africa'.

   d   In 1948, Parliament passed the British Nationality Act. This meant that all the people of the Empire – now called the Commonwealth – had full British citizenship, which meant they could have a British passport and migrate to live and work in Britain.

Historians use the term 'causes' – or reasons – to describe the things that made events happen. When historians try to work out different causes of historical events, they need to be able to justify *why* they think one cause (or reason) is more important than another.

Comparing different causes or reasons

This chapter's assessment asks you to compare the different causes of a historical event – in this case, the causes of the decline of the British Empire.

> Which of the following was the more important reason why the British Empire declined after the Second World War:
> - the impact of two world wars
> - independence movements within the colonies?
>
> Explain your answer with reference to both reasons.

The question asks you to compare two reasons, judge which one is more important, and explain your decision. The steps below show one way to answer this type of question.

TIP: Look back on your work on the decline of the British Empire. Pages 176–183 will be particularly helpful. Pay attention to the two reasons listed.

1 Plan: Look at the two bullet points. Make some brief notes on each of them. For each point, try to note why this reason was more important than the other.

2 Judge: Once you have thought about the two bullet points, you need to decide: Which do you think was the more important reason? What supporting information or details can you provide to back up your choice?

3 Answer: You are asked to decide which bullet point was more important, so make sure you answer the question. Introduce your argument when you start writing your answer.

4 Explain and conclude: You now need to add details to support your decision and explain why you are taking this view. Use your plan to help you add supporting information. Remember to write about *both* bullet points in your answer – try to explain what each point is about, before comparing one to the other. Then, after considering the impact of each reason, it is important to come to a conclusion and explain your choice.

TIP: The question says 'explain your answer with reference to both', so don't forget to do this!

Now, considering all these points, try putting this into practice!

Assessment: Causation

Your challenge is to answer this question comparing different causes or reasons:

> Which of the following was the more important reason why the British Empire declined after the Second World War:
> - the impact of two world wars
> - independence movements within the colonies?
>
> Explain your answer with reference to both reasons. (20)

The steps and example sentence starters below will help you structure your answer.

1   **Plan**: Look at the two bullet points, which are about the reasons for the decline of the British Empire. Make some brief notes on each of them. For each point, try to note why this reason was more important than the other.

2   **Judge**: Which do you think was the more important reason? What supporting information or details can you provide to back up your choice?

3   **Answer**: You are asked to decide which bullet point was more important, so make sure you answer the question. Introduce your argument when you start writing your answer.

> During the reign of Queen Victoria (1837–1901), the British Empire... However, in the latter half of the twentieth century, the empire... When looking at the reasons for the decline of the British Empire, I think that... was a more important reason than... (5)

4   **Explain and conclude**: You now need to add details to support your decision and explain why you are taking this view. Then, after considering the impact of each reason, it is important to come to a conclusion and explain your choice.

> On the one hand, the impact of the two world wars was a key reason why the British Empire declined... (5)

> On the other hand, the independence movements... (5)

> To conclude... was the more important reason for the decline, because... (5)

TIP: For example, do you think that the impact of the First and Second World Wars led to the decline of the empire more than the efforts of the independence movements within some of the colonies? Or vice versa? Why do you think this?

TIP: Remember to write about *both* bullet points in your answer. You might also try to link the bullet points in some way – the independence movements were spurred on by the fact that people in the colonies had fought to defend freedom for Britain, but were getting increasingly frustrated that their own countries were not yet free. They thought it was wrong that they should fight to stop the Nazis occupying other countries, but not fight to stop Britain occupying theirs.

TIP: You will need to go into detail here about how the two world wars contributed to the decline of the British Empire.

TIP: You will need to go into detail here about the work of the independence movements, such as in India (pages 178–179).

TIP: It is important to write a concluding paragraph that sums up what you think. You are being asked to write down your judgement here. This is where it might be possible to link the bullet points – did one bullet point help out the other? If so, do you think that makes it more important – or not?

The fifties

Life was tough in the first few years after the Second World War. Basic goods, such as meat, sugar and clothing, still had to be rationed and few luxuries were available. Even bread was rationed for a while. But, with careful government control, and loans from the USA, things began to improve. Thousands of houses were built for people whose homes had been bombed and there were plenty of jobs. By the early 1950s, Britain had recovered and some people were even calling it a 'golden age'. So what were the 1950s (or 'the fifties') like? What were the new discoveries, ideas and inventions?

Objectives

- Examine and assess key changes, developments, inventions and ideas in Britain in the 1950s.
- Recall key political events and conflicts in the world in the 1950s.

Transport

- Car ownership more than doubled in the 1950s. By 1955, there were around three million car owners in Britain.
- The Mini was launched in 1959. It cost around £500 (about the average yearly salary).
- Britain's first full-length motorway between two major cities was opened between Birmingham and London in 1959.
- In 1952, the first passenger jet aircraft took holidaymakers abroad. In the 1950s, around one million people went on holiday abroad every year.

▼ **SOURCE A** The Mini was designed by Alec Issigonis, a Greek immigrant who moved to Britain when he was 17.

Technology

- Radios and 'record players' were still popular, but the 'must-have' new item was the television. Millions bought a set to watch the live broadcast of the coronation of Queen Elizabeth II in June 1953.
- At first there was just one TV channel – the BBC – but ITV was introduced in 1955. Programmes were shown in black and white only!
- 33 per cent of households had a washing machine, 15 per cent had a fridge and freezer, and ten per cent had a telephone. However, in 1950 around 20 per cent of homes still had no electricity at all.
- The USSR launched the first satellite in 1957, and the first microchip was developed between 1958 and 1959.
- In 1951, UNIVAC I became the world's first electric computer that was available for businesses to buy. It cost up to £1.2 million and was 2.3m wide and 4.3m long.

▼ **SOURCE B** A family watching television in the 1950s. The proportion of families with TVs grew rapidly in the 1950s: 14 per cent in 1952; 21 per cent in 1953; and 31 per cent in 1954.

Entertainment

- Younger people had more money and free time than ever before. A new type of fast and loud music from America became popular – rock 'n' roll. Elvis Presley and Buddy Holly were popular singers.
- Listening to music, dancing, reading, watching television, knitting, cinema visits and playing board games (such as Monopoly and Snakes and Ladders) were popular pastimes. So too were sports such as football, cricket and boxing.
- There were 'crazes' for hula hoops, Lego and yo-yos in the late 1950s.

▶ **SOURCE C** Elvis Presley shown in a poster from a 1957 film. His TV and stage appearances shocked many grown-ups – and his wriggling hips earned him the nickname 'Elvis the Pelvis'. In total, Elvis has sold around 500 million records.

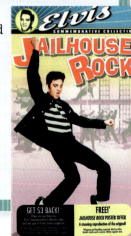

Work and home

- Most of the workforce was employed in 'primary' or 'secondary' jobs. 'Primary' means that workers obtain natural resources (e.g. miners or farmers). 'Secondary' means they make things with the natural resources (e.g. factory workers or food producers).
- Most people shopped at local shops in town centres. They would visit separate shops for bread (bakeries), vegetables (greengrocers) and so on.
- There were around three male workers for every female worker – many women stayed at home as 'housewives'. Around ten per cent of female workers were in management positions.
- Large numbers of settlers came to Britain to work from countries in the British Empire – particularly Jamaica, India and Pakistan – but there were still only around a million people from other cultures living in Britain.

Most popular in UK

Key

 Bestselling music single

 Highest earning film

 Bestselling car

 Most watched television programme

 'Rock Around the Clock' by Bill Haley and His Comets (1955)

 The Ten Commandments (1956)

 Morris Minor

 Wagon Train (a US TV show, shown on ITV)

Timeline

1950s

- 1950 First credit card
- 1952 Polio vaccine developed
- 1953 Structure of DNA discovered and Mount Everest conquered
- 1956 Wireless television remote control introduced
- 1959 Barbie doll goes on sale

Meanwhile...

1952

Britain's population reached 50 million in 1952. At this time the population of the world was 2.5 billion.

Politics and conflict

- Soldiers from the USA, Britain and other powers fought North Korean and Chinese forces in the Korean War (1950–1953).
- Britain, France and Israel fought Egypt over control of the Suez Canal (1956–1957), which runs through Egypt in the Middle East.
- The Cold War continued – a time of threats and tension between the two global superpowers: the USA and the USSR.

Over to You

1 Complete the sentences with accurate terms:

   a In the 1950s, around _____ people went on holiday abroad.

   b The _____ was fought between 1950 and 1953.

   c The Mini motor car was designed by _____ .

   d In the 1950s, only around _____ per cent of female workers were in management positions.

   e Britain's first full-length motorway between two major cities opened in _____ .

2 This chapter is a great opportunity to work in a small group (ideally five). Your challenge is to read through the next 12 pages and work out the answers to the following questions:

   - What are the key changes and developments in transport, entertainment, technology, work and home life, and politics and conflict from the 1950s to the present day?
   - When did these changes happen?
   - Can you suggest reasons for these changes?

   Next:

   - In your group, divide the categories between you, so each person has a category.
   - In no more than 50 words and a few pictures, make notes on your category for the 1950s.
   - Keep your notes safe… and get ready to examine life in the 1960s on the following pages.

   ⭐ NOTE: Top historians working at KS3, GCSE and A Level should be able to analyse change and continuity over large sweeps of time. They should consider developments in areas such as culture, science and technology, war, politics and religion.

The sixties

The 1960s or 'the sixties' was a decade that began on Friday 1 January 1960 and ended on Wednesday 31 December 1969. The sixties saw television and cars become more popular than ever before. Women's skirts became shorter, men's hair became longer and a 'boy band' called the Beatles took the world by storm. There were lots of jobs in the 1960s and young people had money to spend on music, entertainment and clothes. But what great events and inventions might you have seen in the sixties? How was life beginning to change?

Objectives

- Examine and assess key changes, developments, inventions and ideas in Britain in the 1960s.
- Recall key political events and conflicts in the world in the 1960s.

Transport

- By 1960, there were five million cars on Britain's roads, and by the middle of the decade around half of all UK households had access to at least one car.
- 95 per cent of cars sold in Britain were British-made.
- More motorways were made to link Britain's cities, and a national speed limit of 70mph was introduced in 1965.
- In 1966, the first InterCity train was used. It was powered by electricity (rather than steam or diesel), so was much quieter and cleaner. Concorde – the fastest ever passenger jet – made its first test flight in 1969.
- In 1961, 2.6 million people went on holiday abroad.

Transport

- 75 per cent of homes had a television and watching TV became a popular way for families to spend their time. In 1964, BBC2 went on air and was the first UK channel to have colour (1967).
- Lasers, the audio cassette (music tapes) and video tape recorders first appeared.
- The first 'mini-computer' (an early type of PC – personal computer) went on sale in 1965 – and the first public demonstration of the computer mouse, video conferencing and basic email technology soon followed.
- 1961 saw the first human in space (a Soviet named Yuri Gagarin) and in 1969 humans walked on the moon (Americans Neil Armstrong and Buzz Aldrin).

▼ **SOURCE A** Huge crowds greet the Beatles as they arrive at Heathrow Airport, London after a successful US tour, 1964. Songs by the Beatles (such as 'Yesterday') are some of the most covered by other singers ever.

Entertainment

- The 1960s are sometimes called the 'Swinging Sixties' and are associated with the birth of pop music and fashions such as the miniskirt and flared trousers.
- Radio was still popular, but music records sold millions of copies. In 1962, the Beatles, a 'boy band' from Liverpool, released their first single (called 'Love Me Do'). This was the start of 'Beatlemania', a craze that swept the world and made them into the biggest selling group in history.
- Millions of cinema tickets were sold, but television was the big hit of the 1960s. *Coronation Street* and *Doctor Who* were first shown in this decade.

Work and home

- Nearly all houses had electricity so fridges, freezers, TVs and vacuum cleaners became more popular.
- By 1965, more than half the workforce was employed in service industries, rather than in manufacturing (making things). Service industries provide a service, like banking, teaching, healthcare and tourism.
- Around 50 per cent of women aged 16–60 went out to work – and around 15 per cent of female workers were in management positions.
- Lots of new housing estates and high-rise tower blocks were built.
- The word 'teenager' began to be used for 13–19 year olds, and young people became very fashion-conscious!

Politics and conflict

- In the UK, the death penalty was abolished, the Abortion Act made ending a pregnancy legal and the voting age was reduced from 21 to 18.
- The Civil Rights Movement was at its height in America, calling for equal rights for black Americans. In 1964, the Civil Rights Act made racial discrimination illegal in the USA and in 1965 there were equal voting rights for black and white Americans.
- The Cold War continued, and there were major conflicts in the Middle East and Vietnam.

Most popular in UK

 'She Loves You' by the Beatles (1964)

 The Sound of Music (1965)

 Austin 1100

1966 World Cup Final

Timeline

 1960s

1962	First James Bond film
1963	US President John F. Kennedy assassinated
1965	Miniskirt first appears
1966	England wins football World Cup
1967	First heart transplant
1968	US Civil Rights leader Martin Luther King Jr assassinated
1968	Female workers at the Ford Car factory in Dagenham go on strike protesting for men and women to have equal pay. This eventually leads to the Equal Pay Act of 1970

Meanwhile...

 1960

In 1960, Britain's population was around 53 million… and the world's population stood at three billion.

▼ **B** Some typical fashions of the 1960s.

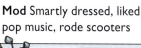
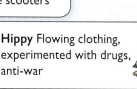

Mod Smartly dressed, liked pop music, rode scooters

Hippy Flowing clothing, experimented with drugs, anti-war

Rocker Liked rock 'n' roll, wore leather jackets, rode motorbikes

Other popular trends Tie-dye, flared jeans, miniskirt, 'mop-top' hair

Over to You

1. Choose five different words to sum up the decade and explain your choices. For example, you might pick the word 'Beatles' and write: 'I have chosen the Beatles because they were a famous "boy band" that took the world by storm in the 1960s. Fans adored them (Beatlemania) and they became the biggest selling group in history – and had the decade's biggest selling pop single.'

2. In your group, continue adding to your notes on your chosen category. Think about:
   - whether there were any big changes between the 1950s and 1960s. If so, in which categories did these changes take place?
   - whether you can make any connections between the categories. For example, what changes in work and home life were caused by changes in technology?

⭐ NOTE: It is important that historians use the correct vocabulary. In this chapter you will have to use words associated with change (such as 'cause', 'effect', 'different'), words associated with time (such as 'decade', '1960s') and words associated with society (such as 'industry', 'leisure', 'population').

8.3 The seventies

The 1970s or 'the seventies' began on Thursday 1 January 1970 and ended on Monday 31 December 1979. The decade is well known for crazy, multi-coloured fashions and new types of music and technology. Jobs became harder to find because many factories closed down, and many British workers who still had jobs kept going on strike. But how were transport, technology, entertainment, work and home life, and politics and conflict changing in the seventies? What were the big news stories in Britain and abroad?

Objectives

- Examine and assess key changes, developments, inventions and ideas in Britain in the 1970s.
- Recall key political events and conflicts in the world in the 1970s.

Transport

- There were now around ten million cars on Britain's roads. However, British consumers were buying more German and Japanese cars as the British car industry went into decline.
- Major developments in air travel, including the introduction of the Boeing 747 (jumbo jet) and Concorde (see **A**), meant that more passengers could travel faster to their holiday destinations than ever before. In 1970, over 5.7 million British people holidayed abroad.

▼ **SOURCE A** Concorde was the first supersonic passenger jet, able to fly from Britain to the USA in under three hours. It first carried passengers in 1976 but was 'retired' in 2003 because of low passenger numbers and high costs.

Most popular in UK

 'Mull of Kintyre' by Wings (1977)

 Star Wars: Episode IV – A New Hope (1977)

 Ford Cortina

 Apollo 13 spacecraft ocean splashdown (1970)

Entertainment

- Over 90 per cent of families had a television, and all three TV stations (BBC1, BBC2 and ITV) were in colour. Families could record programmes on their video cassette recorders.
- Skateboards, roller skates, stunt kites and space hoppers were popular toys.
- Glam rock and punk rock were the big new sounds in music. Disco took the world by storm too. Young people went to 'discotheques' (nightclubs) to dance to this upbeat music with a strong rhythm.

▼ **B** Many 1970s fashions were bold and made a statement.

Glam rocker: Make-up, bright clothing, flares, platform boots, nail varnish. Music by T. Rex, David Bowie, Slade

Punk rocker: Mohican, ripped jeans, Dr. Martens boots, safety pins, offensive t-shirt. Music by the Sex Pistols, the Clash, the Ramones

Meanwhile... 1971

In 1971, the population of Britain was 54 million. In the 1970s, thousands of families emigrated to Australia, New Zealand and South Africa. The world population reached 3.7 billion.

Technology

- The Sony Walkman personal stereo first appeared in 1979, so music lovers could listen to tapes through headphones while on the move.
- In 1972, the Magnavox Odyssey became the first video game console that could be connected to a TV set (see **C**).
- Microwave ovens went on sale in the UK in 1974.

▼ **SOURCE C** The Magnavox Odyssey came with a choice of 11 games, including Simon Says and Shooting Gallery.

Work and home

- The 1970s were known for strikes – by postal workers, lorry drivers and waste collectors, for example. A miners' strike in 1972 disrupted Britain's coal-powered electricity supply. Schools and offices closed down and the government introduced a 'three day week' to save electricity. After seven weeks, the government gave in and the miners won their pay rise.
- The Sex Discrimination Act of 1975 made it illegal to discriminate against women in employment, education and training. It also allowed women to apply for a loan and credit cards. By 1975, around 55 per cent of working-age women had jobs. Around 20 per cent of people in management positions were female.
- 64 per cent of homes now had a washing machine, and 50 per cent of homes had a telephone.
- Foreign nations began to produce goods cheaply and many British factories closed down. Unemployment reached a decade-high 1.5 million in 1979.

▶ **SOURCE D** Rubbish piled up in London, January 1979. This was known as the 'Winter of Discontent' because so many people went on strike – waste collectors, ambulance drivers and even television staff. ITV went 'off air' for 11 weeks!

Politics and conflict

- In 1972, Palestinian terrorists attacked the Munich Olympic Games and killed 11 Israeli athletes.
- In 1973, Britain joined the European Economic Community (now the European Union), a group of European states that traded with each other.
- US troops came home from the Vietnam War in 1973, and the war eventually ended in 1975.
- In 1979, British people elected their first female Prime Minister – Margaret Thatcher.

Timeline   1970s

1970	The Beatles break up
1971	Britain's currency goes decimal – it changes from an older system to the pounds and pennies we use today
1975	Microsoft founded
1976	Apple founded
1977	Queen Elizabeth II celebrates 25 years on the throne. Street parties held all over UK
1978	Last known case of killer disease smallpox occurs in Birmingham, UK. It is later declared eradicated (finally wiped out) in 1980

Over to You

1 Complete the sentences with accurate terms:

  a In the 1970s, there were around _____ cars on Britain's roads.

  b Concorde was able to fly from Britain to the USA in under _____ hours.

  c Margaret Thatcher was elected as Britain's first female _____ in 1979.

  d It became illegal to discriminate against women in employment, education and training in _____.

  e The _____ War finally came to an end in 1975.

2 In your group, each of you should continue adding to your notes on your chosen category. Think about:

  - whether there were any big changes between the 1960s and 1970s

  - whether you can make any connections between the categories. For example, what changes in transport were caused by changes in technology?

The eighties

The 1980s or 'the eighties' was a decade that began on Tuesday 1 January 1980 and ended on Sunday 31 December 1989. This was the decade of the BMX bike and the chunky mobile phone, and saw the birth of CDs, rap music and cheaper games consoles. In politics, Britain's first female Prime Minister, Margaret Thatcher, was in power for the whole decade. But how would you spend your time in the eighties? What impact was technology starting to have on your life? What were the big news events in Britain and around the world?

Objectives

- Examine and assess key changes, developments, inventions and ideas in Britain in the 1980s.
- Recall key political events and conflicts in the world in the 1980s.

Transport

- By the mid-1980s, there were over 15 million cars on Britain's roads, and wearing seat belts in the front seats was made compulsory in 1983.
- The Sinclair C5, a small battery-powered car, was launched in 1985 – but the company went bankrupt after ten months due to poor sales.
- Between 15 and 20 million Brits went on holiday abroad each year – more than half travelled by plane.

Entertainment

- 97 per cent of homes had a television. In 1982, there was another channel to watch – Channel 4. Britain's first satellite service – Sky TV – was launched in 1989.
- The Rubik's Cube, BMX bikes, Cabbage Patch dolls and *Star Wars* toys were popular. Nintendo launched its 100 million-selling Game Boy hand-held games console in 1989. Keeping fit (including jogging and aerobics classes) also became very fashionable.
- In 1984, pop musicians Bob Geldof and Midge Ure brought pop stars together to record the charity single 'Do They Know It's Christmas?' to raise money for victims of a famine in Ethiopia.
- The 1980s saw the rise of hip hop and rap music. Another music trend was the New Romantics, typified by bands such as Duran Duran and Adam and the Ants, who wore elaborate clothes and lots of make-up. Madonna was the most successful female singer of the decade.

▼▶ **SOURCE A & B** Adam and the Ants (below left) dressed as flamboyant pirates and had two drummers. Madonna (below right) was the biggest-selling female pop star of the 1980s, with nearly 20 Top 10 hits.

Technology

- By 1980, more than one million personal computers had been sold around the world.
- In 1982, the first CDs (compact discs – new versions of music records) went on sale, and in 1984 the Apple Macintosh was launched (costing around £4800 in today's money).
- In 1985, the Nintendo Entertainment System featuring the Super Mario Brothers went on sale. Microsoft Windows was launched the same year.
- Mobile phones were introduced but they were very large and expensive.
- In 1989, the World Wide Web was invented by British scientist Tim Berners-Lee.

▼ **SOURCE C** An early mobile phone. You had to carry the large battery pack around with you!

Work and home

- By 1985, over 60 per cent of working-age women had jobs. Around 25 per cent of people in management positions were female.
- By the mid-1980s, over 80 per cent of homes had a telephone.
- Supermarkets began to move from town centres to out-of-town retail parks.
- Only 43 per cent of cars sold in Britain were British-made. By 1980, one in eight cars sold in Britain were Japanese.
- In 1984, three million people were unemployed – the highest level of the decade. Many had lost jobs because British factories closed down when cheaper foreign goods were imported. There was also increased automated manufacturing, so fewer workers were needed to operate equipment.

Most popular in UK

 'Do They Know It's Christmas?' by Band Aid (1984)

 E.T. The Extra-Terrestrial (1982)

 Ford Escort

 EastEnders Christmas Day episode (1986)

▼ **SOURCE D** The Berlin Wall, the barrier that had divided East and West Berlin since 1961, began to be destroyed in November 1989.

Politics and conflict

- In 1982, Argentina invaded the Falklands, a group of islands in the South Atlantic Ocean governed by Britain. On Prime Minister Margaret Thatcher's orders, Britain and Argentina went to war for ten weeks until Argentina withdrew from the islands.
- In 1984, a major miners' strike against the government's mine closures began, ending in 1985 with defeat for the miners.
- Conflict continued in Northern Ireland between those wanting to remain part of the UK and others who wanted an independent united Ireland.

Timeline

1980 John Lennon (one of the Beatles) assassinated
1981 Many millions watch televised wedding of Prince Charles and Lady Diana Spencer
1983 US singer-songwriter Madonna releases her first single ('Holiday').
1984 Huge poison gas leak in Bhopal, India, kills nearly 4000 and injures 500,000
1985 TV soap opera *EastEnders* starts
1986 Space Shuttle Challenger explodes on takeoff
1987 DNA evidence first used to convict criminals
1989 Destruction of the Berlin Wall begins; this boundary split the Soviet-controlled eastern part of Berlin from the western half

Meanwhile....

In 1981, Britain's population hit 56 million. The world population reached 4.5 billion in the 1980s.

Over to You

1 Choose five different words to sum up the decade. For each word you have chosen, explain why you picked it.

2 In your group, each of you should continue adding to your notes on your chosen category. Think about:
- whether there were any big changes between the 1970s and 1980s
- whether you can make any connections between the categories. For example, what changes in work and home life were caused by changes in transport?

The nineties

The 1990s or 'the nineties' began on Monday 1 January 1990 and ended on Friday 31 December 1999. The decade saw the end of the Cold War and the launch of the National Lottery and 24-hour shopping. Mobile phones became much smaller, cheaper and more popular, and the Internet began to change from something that a few 'experts' used, to something that would play a key part in millions of people's lives. But what was life like in the nineties? And how was it changing?

Objectives

- Examine and assess key changes, developments, inventions and ideas in Britain in the 1990s.
- Recall key political events and conflicts in the world in the 1990s.

Transport

- There were around 20 million cars on Britain's roads by 1990 – and around 20 per cent of families had access to more than one car.
- Britain was directly linked to France in 1994 when the Channel Tunnel rail service began.
- In the 1990s, around 20 to 25 million people took holidays abroad every year.

▼ **SOURCE A** French and British Channel Tunnel engineers commemorate the linking of the two countries in 1990.

Entertainment

- Watching television was one of the most common activities for all age groups in the UK.
- Spending time with family and friends, listening to music, shopping, reading, sport and exercise remained popular. British bands such as Oasis, Blur and the Spice Girls made a big impact in both the USA and Europe.
- Cinema trips increased in popularity after a decline in the 1980s.
- Home computers (PCs) and games consoles (both hand-held *and* linked to the TV) were the 'must-have' goods of the decade for younger people.

▼ **SOURCE B** The Spice Girls in 1997 – one of the biggest selling girl groups in history with over 100 million records sold.

Technology

- Mobile phones became smaller, cheaper and much more popular.
- In 1991, the World Wide Web was first made available to the public. Soon three million people in the UK were connected to the Internet, and by 1996 that figure had risen to ten million. By 1998, there were 130 million users worldwide.
- In 1994, Sony launched the first of its PlayStation consoles.
- The 1990s saw the popularity of digital cameras, satellite television, email and text messaging soar. The first text was sent in December 1992 (it read 'merry Christmas'). The Pentium processor (the most widely used microchip in PCs), MP3 players (portable music players) and DVDs became available too.

▼ **SOURCE C** A selection of technology on sale in the 1990s.

Work and home

- By the mid-1990s, 12 million women were at work (and 15 million men). This was around 70 per cent of women of working age (16–60), and 37 per cent of management positions were held by women.
- Over 65 per cent of all workers were in the service industries such as teaching, healthcare, retail, banking and tourism. Some jobs began to be moved abroad, such as in call centres.
- 56 per cent of employees worked with computers or automated equipment, and 12 per cent were self-employed.
- Virtually all homes had at least one TV, a washing machine and access to a phone (landline or mobile).
- Out-of-town shopping centres became popular – and 24-hour shopping and Sunday trading were introduced.

Most popular in UK

 'Candle in the Wind' by Elton John, rewritten after the death of Princess Diana in 1997

 Titanic (1997)

 Ford Fiesta

 Funeral of Diana, Princess of Wales (1997)

Timeline
1990s

1990   Hubble telescope launched into space
1991   South Africa ends racist Apartheid laws
1994   Nelson Mandela elected president of South Africa
1997   First Harry Potter novel published (*Harry Potter and the Philosopher's Stone*)
1999   Euro currency introduced

▼ **SOURCE D** Nelson Mandela, South Africa's first black president, elected in 1994 after the racist social and political system there (known as 'Apartheid') was finally abolished in the early 1990s.

Politics and conflict

- In the late 1980s, relations between the USSR and the USA began to improve. In 1989, some countries that were heavily influenced by the USSR (such as Czechoslovakia, Hungary and East Germany) had begun to reject Soviet control. By 1991, the USSR had lost its grip on these and other areas. The system used to control these areas – communism – collapsed. The Cold War was over.
- In 1990, Iraq invaded Kuwait, and the USA responded by sending in troops to fight Iraq in what became known as the Gulf War. Eventually, the Iraqis withdrew.
- As a member of the UN and NATO, Britain joined other countries in sending its troops to help in several peacekeeping operations (such as in the Balkan region of Europe). In 1997, the Labour Party came to power in the UK, after 18 years of Conservative Party rule.
- On Good Friday (10 April) 1998, British and Irish politicians finally came to an agreement about how Northern Ireland should be governed. Similar to Wales and Scotland, Northern Ireland was to have an Assembly to run its daily affairs. This 'Good Friday Agreement' didn't solve all the problems, but it was a huge step towards peace.

Meanwhile...
1990s

In 1991, Britain's population stood at 59 million. By 1997, 16 per cent were aged 65 or over and seven per cent were over 75 – mainly because of medical improvements. The world population at this time was around 5.5 billion.

Over to You

1 Complete the sentences with accurate terms:
   a Britain was directly linked to France in 1994 when the _____ _____ opened.
   b By the 1990s, over 65 per cent of all workers were in the _____ industries.
   c The first text message was sent in _____.
   d In 1994, _____ _____ was elected President of South Africa.
   e The first _____ _____ book was published in 1997.

2 In your group, each of you should continue adding to your notes on your chosen category. Think about:
   - whether there were any big changes between the 1980s and 1990s
   - whether you can make any connections between the categories. For example, what changes in work and home life or entertainment were caused by changes in technology?

The noughties

The decade that began on Saturday 1 January 2000 and lasted until Thursday 31 December 2009 is known as the 2000s or 'the noughties'. The start of the twenty-first century saw some dramatic changes in the way people lived. Since 1901 the British population had grown from 41 million to over 64 million, which led to ever-expanding towns and cities and increased pressure on services such as healthcare and power supplies. Advances in technology also changed people's lives in all sorts of new ways – at home, at work and at school. So, how exactly did transport, entertainment, technology, work and home life, and politics and conflict change in the 'noughties'?

Objectives

- Examine and assess key changes, developments, inventions and ideas in Britain in the 2000s.
- Recall key political events and conflicts in the world in the 2000s.

Transport

- By 2000, there were over 25 million cars on Britain's roads, with 77 per cent of households owning at least one car.
- Traffic congestion rose and some cities introduced 'congestion charges' to try to reduce traffic. London introduced the scheme in 2003.
- In the 2000s, around 35 million British people took holidays abroad.
- In 2004, plans were announced by a company called Virgin Galactic to offer tourist flights into space. A seat on the space flight could cost around £150,000.

▼ **SOURCE A** A Virgin Galactic spaceship, pictured during a test flight in 2018.

Fact ✓

Globalisation – the spread of large brands all over the world – happened in the 2000s. 'Multinational' companies – businesses that offer products and services that are the same throughout the world – are the main drivers of globalisation and include companies such as McDonald's, Coca-Cola, Nike and Disney.

Entertainment

- Virtually all homes had a television (over 98 per cent in 2005) and there were now a huge variety of channels to view and 'on demand' choices via satellite or broadband connections. The average UK citizen watched TV for just over three hours a day, and it was the top leisure activity for eight out of ten people.
- Reading (via 'e-readers' as well as books), sport and exercise, shopping (in store and online), listening to music (especially via media players such as iPods), cinema visits and socialising with friends were very popular.
- The rise in the use of the Internet led to the popularity of social media sites such as Facebook (founded in 2004) and Twitter (2006).

Technology

- In 2001, Apple launched the hugely successful iPod, a portable music player. This was followed by the iPhone, a smartphone, in 2007.
- In 2000, 25 per cent of households in the UK had Internet connection, rising to 55 per cent in 2005 and 73 per cent by the end of the decade. In 2005, around 30 per cent of people used the Internet every day, rising to 60 per cent by 2010.
- In 2000, around 40 per cent of adults owned a mobile phone, doubling to over 80 per cent by the end of the decade.

▶ **SOURCE B** Steve Jobs, co-founder of Apple, holding up the first iPhone in 2007.

Work and home

- In 2000, around 44 per cent of UK homes had a home computer (PC), rising to 75 per cent by the end of the decade.
- Out-of-town shopping centres and supermarkets were still very common, but online shopping started to increase in the 2000s. By 2010, it was estimated that approximately seven per cent of all goods were bought online.
- All the TVs, dishwashers and mobile phone chargers in our homes meant that demand for electricity increased dramatically – so too did the amount of polluting gases given off by the creation of this energy. In the 2000s, the government announced schemes that would try to use alternative sources of energy that create less pollution (such as wind farms).
- Throughout the 2000s, the percentage of women of working age (16–60) with a job remained constant at around 75 per cent. Around 40 per cent of management positions were held by women.

Timeline

2000 McDonald's opens its 1000th British restaurant (inside the Millennium Dome)

2004 Four terrorist bombs kill 191 people and injure nearly 2000 on trains in Madrid, Spain.

2004 The Boxing Day Tsunami kills at least 280,000 people in Southeast Asia

2005 YouTube, the video-sharing platform, founded

2007 A financial crisis led to closure of several banks and an increase in unemployment and failed businesses

2009 Barack Obama becomes first African-American President of the USA

▼ **SOURCE C** Barack Obama (with his wife Michelle) being sworn in as US President in January 2009.

Meanwhile...

By the mid-2000s, Britain's population had reached 61 million. Twelve per cent were aged over 85 and one in 12 were born overseas. At this time there were more pensioners in the UK than teenagers. The world's population hit six billion in 2000… and was nearly seven billion by the end of the decade.

Politics and conflict

- In 2001, terrorists attacked the USA, including destroying the World Trade Center in New York. A 'war on terror' began soon after when US-led forces invaded Afghanistan to search for terrorist bases.
- British soldiers began fighting in Iraq in 2003 as part of the 'war on terror', although Iraq had no links to the World Trade Center attacks.
- In 2005, terrorists attacked tube trains and a bus in London, and in 2006 many people died in terrorist attacks in Mumbai, India.
- In 2005, Irish nationalist group the IRA announced it was giving up its terror campaign and promised to find peaceful methods to unite Ireland.

▶ **SOURCE D** Troops from the UK, pictured in Iraq in 2003 during the 'war on terror'.

Most popular in UK

 'Evergreen' by Will Young (2002)

 Avatar (2009)

 Ford Focus

 Only Fools and Horses Christmas Day episode (2001)

Over to You

1 Choose five different words to sum up the decade. For each word you have chosen, explain why you picked it.

2 In your group, each of you should continue adding to your notes on your chosen category. Think about:
- whether there were any big changes between the 1990s and 2000s
- whether you can make any connections between the categories. For example, what changes in work and home life or entertainment were caused by changes in technology?

The decade that began on Friday 1 January 2010 and lasted until Tuesday 31 December 2019 is also known as the 'teens' or the 'twenty-tens'. It was a decade that saw the continued growth of the Internet with its widespread use in banking, shopping, education, news, entertainment and media. It was also a decade of complex conflicts, continued efforts to combat pollution and climate change and shifting attitudes to various groups within society. So what changed in British society in the twenty-tens? What were the big news stories in Britain and abroad?

Objectives

- Examine and assess key changes, developments, inventions and ideas in Britain from 2010 to 2019.
- Recall key political events and conflicts in the world in the 2010s.

Transport

- By 2010, there were over 30 million cars on Britain's roads. By the end of the decade this had risen to 33 million, with 78 per cent of households owning at least one car.
- Traffic congestion continued to be a major issue on Britain's roads. Many schemes were tried to combat the problem, including improvements to public transport, and new road layouts.
- There was a move towards types of transport that do not pollute the environment, such as electric and hybrid (combined electric and petrol/diesel engines) cars.
- In the 2010s, between 55 and 60 per cent of people (around 37 million) went on holiday abroad each year. In a 2014 survey, 8 per cent in the UK said they could not afford to go on holiday at all.

▼ **SOURCE A** In 2018, one in every 12 new cars purchased in the UK was either electric or hybrid.

Entertainment

- The decade saw a slight drop in TV ownership – from a high of 98 per cent in 2005 to 95 per cent in 2019. This was partly due to an increase in the use of smartphones and tablets to watch programmes online, rather than on TV.
- Adults spent an average of 17 hours a week on their smartphone or tablet (around ten times longer than they spent exercising). Of this time, around 12 hours were spent using social media platforms such as Facebook, Twitter, Instagram and Snapchat.
- Health and fitness, reading, shopping, listening to music, cinema visits and socialising were still very popular.

Timeline

2010s

2010	Haiti earthquake, the deadliest natural disaster of the decade, kills an estimated 200,000–250,000 people
2012	London hosts the Olympic Games
2014	Gay marriage becomes legal in England, Wales and Scotland. (It becomes legal in Northern Ireland in January 2020.) The whole decade sees a shift in attitudes towards LGBTUA+ rights
2016	The Paris Agreement is signed by 195 countries, promising to make efforts to combat climate change.
2016	People in the UK voted to leave the EU (known as 'Brexit', meaning 'British Exit')
2019	An outbreak of COVID-19 (a respiratory disease) is identified in China. It is recognised as a **pandemic** by the World Health Organisation (WHO) in March 2020.

Meanwhile...

2010s

By 2019, Britain's population had reached around 67 million – but by the end of the decade the speed at which the population was growing was beginning to slow down. The world's population hit seven billion in 2011, and was around 7.7 billion at the end of the decade.

Technology

- In 2010, 73 per cent of UK households had Internet connection, rising to 90 per cent by the end of the decade. In 2010, around 60 per cent of people used the Internet every day, rising to 87 per cent by 2019.
- In 2010, 80 per cent of adults owned a mobile phone, rising to 95 per cent by the end of the decade. It was estimated in 2019 that around 86 per cent of 12–18 year olds regularly used a mobile.
- The widespread use of the Internet led to great changes in many areas – from how people accessed news to how they banked and shopped. Online gaming and social media were very popular in the 2010s.

Work and home

- In 2010, 77 per cent of UK homes had a home computer (PC), rising to 88 per cent by the end of the decade.
- Out-of-town shopping centres and supermarkets remained common, but online shopping grew in the 2010s.
- In 2019, it was announced that non-fossil fuel sources of energy provided more electricity to UK homes and businesses than fossil fuel energy for the first time ever.
- The percentage of women of working age (16–64) with a job rose slightly from around 65 per cent to nearly 72 per cent. Around 40 per cent of management positions were held by women.
- The economic crisis, which began in the 2000s, continued into the 2010s.

Politics and conflict

- Beginning in 2010, there was a series of protests against the governments of several countries in North Africa and the Middle East. The Arab Spring, as it was known, led to government changes in countries such as Tunisia and Egypt. However, in some cases the protests led to civil war, for example in Syria, Iraq and Libya.
- Terror attacks continued during the 2010s, with major attacks in the UK, France, New Zealand, Nigeria, Norway, Sri Lanka and Turkey.
- There was a huge increase in the number of migrants travelling to Europe. Most were fleeing poverty and war, while others came looking for better living conditions and work. How to deal with the 'migrant crisis' (as it became known) was a major political issue in many European nations.
- In 2016, a vote was held in the UK to decide whether or not to continue being a member of the European Union – 52 per cent of voters chose to leave it.

▼ **SOURCE B** Refugees and migrants from Syria attempting to get into Greece in 2015.

Most popular in UK

 'Shape of You' by Ed Sheeran (2017)

 Star Wars: Episode VII – The Force Awakens (2015)

Ford Fiesta

The Closing Ceremony of the London 2012 Olympic Games

Over to You

1 Complete the sentences with accurate terms:

   a By the end of the 2010s, there were around _____ cars on Britain's roads.

   b In 2012, the Olympic Games were held in _____ .

   c In 2016, a Britain voted to leave the _____ .

   d The Paris Agreement of 2016 aimed to combat _____ change.

   e The series of protests in several countries in North Africa and the Middle East was known as the Arab _____ .

2 In your group, each of you should continue adding to your notes on your chosen category. Each member of your group should now have a full set of notes on one of the categories from the 1950s to the present day.

3 In your group, use all of your notes to create a presentation to highlight the key changes in each category from the 1950s to the present day. Think about:

   - what the changes were
   - when the changes happened
   - reasons for the changes
   - links between any of the changes; for example, did changes in one category lead to changes in another?
   - which category changed the most… and the least.

What is 'terrorism'?

On the morning of 11 September 2001, 19 terrorists hijacked four American passenger planes. After taking control, the hijackers flew two of the aircraft straight into the two tallest buildings in New York City – the Twin Towers of the World Trade Center – two skyscrapers containing thousands of office workers (see **A**). This major event (often known as the 9/11 attacks) shocked the world – and it was one of many tragic and violent acts that have been carried out by different terrorist groups across the globe, for various reasons. What is terrorism, and how are countries combating it?

Objectives

- Define the word 'terrorism' and analyse how terrorists operate in today's world.
- Examine methods to combat terrorism.

Further attacks

After two planes crashed into the World Trade Center, a third passenger plane was flown into the Pentagon building in Washington, the headquarters of the US army, navy and air force. Half an hour later a fourth plane crashed in a field near Pennsylvania, not far from Washington. Many experts believe it was heading for the White House, the home of the US President. The fourth flight never made it because some of the passengers fought with the hijackers to stop them reaching their target.

The US President, George W. Bush, was visiting a school when he heard of the first attacks. In a statement a few minutes later, he said, 'Today we have had a national tragedy. Two airplanes have crashed into the World Trade Center in an apparent terrorist attack on our country.'

So what is terrorism – and why is it used?

Terrorism can generally be defined as the use of violence and intimidation for political, economic, social or religious reasons. Terrorists want to change the way governments and societies behave by using threats, fear, damage and bloodshed – in other words, terror.

Terrorism has been used for many, many years to try to achieve a wide variety of different aims and objectives. Terrorists don't usually represent a large proportion of the population, and while some of them may have tried peaceful methods to make change, they feel the need to resort to violence and fear to make their aims known.

▶ **SOURCE A** The moments immediately after a second passenger plane hit the Twin Towers of the World Trade Center on 11 September 2001.

Why did the 9/11 attacks occur?

The attacks on the World Trade Center and the Pentagon in September 2001 were part of a series of attacks by a terrorist group named al-Qaeda. This group's members, who were led at the time by a millionaire named Osama bin Laden, are all followers of Islam but have very strict, extremist beliefs that are different from the vast majority of Muslims. They believe they are fighting against enemies of their religion.

The USA, in particular, is seen as one of al-Qaeda's greatest enemies. Other terror groups, with similar beliefs to al-Qaeda, have attacked American targets, too. They dislike the USA because they believe it interferes too much in the Middle East – an area including Iran, Iraq, Israel-Palestine, Jordan, Kuwait, Saudi Arabia and Syria.

For many years, the USA has built naval and air bases in some Middle Eastern countries, most notably Saudi Arabia. Many groups have found this presence threatening. In recent years, terror groups (such as al-Qaeda) have targeted the USA because they believe the USA has helped so-called 'enemies of Islam' during wars against Muslim nations in the Middle East. These terror groups want to get rid of US influence in the Middle East and are prepared to use terrorism either to frighten the USA into leaving or to anger America so much that it starts a holy war against all Muslim states. This, these groups hope, will end with 'final victory' for Islam.

The impact of the 9/11 attacks

The 9/11 attacks caused international outrage, and led to the US President declaring a 'war on terror'. At this time, a group called the Taliban were in control of Afghanistan, and it allowed al-Qaeda to operate there. So, in October 2001, US forces invaded Afghanistan to search for terrorist bases. Troops from other countries, including the UK, became involved too. The Taliban was quickly removed from power in Afghanistan, but continued to operate there and be a major threat to the new government that replaced it.

Later on...   2011

In 2011, ten years after the 9/11 attacks, Osama bin Laden was eventually found by US soldiers in Pakistan, where he was shot and killed.

Earlier on...   1790s

The word 'terrorist' was first used in the 1790s to refer to the extreme methods (known as the Reign of Terror) used during the French Revolution by the revolutionaries against their opponents.

▼ **SOURCE B** The gaping hole in the side of the USS *Cole*, following an al-Qaeda attack in October 2000 in Aden harbour, Yemen, in the Middle East. Seventeen US sailors were killed and 39 injured.

Over to You

1   a   In your own words, explain what is meant by the word 'terrorism'.

    b   What is a 'terrorist'?

2   Why do you think the 9/11 terrorists might have been targeting:
    • the World Trade Center
    • the Pentagon
    • the White House?

3   Write a sentence or two to explain the following terms:
    a   al-Qaeda
    b   war on terror

What are the different reasons and methods for terrorist attacks?

Terrorists come in different forms: various individuals or groups of people, including countries and governments sometimes, have practised terrorism. They have targeted their own country, or foreign countries, for all sorts of different reasons. For example, in the last few years, you may have encountered news reports of terrorism carried out in the UK, Norway, France, Russia, the USA, Nigeria, India, Pakistan and the Middle East.

- Sometimes governments can use terror tactics against their own people, in order to make them act in a particular way and follow their political beliefs. In Nazi Germany, for example, people were arrested, imprisoned, tortured and executed to create a climate of fear so that people would follow Nazi rules and beliefs.

- Terror tactics have been used by one or both sides in relation to land and territory. This has happened in Vietnam, Algeria and Northern Ireland, for example. Sometimes, the dispute over possession of land can lead to many decades of conflict and terror, such as in the Middle East between Palestinians and Israelis.

- Terror attacks can also be committed by one or two individuals with their own personal beliefs or agenda. In 1995, for example, two men detonated a bomb outside a government building in Oklahoma City, USA, because they were unhappy with the way the US government had handled a siege two years earlier.

- In the twenty-first century some of the most extreme and destructive terror attacks have been carried out by individuals and groups with extreme religious views.

Fact ✔

The IRA was an Irish nationalist group that was prepared to use terror tactics to get British influence out of Ireland. In 2005 it announced it would use peaceful methods to achieve its aims instead, and dismantled its weapons and bombs.

▼ **SOURCE C** The devastation caused by a terrorist bomb that was set off outside a US government building in Oklahoma City in April 1995.

▼ **SOURCE D** The remains of a London bus after terrorist attacks on 7 July 2005. Three men with links to al-Qaeda blew themselves up on London tube trains, while a fourth exploded his bomb on this bus in Upper Woburn Place. In total, over 50 people were killed and 700 injured.

Terrorists use a variety of methods to cause disruption, destruction and death. These include:

- **Bombs:** These can be hidden in busy places, on trains, buses, and even planes. A timer is sometimes used to set off the explosion.

- **Chemical attack:** Poison gas can sometimes be used. In Tokyo, Japan, 12 people were killed in 1995 when the nerve gas sarin was released on the underground train system. In 2001, a killer disease called anthrax was used as a terror weapon in the USA. Anthrax bacteria, in the form of white powder, was sent through the US mail system.

- **Hijacking:** Terrorists can take control of boats, planes and buses. They use the passengers as hostages or use the vehicle as a weapon.

- **Letter bomb:** Explosives in an envelope or parcel that blow up when it is opened. This is a common method used by extreme animal rights groups.

- **Mortar bomb:** A bomb fired through a metal tube or pipe. It flies only a short distance (around 50–200m) but can be made cheaply. For example, the IRA (Irish Republican Army) used mortar bombs to attack 10 Downing Street, the home of the Prime Minister, in 1991.

- **Suicide bomb:** Explosives are attached to the bomber's body. They approach their target and explode the bomb. In 2017, a suicide bomber set off a bomb at Manchester Arena as people were leaving a music concert, killing 23, including the bomber, and injuring 260.

- **Knife and gun attacks:** Individuals or small groups gather weapons and attack citizens in public places – on bridges, in markets, cafés and theatres, for example.

- **Cyberterrorism:** These are terrorist activities involving the use of computers to cause fear and disruption. Examples might include disrupting air traffic control computers, banking or electric power systems.

- **Vehicle-ramming attacks:** In this type of attack, a terrorist will deliberately drive a vehicle into a building, crowd of people, or another vehicle. In 2016, a lorry was deliberately driven into crowds in Nice, France, killing 87 people, including the driver, and injuring 458 others.

Fact ✓

A person who commits acts of terror alone, without assistance from any group is often called a 'lone-wolf terrorist'. However, they may be influenced by the beliefs of a group and may act in support of it.

Stopping terrorism

Stopping terrorists is not easy. However, many methods have been tried, including attacking the bases where terrorists are believed to be and increasing security in public places. In the UK, for example, the public are consistently asked to be on their guard and report any 'suspicious packages' to the police (see **E**).

▼ **SOURCE E** A British anti-terrorism poster.

Fact ✓

It is important to remember that despite the news focusing on terrorism all around the world, the risk of death from terrorist activities is actually quite small compared to other types of deaths, such as from illness related to smoking, or road traffic accidents.

Over to You

1 Make a list of reasons why some people, or terror groups, might carry out acts of terrorism.

2 In your own words, explain the different methods used by terrorists to cause disruption, destruction and death.

Source Analysis

1 Look at **Sources D** and **E**. How useful are these sources to a historian studying terror methods used by terrorists?

🔄 Quick Knowledge Quiz

Choose the correct answer from the three options:

1 Britain's first full-length motorway was opened between which two cities in 1959?

   a Birmingham and London
   b Manchester and Liverpool
   c Cardiff and Glasgow

2 Which of the following wars was fought between 1950 and 1953?

   a Falklands War
   b Korean War
   c Vietnam War

3 Which British TV channel first went on air in 1964?

   a BBC1
   b BBC2
   c ITV

4 What was the name of the first game console that could be connected to a TV set?

   a Sony PlayStation
   b Nintendo Game Boy
   c Magnavox Odyssey

5 In which year did Margaret Thatcher become Britain's first female Prime Minister?

   a 1977
   b 1978
   c 1979

6 The World Wide Web was created by which British scientist in 1989?

   a Tim Berners-Lee
   b Stephen Hawking
   c Rosalind Franklin

7 The world's first text message was sent in December 1992. But what did it say?

   a Happy Birthday
   b merry Christmas
   c Happy New Year

8 In which year did Apple first create the iPhone?

   a 2005
   b 2007
   c 2009

9 The UK's decision to leave the European Union after a public vote in 2016 became known by what name?

   a Brexit
   b Backstop
   c Maastricht Treaty

10 When were the Twin Towers of the World Trade Center in New York attacked by terrorists?

   a 9 September 2001
   b 11 September 2011
   c 11 September 2001

 **Literacy Focus**

Chronology and spelling

1   Look at the following six statements about events that took place in the decades between the 1950s and today. You may notice that the order of events is all mixed up and each statement contains two spelling mistakes. Write them out in the correct order, making sure you correct the spelling errors.

- Iraq invaded kuwait and the USA responded by sending in troops to fight Iraq in what became nown as the Gulf War.
- Milions of people bought a TV set to watch the live broadcast of the coronation of Quean Elizabeth II.
- Argentina invaded the Falklands, a group of irelands in the South Atlantic Ocean govened by Britain.
- Glam rock and punk rock wear the big new sounds in music. Disco tuck the world by storm too.
- Apple launched the hugely succesful iPod, a portable music player. This was followed by the iPhone, a smartfone.
- The Civil Rights Movement was at its hieght in America, calling for equel rights for black Americans.

Vocabulary check

2   In each group of historical words, phrases or names below, there is an odd one out. When you think you have identified it, write a sentence or two to explain why you think it doesn't fit in with the other words in its group. The first one has been done for you:

a   Korean War   (Crimean War)   Vietnam War   Falklands War

> I have chosen the Crimean War because this war was not fought in the twentieth century. The Korean, Vietnam and Falklands Wars were all fought in the years since 1945 – so in the twentieth century.

NOTE: Remember, though, there might be other answers! For example, you might say that the Falklands War is the odd one out because the other three wars involved more than two nations in the conflict – whereas the Falklands War was only between Argentina and Britain. The point of this exercise is not just to get you to think carefully about the events covered in the task, but to get you to *justify* your choices with a reason.

b	Morris Minor	Ford Fiesta	Rolls-Royce	Austin 1100
c	Mod	New Romantic	Hippy	Rocker
d	PlayStation	Nintendo	Apple	Virgin Galactic
e	The Beatles	Oasis	Blur	The Spice Girls
f	credit card	Barbie doll	remote control	Twitter

Comparing interpretations

When analysing different interpretations, a good historian should firstly work out what is being said, or what message the person who created the interpretation is trying to get across, before comparing the different interpretations.

Here is one way to compare two interpretations.

1 **Think about the content:** First you need to understand what the person is saying and/or showing in each interpretation. What is the content of **Interpretation A** saying? What is the content of **Interpretation B** saying?

2 **What are the main differences?** Now that you understand what each interpretation is saying, compare them. Find the ways in which the content of the interpretations is different.

3 **Think about the writers:** Look at the captions. What can they tell you about why the two interpretations might show different opinions about the topic?

4 **Why are there differences?** Can you suggest reasons why the two people who made the interpretations might have different opinions about the topic?

Assessment: Interpretation analysis

The following assessment focuses on two different interpretations of British Prime Minister Margaret Thatcher. In 1979, Thatcher became Britain's first ever female Prime Minister. She won three elections and remained Prime Minister until 1990, longer than any other twentieth-century British leader. But Thatcher was a very controversial figure. When she died in 2013 over 50,000 people lined the streets of London to pay their respects and throw white roses as her coffin passed by on its way to a service in St Paul's Cathedral... but later that week the song 'Ding-Dong! The Witch is Dead' from the film *The Wizard of Oz* reached Number 2 in the UK singles charts after people began downloading it to 'celebrate' her death! So why did Thatcher divide opinion?

Your challenge now is to answer this question about analysing interpretations:

Interpretations A and **B** both provide views on Prime Minister Margaret Thatcher. How do they differ, and what might explain the differences? (20)

Assessment: Interpretation analysis

▼ **INTERPRETATION A** David Cameron was Britain's Prime Minister from 2010 to 2016. He made this short speech shortly after Thatcher's death in 2013. He belonged to the same political party as Thatcher did – and actually worked for her, in 1988, in one of his first jobs.

'Margaret Thatcher didn't just lead our country – she saved our country. She took a country that was on its knees and made Britain stand tall again. We can't deny that Lady Thatcher divided opinion. For many of us, she was, and is, an inspiration. For others she was a force to be defined against [reckoned with]. But if there is one thing that cuts through all of this – one thing that runs through everything she did – it was her lion-hearted love of this country.'

▼ **INTERPRETATION B** David Douglass is a writer who worked as a coal miner in Durham and South Yorkshire. He was an important member of an organisation called the National Union of Mineworkers that fought against the closing of coal mines by Thatcher's government in the 1980s.

'I will not be shedding any tears over her. I wouldn't normally take comfort in anyone's death, but the woman shed no tears over our communities or the poverty she caused. An entire generation was thrown on the scrapheap, and sons and grandsons are still suffering now. Thatcher's legacy has been unemployment, crime, poverty, low levels of life expectancy, heroin addiction – the list goes on in places where she ripped the heart out of the community... a lot of people have no idea of the damage that woman inflicted on this country.'

The sentence starters below show one way to structure an answer to this question.

1 **Think about the content.**

One way that Interpretation A is different from Interpretation B is that A writes... (You can quote the interpretation if you like.)	(2)
On the other hand, B writes...	(2)
This means they are different because A focuses more on...	(2)
However, B focuses more on...	(2)

2 **Think about the creators.**

One reason the creators have different views is...	(2)
The writer of A is...	(2)
This means...	(3)
However, the writer of B is...	(2)
This means...	(3)

TIP:
- It is always important to read about the author. Think about why they might say positive or negative things about Thatcher.
- How do they describe Thatcher? Are they mainly complimentary – or not?

TIP:
- What impression of Thatcher do you get from what the authors have written?
- How does this make you feel about Thatcher? Remember, the authors have chosen to say this, so they are intending for you to feel this.

TIP: Is there any reason you can think of why Douglass might have strong opinions about what happened in the coal mining areas?

TIP: Douglass is talking about the area in which he lived and worked. Might a person who lives in an area affected by the closure of coal mines have a different opinion from someone who does not? What do you think?

TIP: What is each interpretation saying? Make a list of the ways they are different. What is the main difference?

TIP: What can the captions tell you about why the two interpretations might show different opinions? People tend to say what they say and think what they think because of their beliefs, background, upbringing and influences. Can you think of reasons why the two people here might have written what they have written?

How has Britain changed between 1901 and the present day?

The world we live in is always changing. Sometimes small changes, inventions or discoveries that might not seem very significant at the time can add up to large changes over a long period. For example, few people would have predicted the huge impact that the invention of the aeroplane or television or the Internet would have had. The next few pages highlight some of the key changes and innovations that took place during the period this book covers – 1901 to the present day.

Objectives

- Examine some of the key changes in British life since 1901.
- Judge how far Britain has changed since 1901.

Step 1

Meet Robert, a young man living in 1901, around the time of Queen Victoria's death. Have a look at what life was like for Robert at the time.

> Voting in elections for Parliament is for men only... not women! In fact, it is very much a 'man's world' in politics and business. Many jobs (such as teaching) expect women to leave if they get married. Many men think a woman's place is in the home, looking after her husband and their children. And even if women do the same jobs as men (like factory work), they get paid less.

> The average age of death for a man is 49, and 52 for a woman. It is much lower in very poor areas, though – in some parts of London it's 30!

> School is compulsory up to the age of 14... and in the workplace there is a ratio of five male workers to every woman.

> In addition to sports such as football, cricket and horse racing, popular pastimes are cycling, indoor games (such as cards), trips to the theatre for variety shows... and evenings in the pub!

> Britain is the most powerful nation on earth, ruling over more land, selling more goods and making more money than any other.

> Getting around is much faster than it used to be. Lots of people still walk, but we have trains too – and even a new thing called a 'motor car'.

> In old age people are looked after by their families, or they use their savings or charity donations.

> One of the greatest luxuries is the motor car. In 1901, there is only one car for every 900 people. And people save hard to buy things like a gramophone (to play music records), a piano, electric lighting or a new stove or 'cooker'.

> The most common causes of death are heart disease and illnesses that affect breathing, such as bronchitis and pneumonia.

> People communicate by talking to each other! And we write letters or use telegrams, which are short messages sent via telegraph (a system for transmitting messages along a wire). These telegrams are then typed and delivered by hand.

> The average couple have four children – but for every 1000 babies born, 150 will die before their first birthday.

Step 2

Now you've met Robert and got to know a little about his life, study some of the key developments, discoveries and advances of the following century and beyond.

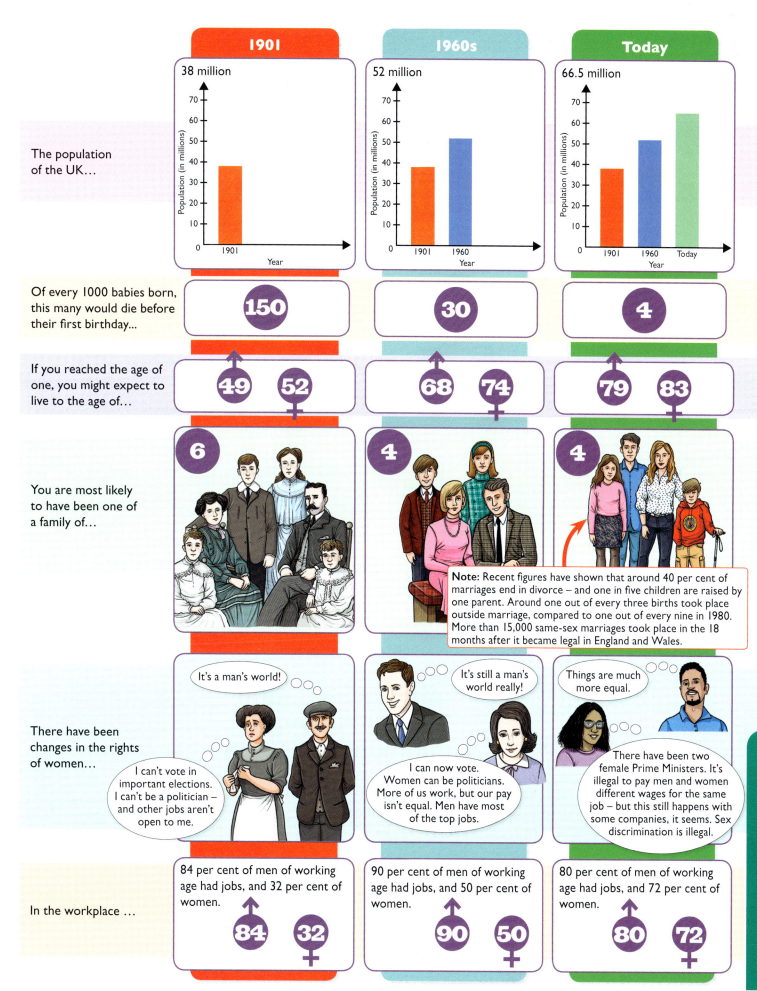

	1901	1960s	Today
You would go to school from the age of five until…	14 years old 	15 years old 	16 years old, and another two years in education 
The main forms of communication were…	Word of mouth, newspapers/magazines, telegrams, letters 	Word of mouth, newspapers/magazines, letters, radio, telephone, television 	Word of mouth, social media, newspapers/magazines, TV, email, telephone, radio, letters
This is how those in need might be looked after…	Savings, families or charity	Savings or small pension, some benefits and the NHS 	Savings, pension, many benefits including the NHS 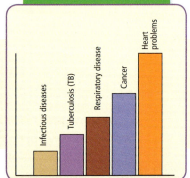
The most common causes of death were…			
Common leisure activities were…			
The British Empire…			

1901 – The most common causes of death were…
Infectious diseases · Cancer · Tuberculosis (TB) · Heart problems · Respiratory disease

1960s – The most common causes of death were…
Liver disease · Respiratory disease · Cancer · Stroke · Heart problems

Today – The most common causes of death were…
Infectious diseases · Tuberculosis (TB) · Respiratory disease · Cancer · Heart problems

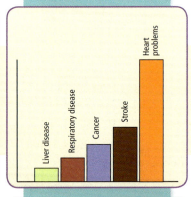

COLLECT PENSION
DOLE MONEY
DISABILITY ALLOWANCE HERE

PENSION · MATERNITY DAY · NHS · CARE HOME · DISABILITY LIVING ALLOWANCE · JOBSEEKER'S ALLOWANCE

THE SALVATION ARMY

► **SOURCE A** A table showing where the UK ranks compared to other countries and states in the world in several different categories.

Category	UK ranking/Number of countries surveyed
Life expectancy	**35**/224*
Infant mortality rate	**185**/225*
Spending on education	**36**/173*
Literacy	**14**/79**
Daily calorie intake	**19**/174***

* Data from CIA World Factbook, 2020
** Data from 2019 Pisa tests
*** Data from the Food and Agriculture Organization of the United Nations, 2017

Step 3

Now it's time to meet Amina, a young woman who lives in the modern world. Based on all the changes you've studied so far on these pages, think about the answers to the questions dotted around her. You might want to work with a partner or in a small group for this.

Is it a more 'caring' society that looks after vulnerable people?

How have women's rights changed?

Has education changed at all?

Is Britain a healthier place?

What type of luxury goods do people desire today – and how are they different from the luxuries of 1901?

How has the way people spend their spare time changed?

Have families and family life changed between 1901 and today?

Has the motor car become popular? And what other types of transport are commonly used?

How has the British Empire changed?

How has the way people communicate with each other changed?

Over to You

1 **a** Draw two spider diagrams called 'Britain in 1901' and 'Britain today'. Surround each spider diagram with facts and figures about Britain at these times.

   b Write a paragraph about the changes that took place in Britain between 1901 and today.

   c Of all the changes mentioned in your paragraph, which do you think was the most important? Give reasons for your choice. See if other people in the class agree with you.

   d When would you rather have lived: 1901 or today? Again, give reasons for your choice.

2 A recent survey showed that around seven out of ten British people were happy with their lives and proud to be British. Why do you think so many people were proud to be British?

Fact ✓

You will have noticed that during any one period of time, some things change and other things stay the same (continuities). Understanding the pace of changes is important – knowing that some changes happen quickly and some happen slowly. You should be able to pick out areas of life where change happened rapidly and areas of life where change happened slowly between 1901 and today.

Change and Continuity

1 Explain two ways in which the rights of women in 1901 were different from the rights of women today.

⟳ Quick Knowledge Quiz

Choose the correct answer from the three options:

1 Which queen died at the beginning of the twentieth century?

  a Queen Elizabeth

  b Queen Victoria

  c Queen Mary

2 In 1901, of every 1000 babies born, approximately how many would die before their first birthday?

  a 15

  b 150

  c 350

3 In today's Britain, of every 1000 babies born, approximately how many would die before their first birthday?

  a 150

  b 15

  c 4

4 What happened to the average age of death for both men and women in the years from 1901 to the present day?

  a increased

  b decreased

  c stayed the same

5 In 1901, school was compulsory up to what age?

  a 14

  b 15

  c 16

6 By the 1960s, the school leaving age had risen to what age?

  a 15

  b 16

  c 18

7 What has consistently been one of the country's most common causes of death from 1901 to today?

  a infectious diseases

  b tuberculosis

  c heart problems

8 What health organisation would people be able to use in the 1960s and today that they would not have been able to use at the beginning of the twentieth century?

  a NHS

  b WHO

  c CIA

9 In 1960, what proportion of men of working age had jobs?

  a 50 per cent

  b 70 per cent

  c 90 per cent

10 According to recent figures, how many marriages end in divorce?

  a 10 per cent

  b 40 per cent

  c 70 per cent

 **Literacy Focus**

Weighing evidence

Here are two examples of strong opinions about the twentieth century.
Read them carefully.

> The twentieth century has been one of the most amazing periods of development for the human race. Our knowledge about the world and the universe has grown. It has enabled new technology to be developed that has wiped out diseases and saved millions of lives that would have been lost in the past. In countries like Britain, education, healthcare and a basic income are guaranteed for just about everyone. Minority groups have had their basic rights recognised and courts are used to protect everyone's civil rights.

> However, at the same time, this new knowledge and technology have been used to organise genocide on a scale unimaginable in the past. Communist and fascist governments killed millions in the first half of the twentieth century and dictatorships continue to kill people all around the world today. The healthcare and lifestyle we have in Britain are enjoyed by a minority of people in the world and, by the end of the twentieth century, one in five children were still hungry.

1   While both of these statements are true, they are very different. Each person has a different opinion about the twentieth century and they have chosen certain facts to support their own view. Look through the work you have completed about the twentieth century and copy and complete the following table with additional information for each agreement.

Evidence for progress	Evidence for destruction

2   As you have probably worked out, the twentieth century was both a century of progress and a century of great destruction. Write a paragraph that sums up the century. You might agree with one of the opinions more than the other – explain why in your paragraph.

9 History skill: Change

During any period in history, there are usually things that are changing and things that are staying the same (known as 'continuities'). Sometimes there can be dramatic changes in one area of life, but very little change in another.

Historians sometimes don't agree with each other about which areas of life experienced the biggest changes in a historical period. However, whatever your opinion might be, it is important to try to argue your point in a structured and detailed way, and back up your views with evidence and facts!

> **TIP:** For example, there have been major changes in the way we communicate with each other in the years between 1901 and the present day.

Responding to questions about change

One way of thinking about a question on change is:

1 **Plan:** Study the question. Do you agree or disagree with it? What do you know about that area of change in this period of history? Also, make some notes about *other* changes in this period. There will likely be different areas of change, but some may be bigger (made more impact on people, or affected more people) than others.

> **TIP:** You could create a mind map to help you organise your ideas about all the areas of change.

2 **Judge:** Once you have thought about the different changes, you need to decide: which do you think was the largest or most important change? List in bullet points the reasons for your choice.

> **TIP:** Do you strongly agree with it? Do you not agree with the statement at all? Or do you only slightly agree? There is no right answer for this, it is all down to what you think!

3 **Answer:** Remember to focus on the question asked. So, after steps 1 and 2, decide *how far* you agree with the statement given in the question.

> **TIP:** To explain your judgement and your reasons, you can use phrases like:
> - This was a change because...
> - This had not been seen before...
> - This can be seen through...

4 **Explain** and conclude: You now need to add details/reasons to support your decision and explain why you are taking this view. Use your plan to help you add detail. Try to refer to other areas of change when answering this question.

> **TIP:** You will need to use examples in your answer. For instance, instead of simply saying 'Women's rights changed', you could say 'Women's rights changed greatly. For example, in the early twentieth century, voting in elections for Parliament was for men only, and many jobs (including teaching, for example) expected women to leave if they got married. However, in today's world...'

Assessment: Change

Now that you have reached the end of this book, you can consider the changes in the period you have been studying – from 1901 (the end of the Victorian period) to the present day. Your challenge is to answer this question:

> How far do you agree that the way people communicate with each other has seen the greatest change between 1901 and the present day in Britain? Give reasons for your answer. (20)

The steps and sentence starters below show you one way to structure an answer to this question.

1 **Plan**: Study the question. It suggests that communication has seen the greatest changes between 1901 and the present day in Britain. Do you agree with this? What do you know about communication in this period?

There may be other areas of change in this period that are important too. Create a mind-map and add details to it to help you.

2 **Judge**: Look at your mind-map. Which of the areas you have covered do you think changed the most? Make a list of the areas – from the one that you think saw the most change, to the one you think saw the least.

3 **Answer**: Now that you've made your judgement, **answer the question directly**. Remember that the question asks you *how far* you agree with it.

> I... that communication saw the largest change between 1901 and the present day in Britain...

4 **Explain and conclude**: Finally, add some **details and reasons** to support *why* you think what you think. Try to refer to other areas of change.

> In 1901, the main methods of communication were...
> In the modern world...
> So, the key changes in communication have been... (5)

> There were other changes that were important too. Another area of change was... (5)

> Yet another area of change was... (5)

> In conclusion, I (strongly agree/agree to a certain extent/disagree) that communication saw the largest change between 1901 and the present day in Britain, because... (5)

TIP: Look at the diagram on page 216 to help you.

TIP:

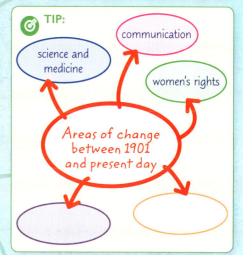

TIP: Remember, you are being asked to judge whether communication changed more than any other areas – so make sure you compare it with other changes, and see which areas haven't changed that much or have changed lots!

TIP: You could pick one of the phrases below that fits best with your judgement:

strongly agree

don't agree very much

agree to a certain extent

TIP: Don't just write what changed – try to explain the *impact* of the change too.

TIP: You are being asked to compare the changes in the way people communicated to changes in other areas – so it's vital you write about other areas.

TIP: Remember to conclude your answer. Explain *how far* you agree.

Glossary

abdicate when a king or queen has given up their throne

Aboriginal people the original people of mainland Australia

alliance agreement between countries to support each other in war

ally another country that will defend you if attacked – or help you if you decide to attack

annex when an area of land or a country is added to another country or area, usually by force or without permission

antibiotic a chemical substance that kills bacteria and cures infections

antisemitism the strong dislike or cruel and unfair treatment of Jewish people

Anzac the collective term for men from Australia and New Zealand who fought in the First and Second World Wars (Australian and New Zealand Army Corps)

appeasement the policy of giving someone what they want in the hope that they will stop their demands

area bombing releasing bombs over a whole town or city

armed forces soldiers, sailors and air crew who fight in wars

armistice the ceasefire that ended the First World War on 11 November 1914

arms race a competition between countries for superiority in the development and build-up of weapons

Aryan (in Nazi thinking) a person of German or Scandinavian origin (not Jewish), usually fair-haired and blue-eyed; the Nazis believed that Aryans were superior to all other races

assassinate to murder an important person, usually for political or religious reasons

assembly line a system using workers and machines in a factory to make goods in stages

asylum protection or safety, given by a government to someone who has been forced to leave their own country for their safety or because of war

assimilation the process of becoming part of a group, country or society by taking in its language, culture and customs and so becoming like the majority of people in that group, country or society

Blitz German air raids on major British cities in 1940–1941

Blitzkrieg intense German military campaign using tanks, aircraft and troops to try to bring about a swift victory

bomber an aircraft designed to carry and drop bombs

British Empire the collection of countries and colonies (areas) that Britain ruled over; at its height, Britain ruled over 56 colonies around the world

cause the reason why something happens

capitalism an economic and political system where businesses are run by private owners rather than the government with the aim of making a profit

censor to delete sensitive information in a publication

censorship limiting access to information, ideas or books in order to prevent knowledge

Cold War the term used to describe tensions between East and West after the Second World War up to 1991

collaboration working together to achieve something

collective security the idea of 'safety in numbers' that a country or area is stronger as part of a unified team

colony an area of land controlled by another country

Commonwealth an international association consisting of the UK together with countries that were previously part of the British Empire

communism a political theory created by Karl Marx in which all property is publicly owned and each person works and is paid according to their abilities and needs

conscientious objector a person who believes that war is wrong and refuses to fight

conscription the government policy of forcing people to join the armed forces in wartime

consequence the impact or results of something that has happened

consumer goods items bought by people for their own use

court martial a military court for trying soldiers accused of breaking the rules

cowardice lack of courage

currency the system of money used by a country or group of countries

death toll the number of people killed in war or a natural disaster

democratic a system of government in which people vote to choose their politicians

desertion illegally leaving a military position without permission

dictator a person in complete control of a country

dictatorship a country governed by a dictator, who passes very strict laws; the people who live there have no say in how the country is run

distress flare a small explosive device that produces a bright flame; they are fired into the air when a ship requires assistance

dole money given to unemployed people by the government

enlist to join the armed services – army, navy or air force

eugenics the study of how to influence or 'improve' the mental and physical characteristics of the human race by choosing who may become parents

Euro the money system used by many countries in the European Union

evacuation moving from a dangerous place to a safer place. For example, being taken from places at risk during war, such as cities, to safer places, such as the countryside

fascism an anti-democratic system of government developed by Mussolini in Italy and Hitler in Germany

fighter a fast military aircraft designed for attacking other aircraft

firestorm an intense fire caused by bombing in which strong air currents are drawn into the blaze, making it burn more fiercely

firing squad a group of soldiers who are ordered to shoot and kill prisoners

flapper a middle- or upper-class woman who cut her hair shorter and wore shorter dresses; flappers smoked and drank openly – and shocked the older generation

foreign affairs political matters connected with other countries

Free Corps ex-soldiers who joined the government to end the Spartacist Uprising; they also formed part of the Kapp Putsch in 1920

front an area where fighting takes place between two sides

Führer German word for supreme leader

Gestapo the secret police in Nazi Germany

ghetto a small, restricted area of a town where Jews were forced to live by the Nazis

Great Depression the period of high unemployment in the 1930s when many businesses failed

guerrilla attack quick, devastating, hit-and-run raid on troops and supply lines

hand grenade a small bomb thrown by hand

hereditary passed on from parents to their children

Holocaust the commonly known name for the Nazis' attempt to wipe out the Jewish race

home front the civilian population of a nation whose armed forces are engaged in war abroad

human rights the basic rights that it is generally considered all people should have, such as education, justice and freedom of speech

hyperinflation a sudden, dramatic rise in prices

immigrant person who has come to a different country in order to live there permanently

imperialism a policy of extending a country's power and influence over other countries, or a desire for control over other countries

immunisation a method of protecting a person or animal from disease, usually by giving them a vaccine

incendiary bomb a bomb designed to start fires

infantry soldiers who fight on foot

interpretation historical evidence created much later than the period studied, produced by people with a particular opinion about an event in the past

Irish Republican Army also known as the IRA, which fought for Irish independence from Britain

Iron Curtain a term coined by Winston Churchill to describe an imaginary barrier between the communist countries of the Soviet bloc and the West after the Second World War

long-term describes an event or situation in the past that leads to an effect sometime later

Luftwaffe German air force

Māori a member of the race of people who were the original people living in New Zealand

martyr someone who is prepared to die for their beliefs

mass produce to make goods in huge numbers, often for cheaper than before

militant someone who supports or uses confrontational or violent methods to support a political or social cause

militarism the belief that a country should have great military strength in order to be powerful

multicultural containing several cultural or ethnic groups within a society

munitions military weapons, ammunition and equipment

National Insurance compulsory payments by employees and employers to provide state assistance for people who are sick, unemployed or retired

nationalise to transfer an industry such as coal mining from private to state ownership or control

nationalism a strong attachment to a particular country, or nation

nationalist a person with strong beliefs about their nation. and who wants political independence for their nation

neutral not supporting or helping either side in a conflict or disagreement

no man's land the wasteland between the trenches of the Allied and German forces during the First World War controlled by neither side

Pacific Islander a person who originates from the Pacific Islands, which include countries within the Oceanic regions of Polynesia, Melanesia and Micronesia

pals battalion a group of friends or co-workers who enlisted to fight in the First World War together

pandemic a disease that has spread across a large region – for example, multiple continents, or worldwide

pardon to remove the blame from someone wrongly accused of a crime, such as desertion in wartime

partition when a region or country is divided into separate parts

patriotic showing love for your country and being proud of it

persecution the unfair or cruel treatment of someone (or a group of people) over a long period because of their race, religion or political beliefs

poverty the state of being extremely poor

precision bombing carefully targeted bombing of specific locations such as docks, air bases and munitions factories

propaganda false or misleading information used to spread a certain point of view

public health the health and wellbeing of the population as a whole, in a particular place at a particular time

putsch German word for revolution or rebellion

radar a detection system that uses radio waves to determine the range, angle and speed of objects

rationing officially limiting the amount of items such as food allowed to each person during wartime

rearmament restocking a country's supply of weapons and armed forces

referendum a vote in which all the people in a country or an area are asked to decide an important political or social question

refugee person who has been forced to leave their country in order to escape war, persecution or natural disaster

reparations money paid by a country that has lost a war, for the damage and injuries it has caused

scapegoat a person who is blamed for wrongdoings or mistakes

secular not connected to religious or spiritual matters

shell a bomb that is fired a long distance by artillery (heavy guns)

shell shock a nervous condition suffered by some soldiers exposed to the noise and chaos of battle

short-term describes an event or situation that leads to an immediate effect

shrapnel fragments of a bomb or shell that are thrown out when it explodes

single market an association of countries trading with each other without restrictions or taxes

significance something (like an individual, event or development) that makes an impact at the time and continues to make an impact many years later; historians are often asked to judge the significance of something

skin graft a surgical operation in which a piece of healthy skin is transplanted to a new place on a patient's body (or to a different individual)

social security financial help from the government for people with little or no money

SOS an international code signal of extreme distress, used especially by ships

source historical evidence from the period studied, created by someone who was directly involved with an event or an eyewitness to an event; sources provide information historians need to create interpretations

space race the competition between the USA and the USSR to explore space

Spartacist member of a Communist group that wanted a revolution similar to the one in Russia; they revolted against the German government in 1919

stalemate a situation in which further progress by opposing sides in a war seems impossible

sterilise deprive of the ability to produce children, usually by removing or blocking the sex organs

strike a refusal to work organised by a group of workers as a form of protest, usually in an attempt to improve pay or conditions

suffragette campaigner for the right of women to vote, who organised often-violent protests to press their cause

suffragist campaigner for the right of women to vote, who used peaceful means of protest

superpower one of the world's two most powerful nations in the Cold War period after the Second World War, the USA and the USSR

synagogue a building in which Jews meet for religious worship

treaty an official written agreement between countries or international organisations

Torres Strait Islander people the original people of the 274 islands off the north coast of Australia, in the Torres Strait

trench a deep narrow hole dug in the ground; during wars trenches are dug by soldiers and used as places from which they can attack the enemy while staying hidden

trench foot a foot disease common among First World War troops who stood in cold and wet conditions for long periods

unionist a person, especially a member of a Northern Ireland political party, who is in favour of the union of Northern Ireland with Britain

viceroy a ruler who leads a colony on behalf of a monarch

war pension an amount of money, regularly paid to the wives of soldiers killed during warfare

welfare state system whereby the state protects the health and wellbeing of its citizens with free healthcare, pensions and other benefits

Zeppelin a large German airship

Index

OXFORD
UNIVERSITY PRESS

Great Clarendon Street, Oxford, OX2 6DP, United Kingdom

Oxford University Press is a department of the University of Oxford.

It furthers the University's objective of excellence in research, scholarship, and education by publishing worldwide. Oxford is a registered trade mark of Oxford University Press in the UK and in certain other countries

British Library Cataloguing in Publication Data

Data available

978-0-19-849466-9

10 9 8 7 6 5 4 3

Paper used in the production of this book is a natural, recyclable product made from wood grown in sustainable forests.

The manufacturing process conforms to the environmental regulations of the country of origin.

Printed in Italy by L.E.G.O. S.p.A.

Acknowledgements

The publisher would like to thank the following for permissions to use copyright material:

Max Arthur: the words of S C Lang in *Forgotten Voices of the Great World War* (Ebury Press, 2002, 2006), copyright © Max Arthur and Imperial War Museums 2002, used by permission of the Random House Group Ltd a division of Penguin Random House UK; **Associated Press**: news report, *British Movietone News*, 6 June 1940, copyright © AP Archive/ British Movietone, used by permission of The Associated Press; **J F Aylett**: *In Search of History:Twentieth Century* (Hodder Education, 1986), copyright © J F Aylett 1986, used by permission of Hodder Education; **Liz Bellamy** and **Kate Moorse**, The Schools History Project: Table 'Women's Work in 1914 and 1931', in *Discovering the Past: The Changing Role of Women* (Hodder Education, 1996), used by permission of Hodder Education; **Vera Brittain**: *Testament of Youth: An Autobiographical Study of the Years 1900-1925* (Gollancz 1933/Penguin 1989), used by permission of Mark Bostridge and T J Brittain-Catlin, literary executors for the Estate of Vera Brittain 1970; **Ruth Brocklehurst**: *Usborne History of Britain* (Usborne, 2008), copyright © Usborne Publishing Ltd 2008, used by permission of Usborne Publishing, 83-85 Saffron Hill, London EC1N 8RT, UK, www.usborne.com; **Alan Bullock**: *Hitler: A Study in Tyranny* (abridged edition, Penguin, 1962), copyright © Alan Bullock 1962; and 'Hitler and the Origins of the Second World War' in Edmonde Manning Robertson (Ed): *The Origins of the Second World War: Historical Interpretations* (Palgrave Macmillan, 1971) used by permission of Curtis Brown Group Ltd, London on behalf of the Estate of Baron Bullock ; **Adrian Caesar**: *Dividing Lines: Poetry, Class and Ideology in the 1930s* (Manchester University Press, 1991), reproduced by permission of the University of Manchester through PLSclear; **David Cameron**: Tribute to Margaret Thatcher, in *The Spectator,* 8 April 2013 used by permission of David Cameron via Curtis Brown Ltd, London; **Winston S Churchill**: 'Blood, toil, tears, and sweat', 13 May 1940, House of Commons; 'Wars are not won by evacuations', 4 June 1940, House of Commons; and 'Never Give In!', 29 Oct 1941, Harrow School; copyright © The Estate of Winston S Churchill, used by permission of Curtis Brown, London, on behalf of the Estate of Winston S Churchill; **Catriona Clarke**: 'Breaking the Mould - the story of penicillin', Wellcome Sanger Institute, 6 June 2019, used by permission of the Wellcome Sanger Institute; **David Douglass**: 'Thatcher will never be forgiven for the devastation she caused in Sheffield', *The Star,* 9 April 2013, used by permission of the SWNS Media Group for The Star;

The Oxford Impact Framework is a systematic approach to evaluating the impact of Oxford University Press products and services. It was developed through a unique collaboration with the National Foundation for Educational Research (NFER) and is supported by the Oxford University Department of Education.

OXFORD IMPACT FRAMEWORK
EVALUATING EDUCATIONAL PRODUCTS AND SERVICES FROM OXFORD UNIVERSITY PRESS

CREATED WITH  SUPPORTED BY

Pamela Duncan and **Juliette Jowit**: 'Is the NHS the world's best healthcare system?', *The Guardian,* 2 July 2018, copyright © Guardian News & Media Ltd 2018, 2020, used by permission of GNM Ltd.; **Kate Eggleston**: 'The State Schoolgirl' in Jonathan Croall: *Don't You Know There's a War On?: The People's Voice 1939-45* (Hutchinson, 1989), copyright © Jonathan Croall 1989, used by permission of the publishers, Taylor & Francis Group, Informa Ltd, through PLSclear; **Dwight D Eisenhower**: *Crusade in Europe* (Johns Hopkins University Press, 1948), copyright © 1948 by Penguin Random House LLC, used by permission of Doubleday, an imprint of the Knopf Doubleday Publishing Group, a division of Penguin Random House LLC. All rights reserved; **Hilma Geffen**: interviewed by Dr Jon Fishbane, 15 February 1985, from The Voice/Vision Holocaust Survival Oral History Archive, University of Michigan-Dearborn, copyright © The Regents of the University of Michigan, used by permission of the Voice/Vision Archive; **Muriel Green**: diary entry 23 Nov 1939, copyright © The Trustees of the Mass Observation Archive, used by permission of Curtis Brown Group Ltd, London on behalf of The Trustees of the Mass Observation Archive; **Nick Higham**: 'Dunkirk: The Propaganda War', BBC News, 2 June 2000, used by permission of Nick Higham and of the BBC; **Ian Hislop**: commentary on *Not Forgotten: Soldiers of Empire*, Channel 4 television, November 2009, used by permission of Casarotto Ramsay & Associates Ltd on behalf of Ian Hislop; **Hendrik Karsten Hogrefe**: 'Nazi aggression: planned or improvised?', *Historian* Magazine, 3 Jan 2012, used by permission of the Historical Association; **Richard Holmes**: *World at War* (Ebury Press, 2007, 2011), copyright © Richard Holmes 2007, used by permission of The Random House Group Ltd, a division of Penguin Random House UK; **Boris Johnson**: 'Churchill embodied Britain's greatness', *The Telegraph,* 23 Jan 2015, copyright © Telegraph Media Group Ltd 2015, used by permission of TMG Ltd; **Bernard Kops**: *The World is a Wedding* (Five Leaves, 2008), copyright © Bernard Kops 1963, 2008, used by permission of the author; **Caroline Lang**: interview with Anita Bowers in *Keep Smiling Through: Women in the Second World War* (CUP, 1989), used by permission of Cambridge University Press; **Jennie Lee**: *My Life with Nye* (Jonathan Cape, 1980), used by permission of the Random House Group Ltd a division of Penguin Random House UK; **Bill Kristol**: interview with Garry Kasparov, from www.conversationswithbillkristol.org, 2016, used by permission of The Foundation for Constitutional Government, Inc.; **Linda McDowell:** 'How Caribbean migrants helped to rebuild Britain', Windrush Stories, The British Library, 4 Oct 2018, used by permission of Professor McDowell; **Margaret Macmillan**: comment made on a history website in 2004, used by permission of Professor MacMillan; **A W Martin** and **Patsy Hardy** (Eds): *Dark and Hurrying Days: Menzie's 1941 Diary* (1993), National Library of Australia, Prime Ministerial History, used by permission of the National Library of Australia; **Henry Metelmann**: *Through Hell for Hitler* (Spellmount, 2002), used by permission of The History Press; **David Olusoga**: 'Wake up, Britain. Should the empire really be a source of pride?', *The Guardian,* 23 Jan 2016, copyright © Guardian News & Media Ltd 2016, 2020; 'Lost empire: it's a myth that Britain stood alone against Hitler', theguardian.com, 2 Sept 2019, copyright © Guardian News & Media Ltd 2019, 2020; used by permission of GNM Ltd; **Gerry Oram**: extract from a BBC report, 12 Nov 2018, used by permission of Dr Gerard Oram; **Dr Matt Perry** reported in David Martin: '80 years ago today: the Jarrow Crusade set off - did it achieve anything?', *Newcastle Chronicle,* 5 Oct 2016, used by permission of Reach Publishing Services Ltd; **Frederick Rebman** interviewed by author, used with his permission; **Andrew Roberts**: 'On Churchill and the Craft of Biography', interview by Russ Roberts on Econ Talk, The Library of Economics and Liberty, 19 July 2019, used by permission of Andrew Roberts; **Seebohm Rowntree**: *Poverty: A Study of Town Life* (1901), used by permission of the Joseph Rowntree Foundation; **Vita Sackville West**: letter (1942) from *Vita and Harold: The letters of Vita Sackville-West and Harold Nicolson* edited by Nigel Nicolson (Weidenfeld and Nicolson, 1992), copyright © Nigel Nicolson 1992, used by permission of Curtis Brown Ltd, London on behalf of Nigel Nicolson; **Dominic Selwood**: 'Dresden was a civilian town with no military significance. Why did we burn its people?', *The Telegraph,* 13 Feb 2015, copyright © Telegraph Media Group Ltd 2015, used by permission of TMG Ltd.; **Anthony Storr**: *Churchill's Black Dog and Other Phenomena of the Human Mind* (Collins, 1989), copyright © Anthony Storr 1989, used by permission of HarperCollins Publishers Ltd; **A J P Taylor**: *Origins of the Second World War* (Hamish Hamilton, 1961, Penguin, 1964, 1987, 1991), copyright © A J P Taylor 1961, 1963, used by permission of Penguin Books Ltd, a division of Penguin Random House UK.

Cover: Matthew Hollings

Artworks: Moreno Chiacchiera via Beehive Illustrations, Rudolf Farkas via Beehive Illustrations, Martin Sanders via Beehive Illustrations, QBS Learning

Photos: Throughout: Paladin12/Shutterstock; **Throughout:** Paladin12/Shutterstock; **Throughout:** Paladin12/Shutterstock; **p7 (T):** smatch/Shutterstock; **p6:** trucic/Shutterstock; **p7 (B):** agolndr/Shutterstock; **p9 (L):** Liverpool Record Office; **p9 (R):** London Stereoscopic Company/Getty images; **p10 (T):** Science History Images/Alamy Stock Photo; **p10 (B):** The Granger Collection/Alamy Stock Photo; **p11:** Everett Collection Inc/Alamy StockPhoto; **p12:** V&A Images/Alamy StockPhoto; **p13 (L):** Pictorial Press ltd/Alamy Stock Photo; **p13 (R):** Art Collection 3/Alamy Stock Photo; **p14:** London Metropolitan Archives, City of London/Catalogue No: SC/PHL/02/0423/3350C Collage no 204983; **p16-p17:** Sueddeutsche Zeitung Photo/Alamy Stock Photo; **p18 (L):** Chronicle/Alamy Stock Photo; **p18 (R):** Granger, NYC/Topfoto; **p19 (L):** Underwood & Underwood/Getty Images; **p19 (R):** Hulton-Deutsch Collection/Getty Images; **p20:** Chronicle/Alamy Stock Photo; **p21, 24:** The Royal Mint; **p23:** World History Archive/Alamy Stock Photo; **p28:** Aaron Wilkes; **p31:** World History Archive/Alamy Stock Photo; **p32:** Shawshots/Alamy Stock Photo; **p33:** Hi-Story/Alamy Stock Photo; **p35 (T):** David Cohen Fine Art/Mary Evans Picture Library; **p35 (B):** Grenville Collins Postcard Collection/Mary Evans Picture Library; **p38 (TL):** Bridgeman Art Library; **p38 (TR):** The Imperial War Museum; **p38 (BL):** GL Archive/Alamy Stock Photo; **p38 (MR):** The Imperial War Museum; **p38 (BR):** Akg-images/Alamy; **p39 (T):** Chronicle/Alamy; **p39 (M):** Military Images/Alamy Stock Photo; **p39 (B):** David Osborn/Alamy Stock Photo; **p40:** British Pathé/ITN; **p41:** David Osborn/Alamy Stock Photo; **p43 (L):** Maurice Savage/Alamy Stock Photo; **p43 (M):** Aaron Wilkes; **p43 (R):** Aaron Wilkes; **p46:** History and Art Collection/Alamy Stock Photo; **p47 (L):** Onslow Auctions Limited/Mary Evans Picture Library; **p47 (R):** Niday Picture Library/Alamy Stock Photo; **p49:** Imperial War Museum; **p50 (L):** Granger Historical Picture Archive/Alamy Stock Photo; **p50 (R):** Glasshouse Images/Alamy Stock Photo; **p51:** Keith Corrigan/Alamy Stock Photo; **p52:** De Luan/Alamy Stock Photo; **p53:** Roger Bamber/Alamy Stock Photo; **p54:** Hulton Deutsch/Getty Images; **p55:** Fotolibra; **p57:** Leonard Raven Hill/Punch 10/12/1919/public domain; **p61:** PRISMA ARCHIVO/Alamy Stock Photo; **p65 (L):** Topical Press Agency/Hulton/Getty Images; **p65 (R):** MUNICIPAL DREAMS; **p67:** Chronicle/Alamy Stock Photo; **p68:** Central Press/Hulton Archive/Getty Images; **p69:** Everett Collection, Inc./Alamy; **p70:** Getty Images; **p73:** World History Archive/Alamy; **p74:** SSPL via Getty Images; **p75:** Popperfoto/Getty Images; **p82:** Granger Historical Picture Archive/Alamy Stock Photo; **p83:** Hemis/Alamy Stock Photo; **p85:** sawshots/Alamy Stock Photo; **p87:** World History Archive/Alamy Stock Photo; **p88:** Mary Evans Picture Library; **p89:** Moviestore Collection Ltd/Alamy Stock Photo; **p90:** World History Archive/Alamy Stock Photo; **p91:** World History Archive/Alamy Stock Photo; **p92 (T):** CTK/Alamy Stock Photo; **p92 (B):** INTERFOTO/Alamy Stock Photo; **p93:** akg-Images; **p94 (T):** CBW/Alamy Stock Photo; **p94 (B):** popperfoto/Getty Images; **p96:** Granger Historical Picture Archive Alamy; **p97:** Photo12/Ann Ronan Picture Library/Alamy Stock Photo; **p99:** Courtesy of University of Wisconsin Digital Collections via Recollection Wisconsin/Public Domain; **p101:** Topfoto/Punch; **p107 (L):** IPW/Getty Images; **p107 (R):** Trinity Mirror/Mirrorpix/Alamy Stock Photo; **p109 (B):** Heritage Image Partnership Ltd/Alamy Stock Photo; **p109 (T):** Chronicle/Alamy Stock Photo; **p110:** Time Life Pictures/getty Images; **p111:** Science History Images/Alamy Stock Photo; **p113 (L):** John Frost Newspapers/Alamy Stock Photo; **p113 (R):** British Cartoon Archvie/SoloSyndication; **p114:** LAPI/RogerViollet/Getty Images; **p115:** Pictorial Press Ltd/Alamy Stock Photo; **p116:** Alamy Stock Photo; **p117:** Imperial War Museum; **p118 (TL):** Fox photos/Hulton/Getty Images; **p118 (TR):** David Osborn/Alamy; **p118 (BL):** Topfoto; **p118 (BM):** DPA/PA Photos;

p118 (BR): Richard Seaman; **p119:** PjrStudio/Alamy Stock Photo; **p120:** IWM; **p121:** incamerstock/Alamy; **p122:** Hulton Deutsch/Getty Images; **p124:** Hulton Archives/Getty Images; **p125:** Imperial War Museum; **p128 (L):** Shawshots/Alamy Stock Photo; **p128 (R):** Mirrorpix/Alamy Stock Photo; **p129 (T):** Pictorial Press Ltd/Alamy Stock Photo; **p129 (B):** incamerastock/Alamy Stock Photo; **p132 (T):** JennyGoodall/Solo syndication; **p132 (B):** DPA/Topfoto; **p133:** Granger Historical Picture Archive/Alamy Stock Photo; **p134 (L):** Ullstein Bild/Topfoto; **p134 (R):** Ullstein Bild/Topfoto; **p136:** Andrew Michael/Alamy Stock Photo; **p137 (TL):** Fremantle/Alamy Stock Photo; **p137 (B):** The National Archives; **p137 (TR):** Fremantle/Alamy Stock Photo; **p139:** Punch Cartoon Library/Topfoto; **p141:** Illustrated London News Ltd/Mary Evans Picture Library; **p142:** Prisma by Dukas Presseagentur GmbH/Alamy Stock Photo; **p145 (T):** Library of Congress; **p145 (B):** World History Archive/Alamy Stock Photo; **p146:** Yuriy Boyko/Shutterstock/DAM; **p150:** wanchai/Shutterstock; **p153:** Shawshots/Alamy Stock Photo; **p155:** Topfoto; **p158:** Granger Historical Picture Archive/Alamy Stock Photo; **p159:** CSU Archives/Everett; **p160:** Keystone Press/Alamy Stock Photo; **p162:** GL Archive/Alamy Stock Photo; **p163:** Granger Historical Picture Archive/Alamy Stock Photo; **p164:** SPUTNIK / Alamy Stock Photo; **p165:** Larry Burrows/Getty Images; **p166:** Pictorial Press Ltd/Alamy Stock Photo; **p167 (T):** INTERFOTO/Alamy Stock Photo; **p167 (B):** Getty Images/staff; **p168:** INTERFOTO/Alamy Stock Photo; **p169:** PA Archive/PA Images; **p170:** Silvan Bachmann/Alamy Stock Photo; **p171 (T):** © Chappatte, NZZ am Sonntag, Switzerland/ www.chappatte.com; **p171 (M):** Anthony Collins/Alamy Stock Photo; **p171 (B):** Paul Brown/Alamy Stock Photo; **p176:** Chronicle/Alamy Stock Photo; **p177:** EggImages/Alamy Stock Photo; **p178:** Mary Evans Picture Library; **p179:** Trinity Mirror/Mirrorpix/Alamy Stock Photo; **p181:** World History Archive/Alamy; **p182:** ALAN OLIVER/Alamy Stock Photo; **p183:** Keystone /Getty Images; **p186:** Contraband Collection/Alamy; **p187:** London Metropolitan University Library Services and Special Collections; **p188 (TL):** Marc Gascoigne/Alamy Stock Photo; **p188 (BL), p190 (R):** JEP Live Music/Alamy Stock Photo; **p188 (TR), p190 (L):** UPI/Alamy Stock Photo; **p188 (BR):** Cal Sport Media/Alamy Live News; **p189:** Jeffrey Blackler/Alamy Stock Photo; **p194 (T):** Heritage Image Partnership Ltd/Alamy Stock Photo; **p194 (BL):** ClassicStock/Alamy Stock Photo; **p194 (BR):** Shawshots/Alamy Stock Photo; **p196:** Photo 12/Alamy Stock Photo; **p198:** Flight Collection /Topfoto; **p199 (L):** INTERFOTO/Alamy Stock Photo; **p199 (R):** BRIAN HARRIS/Alamy Stock Photo; **p200 (L):** Andre Csillag/REX/Shutterstock; **p200 (R):** Alamy Stock Photo; **p200 (M):** Photo Oz/Shutterstock; **p201:** Pictorial Press Ltd/Alamy Stock Photo; **p202 (TL):** qaphotos.com/Alamy Stock Photo; **p202 (TR):** Featureflash Archive/Alamy Stock Photo; **p202 (B-1):** seeshooteatrepeat/Shutterstock; **p202 (B-2):** Photo Oz/Shutterstock; **p202 (B-3):** NOKIA; **p202 (B-4):** robtek/Shutterstock; **p202 (B-5):** Science and Society Photo Library; **p202 (B-6):** robtek/Shutterstock; **p202 (B-7):** SasPartout/Shutterstock; **p203:** Louise Gubb/Contributor/Getty images; **p204 (L):** ZUMA Press, Inc./Alamy Stock Photo; **p204 (R):** David Paul Morris/Stringer; **p205 (T):** Purple Pilchards/Alamy Stock Photo; **p205 (B):** Shutterstock; **p206 (B):** MediaWorldImages/Alamy Stock Photo; **p207 (B):** ZUMA Press, Inc./Alamy Stock Photo; **p206-p207:** tanuha2001/Shutterstock; **p208:** Spencer Platt/Staff/Getty Images; **p209 (B):** American Photo Archive/Alamy Stock Photo; **p209 (BL):** Everett Collection Historical/Alamy Stock Photo; **p210 (T):** BOB DAEMMRICH/AFP via Getty Images; **p210 (B):** Peter Macdiarmid/Getty Images; **p211:** Ray Tang/Shutterstock; **p214:** Tim Graham/Alamy Stock Photo.

Although we have made every effort to trace and contact all copyright holders before publication this has not been possible in all cases. If notified, the publisher will rectify any errors or omissions at the earliest opportunity.

Links to third party websites are provided by Oxford in good faith and for information only. Oxford disclaims any responsibility for the materials contained in any third party website referenced in this work.

From the author: Special thanks to Alison Schrecker, Kate Buckley and Melanie Waldron at OUP for their tireless hard work, sound advice and brilliant suggestions at every stage of this project. In addition, huge thanks also to Sarah Flynn, Janice Mansel-Chan, Emma Jones, Georgia Styring, Marcus Bell and Jade Coyle at OUP, and to Ben Fuller at the Holocaust Educational Trust. As ever, I am particularly indebted to my family – Emma, Hannah and Eleanor – for all their support, patience and kind words.

The publisher would like to thank the following people for offering their contribution in the development of this book: David Rawlings, Lisa Dixon-Eyre, Gabrielle Rowles, James Helling and Melanie Simms.

Relevant sections have been reviewed by the Holocaust Educational Trust (www.het.org.uk). We are very grateful for their valuable input.

Relevant sections have also been reviewed by James Renton from the International Centre on Racism. We are very grateful for his careful review.